A Treasure of Tagore's Writings

Volume One

Tagore's other titles in Srishti

Gitanjali

My Boyhood Days

Mashi & other stories

The Gardener

The Post Office

The Home and the World

Four Chapters

Selected short stories

A Treasure of Tagore's Writings

Volume One

Srishti
PUBLISHERS & DISTRIBUTORS

Srishti Publishers & Distributors
N-16, C. R. Park
New Delhi 110 019
srishtipublishers@gmail.com

First published by
Srishti Publishers & Distributors in 2012

Typeset by EGP at Srishti

Printed and bound in India

Contents

My Boyhood Days 1

Lover's Gift 69

The Post Office 99

Chitra 131

Two Sisters 157

Sacrifice & Other Plays 225

Shesher Kabita 313

MY BOYHOOD DAYS

I

The Calcutta where I was born was an altogether old-world place. Hackney carriages lumbered about the city raising clouds of dust, and the whips fell on the backs of skinny horses whose bones showed plainly below their hide. There were no trams then, no buses, no motors. Business was not the breathless rush that it is now, and the days went by in leisurely fashion. Clerks would take a good pull at the hookah before starting for office, and chew their betel as they went along. Some rode in palanquins, others joined in groups of four or five to hire a carriage in common, which was known as a "share-carriage". Wealthy men had monograms painted on their carriages, and a leather hood over the rear portion, like a half-drawn veil. The coachman sat on the box with his turban stylishly tilted to one side, and two grooms rode behind, girdles of yaks' tails round their waists, startling the pedestrians from their path with their shouts of "Hey-yo!"

Women used to go about in the stifling darkness of closed palanquins; they shrank from the idea of riding in carriages, and even to use an umbrella in sun or rain was considered unwomanly. Any woman who was so bold as to wear the new-fangled bodice, or shoes on her feet, was scornfully nicknamed "memsahib", that is to say, one who had cast off all sense of propriety or shame. If any woman unexpectedly encountered a stange man, one outside her family circle, her veil would promptly descend to the very tip of her nose, and she would at once turn her back on him. The palanquins in which women went out were shut as closely as their apartments in the house. An additional covering, a kind of thick tilt, completely enveloped the palanquin of a rich man's daughters and daighters-in-law, so that it looked like a moving tomb. By its side went the *durwan* carrying his brass-bound stick. His work was to sit in the entrance and watch the house, to tend his beard, safely to conduct the money to the bank and the women to their relatives' houses, and on festival days to dip the lady of the house into the Ganges, closed palanquin and all. Hawkers who came to the door with their array of wares would grease Shivnandan's palm to gain admission, and the drivers of hired carriages were also a source of profit to him. Sometimes, a man who was unwilling to fall in with this idea of going shares would create a great scene in front of the porch.

Our "jamadar" Sobha Ram, who was a wrestler, used to spend a good deal of time in practising his preparatory feints and approaches, and in brandishing his heavy clubs. Sometimes, he would sit and grind hemp for drink, and sometimes, he would be quietly eating his raw radishes, tender leaves and all, when we boys would creep upon him and yell "Radhakrishna!" in his ear. The more he waved his arms and protested the more we delighted in teasing him. And perhaps,—who knows?—his protests were merely a cunning device for hearing repeated the name of his favourite god.

There was no gas then in the city, and no electric light. When the kerosene lamp was introduced, its brilliance amazed us. In the evening the house-servant lit castor-oil lamps in every room. The one in our study-room had two wicks in a glass bowl.

By this dim light my master taught me from Peary Sarkar's First Book. First, I would begin to yawn, and then, growing more and more sleepy, rub my heavy eyes. At such times, I heard over and over again of the virtues of my master's other pupil Satin, a paragon of a boy with a wonderful head for study, who would rub snuff in his eyes to keep himself awake, so earnest was he. But as for me—the less said about that the better! Even the awful thought that I should probably remain the only dunce in the family could not keep me awake. When nine o'clock struck I was released, my eyes dazed and my mind drugged with sleep.

There was a narrow passage, enclosed by latticed walls, leading from the outer apartments to the interior of the house. A dimly burning lantern swung from the ceiling. As I went along this passage, my mind would be haunted by the idea that something was creeping upon me from behind. Little shivers ran up and down my back. In those days devils and spirits lurked in the recesses of every man's mind, and the air was full of ghost stories. One day it would be some servant girl falling in a dead faint because she had heard the nasal whine of Shañk-chunni. The female demon of that name was the most bad-tempered devil of all, and was said to be very greedy of fish. Another story was connected with the thick-leaved *bādām* tree at the western corner of the house. A mysterious Shape was said to stand with one foot in its branches and the other on the third-storey cornice of the house. Plenty of people declared that they had seen it, and there were not a few who believed them. A friend of my elder brother's laughingly made light of the story, and the servants looked upon him as lacking in all piety, and said that his neck would surely be wrung one day and his pretensions exposed. The very atmosphere was so enmeshed in ghostly terrors that I could not put my feet into the darkness under the table without them getting the creeps.

There were no water-pipes laid on in those days. In the spring months of *Māgh* and *Fālgoon* when the Ganges water was clear, our bearers would bring it up in brimming pots carried in a yoke across their shoulders. In the dark rooms of the ground floor stood rows of huge water jars filled with the whole year's supply of drinking water. All those musty, dingy, twilit rooms were the home of furtive "Things"—which of us did not know all about those "Things"? Great gaping mouths they had, eyes in their breasts, and ears like winnowing fans; and their feet turned backwards. Small wonder, that my heart would pound in my breast and my knees tremble when I went into the inner garden, with the vision of those devilish shapes before me.

At high tide the water of the Ganges would flow along a masonry channel at the side of the road. Since my grandfather's time an allowance of this water had been discharged into our tank. When the sluices were opened the water rushed in, gurgling and foaming like a waterfall. I used to watch it fascinated, holding on by the railings of the south verandah. But the days of our tank were numbered, and finally there came a day when cartload after cartload of rubbish was tipped into it. When the tank no longer reflected the garden, the last lingering illusion of rural life left it. That *bādām* tree is still standing near the third-storey cornice, but though his footholds remain, the ghostly shape that once bestrode them has disappeared for ever.

II

The palanquin belonged to the days of my grandmother. It was of ample proportions and lordly appearance. It was big enough to have needed eight bearers for each pole. But when the former wealth and glory of the family had faded like the glowing clouds of sunset, the palanquin bearers, with their gold bracelets, their thick ear-rings, and their sleeveless red tunics, had disappeared along with it. The body of the palanquin had been decorated with coloured line drawings, some of which were now defaced. Its surface was stained and discoloured, and the coir stuffing was coming out of the upholstery. It lay in a corner of the counting-house verandah as though it were a piece of common-place lumber. I was seven or eight years old at that time.

I was not yet, therefore, of an age to put my hand to any serious work in the world, and the old palanquin on its part had been dismissed from all useful service. Perhaps, it was this fellow-feeling that so much attracted me towards it. It was to me an island in the midst of the ocean, and I on my holidays became Robinson Crusoe. There I, sat within its closed doors, completely lost to view, delightfully safe from prying eyes.

Outside my retreat, our house was full of people, innumerable relatives and other folk. From all parts of the house I could hear the shouts of the various servants at their work. Pari, the maid, is returning from the bazaar through the front courtyard with her vegetables in a basket on her hip. Dukhon, the bearer, is carrying in Ganges water in a yoke across his shoulder. The weaver woman has gone into the inner apartments to trade the newest style of saries. Dinu, the goldsmith, who receives a monthly wage, usually sits in the room next to the lane, blowing his bellows and carrying out the orders of the family; now he is coming to the counting house to present his bill to Kailash Mukherjee, who has a quill pen stuck over his ear. The carder sits in the courtyard cleaning the cotton mattress stuffing on his twanging bow. Mukundalal, the durwan, is rolling on the ground outside with the one-eyed wrestler, trying out a new wrestling fall. He slaps his thighs loudly, and repeats his "physical jerks" twenty or thirty times, dropping on all fours. There is a crowd of beggars sitting waiting for their regular dole.

The day wears on, the heat grows intense, the clock in the gate-house strikes the hour. But inside the palanquin the day does not acknowledge the authority of clocks. Our mid-day is that of former days, when the drum at the great door of the king's palace would be beaten for the breaking-up of the court, and the king would go to bathe in sandal-scented water. At mid-day on holidays those in charge of me have their meal and go to sleep. I sit on alone. My palanquin, outwardly at rest, travels on its imaginary journeys. My bearers, sprung from "airy nothing" at my bidding, eating the salt of my imagination, carry me wherever my fancy leads. We pass through far, strange lands, and I give each country a name from the books I have read. My imagination has cut a road through a deep forest. Tigers' eyes blaze from the thickets, my flesh creeps and tingles. With me is Biswanath the hunter; his gun speaks—Crack! Crack!—and there, all is still. Sometimes, my palanquin becomes a peacock-boat, floating far out on the ocean till the shore is out of sight. The oars fall into the water with a gentle plash, the waves swing and swell around us. The sailors cry to us to beware, a storm is coming. By the tiller stands Abdul the sailor, with his pointed beard, shaven moustache and close-cropped head. I know him, he brings *hilsa* fish and turtle eggs from the Padma for my elder brother.

Abdul has a story for me. One day, at the end of *Chaitra*[1] he had gone out in a dinghy to catch fish when suddenly there arose a great *Vaisākh* gale[2]. It was a tremendous typhoon and the boat sank lower and lower. Abdul seized the tow-rope in his teeth, and jumping into the water swam to the shore, where he pulled his dinghy up after him by the rope. But the story comes to an end far too quickly for my taste, and besides, the boat is not lost, everything is saved–that isn't what I call a story! Again and again I demand, "What next?" "Well," says Abdul at last, "after that there were great doings. What should I see next but a panther with enormous whiskers. During the storm he had climbed up a *pākur* tree on the village ghat on the other side of the river. In the violent wind the tree broke and fell into the Padma. Brother Panther came floating down on the current, rolled over and over in the water and reached and climbed the bank on my side. As soon as I saw him I made a noose in my tow-rope. The wild beast drew near, his big eyes glaring. He had grown very hungry with swimming, and when he saw me saliva dribbled from his red, lolling tongue. But though he had known many other men, inside and out, he did not know Abdul. I shouted to him, "Come on old boy", and as soon as he raised his fore-feet for the attack I dropped my noose round his neck. The more he struggled to get free the tighter grew the noose, until his tongue began to loll out...." I am tremendously excited. "He didn't die, did he Abdul?" I ask. "Die?" says Abdul, "He couldn't die for the life of him! Well, the river was in spate, and I had to get back to Bahadurganj. I yoked my young panther to the dinghy and made him tow me fully forty miles. Oh, he might roar and snarl, but I goaded him on with my oar, and he carried me a ten or fifteen hours' journey in an hour and a half! Now, my little fellow, don't ask me what happened

1. March-April.
2. Nor-wester, a very common phenomenon in Bengal in the beginning of the hot weather.

next, for you won't get an answer."

"All right," say I, "so much for the panther; now for the crocodile?" Says Abdul, "I have often seen the tip of his nose above the water. And, how wickedly he smiles as he lies basking in the sun, stretched at full length on the shelving sandbanks of the river. If I'd had a gun I should have made his acquaintance. But my license has expired....

"Still, I can tell you one good yarn. One day, Kanchi the gypsy woman was sitting on the bank of the river trimming bamboo with a bill-hook, with her young goat tethered nearby. All at once the crocodile appeared on the surface, seized the billy-goat by the leg and dragged it into the water. With one jump the gypsy woman landed astride on its back, and began sawing with her sickle at the throat of the "demon-lizard", over and over again. The beast let go of the goat and plunged into the water...."

"And then? And then?" comes my excited question. "Why," says Abdul, "the rest of the story went down to the bottom of the river with the crocodile. It will take some time to get it up again. Before I see you again I will send somebody to find out about it, and let you know." Abdul has never come again; perhaps he is still looking for news.

So much, then, for my travels in the palanquin. Outside the palanquin there were days when I assumed the role of teacher, and the railings of the verandah were my pupils. They were all afraid of me, and would cower before me in silence. Some of them were very naughty, and cared absolutely nothing for their books. I told them with dire threats that when they grew up they would be fit for nothing but casual labour. They bore the marks of my beatings from head to foot, yet they did not stop being naughty. For, it would not have done for them to stop, it would have made an end of my game.

There was another game, too, with my wooden lion. I heard stories of poojah sacrifices and decided that a lion sacrifice would be a magnificent thing. I rained blows on his back–with a frail little stick. There had to be a "mantra", of course, otherwise it would not have been a proper poojah:

"Liony, liony, off with your head,
Liony, liony, now you are dead.
Woofle the walnut goes clappety clap,
Snip, snop, SNAP!"

I had borrowed almost every word in this from other sources; only the word walnut was my own. I was very fond of walnuts. From the words "clappety clap" you can see that my sacrificial knife was made of wood. And, the word "snap" shows that it was not a strong one.

III

The clouds have had no rest since yesterday evening. The rain is pouring incessantly. The trees stand huddled together in a seemingly foolish manner; the birds are silent. I call to mind the evenings of my boyhood.

We used then to spend our evening in the servants' quarters. At that time English spellings and meanings did not yet lie like a nightmare on my shoulders. My third brother used to say that I ought first to get a good foundation of Bengali and only afterwards to go on to the English superstructure. Consequently, while other school-boys of my age were glibly reciting "I am up", "He is down", I had not even started on B, A, D, bad and M, A, D, mad.

In the speech of the *nabobs* the servants' quarters were then called "tosha-khana". Even though our house had fallen far below its former aristocratic state, these old high-sounding names, "tosha-khana", "daftar-khana", "baithak-khana", still clung to it.

On the southern side of this "tosha-khana", a castor oil lamp burned dimly on a glass stand in a big room; on the wall was a picture of Ganesh and a crude country painting of the goddess Kali, round which the wall lizards hunted their insect prey. There was no furniture in the room, merely a soiled mat spread on the floor.

You must understand that we lived like poor people, and were consequently saved the trouble of keeping a good stable. Away in a corner outside, in a thatched shed under a tamarind tree, was a shabby carriage and an old horse. We wore the very simplest and plainest clothes, and it was a long time before we even began to wear socks. It was luxury beyond our wildest dreams when our tiffin rations went beyond Brajeswar's inventory and included a loaf of bread, and butter wrapped in a banana leaf. We adapted ourselves easily to the broken wrecks of our former glory.

Brajeswar was the name of the servant who presided over our mat seat. His hair and beard were grizzled, the skin of his face dry and tight-drawn; he was a man of serious disposition, harsh voice, and deliberately mouthed speech. His former master had been a prosperous and well-known man, yet necessity had degraded him from that service to the work of looking after neglected children like us. I have heard that he used to be a master in a village school. To the end of his life he kept this school-masterly language and prim manner. Instead of saying "The gentlemen are waiting", he would say "They await you", and his masters smiled when they heard him. He was as finicky about caste matters as he was conceited. When bathing he would go down into the tank and push back the oily surface water five or six times with his hands before taking a plunge. When he came out of the tank after his bath Brajeswar would edge his way through the garden in so gingerly a way that one would think he could only keep caste by avoiding all contact with this unclean world that God has made. He would talk very emphatically about what was right and what was wrong in manners and behaviour. And besides, he held his head a little on one side, which made his words all the more impressive.

But with all this there was one flaw in his character as *guru*. He cherished secretly a suppressed greed for food. It was not his method to place a proper portion of food on our plates before the meal. Instead, when we sat down to eat he would take one *luchi*[1] at a time, and dangling it at a little distance ask, "Do you want any more?" We knew by the tone of his voice what answer he desired, and I usually

---

1. Fried pancake known in Hindusthani as *puri*.

said that I didn't want any. After that he never gave us an opportunity to change our minds. The milk bowls also had an irresistible attraction for him—an attraction which I never felt at all. In his room was a small wired foodsafe with shelves in it. In it was a big brass bowl of milk, and *luchis* and vegetables on a wooden platter. Outside the wire-netting the cat prowled longingly to and fro sniffing the air.

From my childhood upwards these short commons suited me very well. Small rations cannot be said to have made me weak. I was, if anything, stronger, certainly not weaker, than boys who had unlimited food. My constitution was so abominably sound that even when the most urgent need arose for avoiding school, I could never make myself ill by fair means or foul. I would get wet through shoes, stockings and all, but I could not catch cold. I would lie on the open roof in the heavy autumn dew; my hair and clothes would be soaked, but I never had the slightest suspicion of a cough. And, as for that sign of bad digestion known as stomach-ache, my stomach was a complete stranger to it, though my tongue made use of its name with mother in time of need. Mother would smile to herself and not feel the least anxiety; she would merely call the servant and tell him to go and tell my teacher that he should not teach me that evening. Our old-fashioned mothers used to think it no great harm if the boys occasionally took a holiday from study. If we had fallen into the hands of these present-day mothers, we should certainly have been sent to the teacher, and had our ears tweaked into the bargain. Perhaps, with a knowing smile they would have dosed us with castor oil, and our pains would have been permanently cured. If by chance, I got a slight temperature no one ever called it fever, but "heated blood". I had never set eyes on a thermometer in those days. Dr Nilmadhav would come and place his hand on my body, and then prescribe as the first day's treatment castor oil and fasting. I was allowed very little water to drink, and what I had was hot, with a few sugar-coated cardamoms for flavouring. After this fast, the *mouralā fish* soup and soft-boiled rice which I got on the third day seemed a veritable food for the gods.

Serious fever I do not remember, and I never heard the name of malaria. I do not remember quinine—that castor oil was my most distasteful medicine. I never knew the slightest scratch of a surgeon's knife; and to this very day I do not know what measles and chicken-pox are. In short, my body remained obstinately healthy. If mothers want their children to be so healthy that they will be unable to escape from the school master, I recommended them to find a servant like Brajeswar. He would save not only food bills but doctor's bills also, especially in these days of mill flour and adulterated ghee and oil. You must remember that in those days chocolate was still unknown in the bazaar. There was a kind of rose lollipop to be had for a pice. I do not know whether modern boy's pockets are still made sticky by this sesamum-covered sugar-lump, with its faint scent of roses. It has certainly fled in shame from the houses of the respectable people of today. What has become of those cone-shaped packets of fried spices? And, those cheap sesamum sweetmeats? Do they still linger on? If not, it is no good trying to bring them back.

Day after day, in the evenings, I listened to Brajeswar reciting the seven cantos of Krittibas' *Rāmayanā*. Kishori Chatterjee used to drop in sometimes while the reading was going on. He had by heart *Pānchāli*[2] versions of the whole *Rāmayanā*, tune and all. He took possession at once of the seat of authority, and superseding Krittibas, would begin to recite his simple folk-stanzas in great style:

"Lakshman O hear me
Greatly I fear me
Dangers are near me."

2. A kind of folk-version very popular in Bengali.

There was a smile on his lips, his bald head gleamed, the song poured from his throat in a torrent of sound, the rhymes jingled and rang verse after verse, like the music of pebbles in a brook. At the same time he would be using his hands and feet in acting out the thought. It was Kishori Chatterjee's greatest grief that Dadabhai, as he called me, could not join a troupe of strolling players and turn such a voice to account. If I did that, he said, I should certainly make my name.

By and by it would grow late and the assembly on the mat would break up. We would go into the house, to Mother's room, haunted and oppressed on our way by the terror of devils. Mother would be playing cards with her aunt, the inlaid parquet floor gleamed like ivory, a coverlet was spread on the big divan. We would make such a disturbance that Mother would soon throw down her hand and say, "If they are going to be such a nuisance, auntie, you'd better go and tell them stories." We would wash our feet with water from the pot on the verandah outside, and climb on to the bed, pulling "Didima" with us. Then, it would begin—stories of the magical awakening of the princess and her rescue from the demon city. The princess might wake, but who could waken me? ... In the early part of the night the jackals would begin to howl, for in those days they still haunted the basements of some of the old houses of Calcutta with their nightly wail.

IV

When I was a little boy, Calcutta city was not so wakeful at night as it is now. Nowadays, as soon as the day of sunlight is over, the day of electric light begins. There is not much work done in it, but there is no rest, for the fire continues, as it were, to smoulder in the charcoal after the blazing wood has burnt itself out. The oil mills are still, the steamer sirens are silent, the labourers have left the factories, the buffaloes which pull the carts of jute bales are stabled in the tin-roofed sheds. But the nerves of the city are throbbing still with the fever of thought which has burned all day in her brain. Buying and selling go on as by day in the shops that line the streets, though the fire is a little choked with ash. Motors continue to run in all directions, emitting all kinds of raucous grunts and groans, though they no longer run with the zest of the morning. But in those old times which we knew, when the day was over whatever business remained undone wrapped itself up in the black blanket of the night and went to sleep in the darkened ground-floor premises of the city. Outside the house the evening sky rose quiet and mysterious. It was so still that we could hear, even in our own street, the shouts of the grooms from the carriages of those people of fashion who were returning from taking the air in Eden Gardens by the side of the Ganges.

In the hot season of *Chaitra* and *Vaishākh* the hawkers would go about the streets shouting "I-i-i-ce". In a big pot full of lumps of ice and salt water were little tin containers of what we called "kulpi" ice—nowadays, ousted by the more fashionable ices or "ice-cream".

No one but myself knows how my mind thrilled to that cry as I stood on the verandah facing the street. Then there was another cry, "*Bela* flowers". Nowadays, for some reason one hears little of the gardeners' baskets of spring flowers–I do not know why. But in those days the air was full of the scent of the thickly strung *bel* flowers which the women and girls wore in their hair-knots. Before they went to bathe, the women would sit outside their rooms with a hand-mirror set up before them, and dress their hair. The knot would be skilfully bound with the black hair-braid into all sorts of different styles. They wore black-bordered Chandernagore sarees, skilfully crinkled before use by pleating and twisting after the fashion of those days. The barber's wife would come to scrub their feet with pumice and paint them with red lac. She and her like were the gossip-mongers of the women's courts.

The crowds returning from office or from college did not then, as they do now, rush to the football fields, clinging in swarms to the foot-boards of the trams. Nor, did they crowd in front of cinema halls as they returned. There was some active interest shown in drama, but alas! I was only a child then.

Children of those times got no share in the pleasures of the grown-ups, even from a distance. If we were bold enough to go near, we should be told, "Off with you, go and play." But if we boys made the amount of noise appropriate for proper play, it would then be, "Be quiet, do." Not that the grown-ups themselves conducted their pleasures and conversation in silence, by any means; and now and again we would stand on the fringe of their far-flung jubilations, as though sprinkled by the spray of a waterfall. We would hang over the verandah on our side of the courtyard, staring across at the brilliantly lit reception-room on the other side. Big coaches would roll up to the portico one after another. Some of our elder brothers conducted the guests upstairs from the front door, sprinkling them with rose-water from the sprinkler, and giving each one a small buttonhole or nosegay of flowers. As the dramatic entertainment proceeded, we could hear the sobs of the "highcaste *kulin* heroine", but we could make out nothing of their meaning, and our longing to know grew intense. We discovered later that though the sobber was certainly high-caste, "she" was merely our own brother-in-law. But in those days grown-ups and children were kept apart as strictly as men and women with their separate apartments. The singing and dancing would go on in the blaze of the drawing-room chandeliers, the men would pull at the hookah, the women of the family would take their betel boxes and sit in the subdued light behind their screen, the visiting ladies would gather in these retired nooks, and there would be much whispering of intimate domestic gossip. But we children were in bed by this time, and lay listening as our maid-servants Piyari or Sankari told us stories—"In the moonlight, expanding like an opening flower..."

V

A little before our day it was the fashion among wealthy householders to run *jātrās* or troupes of actors. There was a great demand for boys with shrill voices to join these troupes. One of my uncles was patron of such an amateur company. He had a gift for writing plays, and was very enthusiastic about training the boys. All over Bengal professional companies were the rage, just as the amateur companies were in aristocratic circles. Troupes of players sprang up like mushrooms on all sides, under the leadership of some well-known actor or other. Not that either patron or manager was necessarily of high family or good education. Their fame rested on their own merits. *Jātrā* performances used to take place in our house from time to time. But we children had no part in them, and I managed to see only the preliminaries. The verandah would be full of members of the company, the air full of tobacco smoke. There were the boys, long-haired, with dark rings of weariness under their eyes, and, young as they were, with the faces of grown men. Their lips were stained black with constant betel chewing. Their costumes and other paraphernalia were in painted tin boxes. The entrance door was open, people swarmed like ants into the courtyard, which, filled to the brim with the seething, buzzing mass, spilled over into the lane and beyond into the Chitpore Road. Then, nine o'clock would strike, and Shyam would swoop down on me like a hawk on a dove, grip my elbow with his rough, gnarled hand, and tell me that Mother was calling me, to go to bed. I would hang my head in confusion at being thus publicly dragged away, but would bow to superior force and go to my bedroom. Outside all was tumult and shouting, outside flared the lighted chandeliers, but in my room there was not a sound and a brass lamp burned low on its stand. Even in sleep I was dimly conscious of the crash of the cymbals marking the rhythm of the dance.

The grown-ups usually forbade everything on principle, but on one occasion for some reason or other they decided to be indulgent, and the order went forth that the children also might come to the play. It was a drama about Nala and Damayanti. Before it began we were sent to bed till half-past eleven. We were assured again and again that when the time came we should be roused, but we knew the ways of the grown-ups, and we had no faith at all in these promises—*they* were adults, and *we* were children!

That night, however, I did drag my unwilling body to bed. For one thing, Mother promised that she herself would come and wake me. For another thing, I always had to pinch myself to keep myself awake after nine o'clock. When the time came I was awakened and brought outside, blinking and bewildered in the dazzling glare. Light streamed brightly from coloured chandeliers on the first and second storeys, and the white sheets spread in the courtyard made it seem much bigger than usual. On one side were seated the people of importance, senior members of the family, and their invited guests. The remaining space was filled with a motley crowed of all who cared to come. The performing company was led by a famous actor wearing a gold chain across his stomach, and old and young crowded together in the audience. The majority of the audience were what the respectable would call "riff-raff". The play itself had been written by men whose hands were trained only to the villager's reed pen, and who had never practised on the letters of an English copy book. Tunes, dances, and story had all sprung from the very heart of rural Bengal, and no pundit had polished their style.

We went and sat by our elder brothers in the audience, and they tied up small sums of money in kerchiefs and gave them to us. It was the custom to throw this money on to the stage at the points where applause was most deserved. By this means the actors gained some extra profit and the family a good reputation.

The night came to an end, but the play would not. I never knew whose arms gathered up my limp body, nor where they carried me. I was far too much ashamed to try to find out. I, a fellow who had been sitting like an equal among the grown-ups and doling out *baksheesh,* to be disgraced in this way before a whole courtyard full of people! When I woke up I was lying on the divan in my mother's room; it was very late, and already blazing hot. The sun had risen, but I had not risen!–Such a thing had never happened before.

Nowadays, the city's pleasures flow on in an unbroken stream. There is always a cinema show somewhere, and whoever pleases may see it for a trifling sum. But in those days entertainments were few and far between, like water holes dug in the sandy bed of a dried-up river, three or four miles apart. Like these too, they lasted only a few hours, and the wayfarers hastily gathered round, drinking from their cupped hands to quench their thirst.

The old days were like a king's son who, from time to time on festive occasions, or according to his whim, distributes rich and royal gifts to all within his jurisdiction. Modern days are like a merchant's son, sitting at the cross-roads on some great highway with many kinds of cheap and tawdry goods spread glittering before him, and drawing his customers by highway and byway from every side.

VI

Brajeswar was the head-servant, and his second-in-command was called Shyam. He came from Jessore, and he was a real countryman, speaking in a dialect strange to Calcutta. He would say "tenārā" and "onārā" for "tārā" and "orā"; "jāti" and "khāti" for "jete" and "khete". He used to call us affectionately "Domani". He had a dark skin, big eyes, long hair glistening with oil, and a strong, well-built body. He was really good at heart, and affectionate and kind to children. He used to tell us stories of dacoits. Dacoity stories filled men's houses then as universally as the fear of ghosts filled their minds. Even today dacoity is not uncommon; murder, assault and looting still take place, and the police still do not catch the right man. But nowadays this is only a news-item, it has none of the fascination of romance. In those days dacoities were woven into stories, and passed from mouth to mouth for long periods. In my childhood men were still to be met with who in their prime had been members of dacoit gangs. They were all past-masters in the science of the *lathi*, and were surrounded by disciples eager to learn the art of single-stick. Men salaamed at the very mention of their names. Dacoity then was usually not a mere matter of rash, headstrong bloodshed. As bodily strength and skill played their part, so did a generous, gallant mind. Moreover, gentlemen's houses often contained an exercise-ground for the practice of *lathi*-fighting, and those who made a name on these grounds were acknowledged as masters even by dacoits, who gave them a wide berth. Many zemindars made a profession of dacoity. There was a story of a man of this class who had stationed his desperadoes at the mouth of a river. It was new moon, and poojah night, and when they returned, carrying a severed head to the temple in honour of Kali Kankali[1], the zemindar clapped his hands to his head and cried out, "What have you done? It's my son-in-law!"

We heard also about the exploits of the dacoits Raghu and Bishu. They used to give notice before they attacked, and there was nothing underhand in their dacoity. When their rallying-cry was heard in the distance, the blood of the villagers ran cold. But their code forbade them to lay hands on women. On one occasion, in fact, a woman even succeeded in "robbing the robbers", by appearing to them dressed as Kali, brandishing the goddess's heavy-curved blade, and claiming their devout offerings.

One day, there was a display of dacoits' wrestling feats in our house. They were all strong young fellows, big-made, dark-skinned, and long-haired. One man tied a cloth round a heavy grain-pounder, seized the cloth in his teeth, and then flung the pounder upwards and backwards over his shoulder. Another got a man to grasp him by his shaggy hair, and then whirled him round and round by a mere turn of his head. Using a long pole as support and lever, they leaped up to the second storey. Then, one man stood with his hands clasped above his bent head, and others shot through the aperture like diving birds. They also showed how it was possible for them to manage a dacoity twenty or thirty miles away, and the same night be found sleeping peacefully in their beds like law-abiding citizens. They had a pair of very long poles with a piece of wood lashed cross-wise in the middle of each as a foot-rest. These poles were called *rang-pā* (stilts). When walking with the tops of the poles held in the hands, and the feet on these footholds, one stride had the value of ten ordinary steps, and a man could run faster than a

1. The destructive aspect of the goddess Kali, pictured with a necklace of skulls.

horse. I used to encourage boys at Santiniketan to practise stilt-walking—though without any idea of committing dacoity! My imagination mingled such pictures of dacoity feats with Shyam's stories with gruesome effect, so that I have often spent the evening with my arms huddled against my pounding heart!

Sunday was a holiday. On the previous evening the crickets were chirping in the thickets outside in the south garden, and the story was about Raghu the highwayman. My heart went pit-a-pit in the dim light and flickering shadows of the room. The next day in my holiday leisure I climbed into the palanquin. It began to move unbidden, its destination unknown, and my mind, enthralled still by the magic of the previous night's romance, knew a thrill of delicious fear. In the silent darkness my pulses attuned themselves to the rhythmic shouts of the bearers, and my body grew numb with terrified anticipation.

On the boundless expanse of plain the air quivers in the heat, in the distance glistens the Kali tank; the sand sparkles, the wide-spreading *pākur* tree leans from the bank of the river over the cracked, ruined *ghāt*. My romance-fed terrors are concentrated on that thick clump of reeds, and in the shade of the tree on that unknown plain. Nearer and nearer we approach, quicker and quicker beats my heart. Above the reeds can be seen the tips of one or two stout bamboo staves. The bearers will stop there to change shoulders. They will drink, and wind wet towels round their heads. And then?...

Then, with a blood-curdling shout, the dacoits are upon us....

VII

From morning till night the mills of learning went on grinding. To wind up this creaking machinery was the work of *Shejadādā*[1], Hemendranath. He was a stern taskmaster, but it is useless now to try to hide the fact that the greater part of the cargo with which he sought to load our minds was tipped out of the boat and sent to the bottom. My learning at any rate was a profit-less cargo. If one seeks to key an instrument to too high a pitch, the strings will snap beneath the strain.

Shejadādā made all arrangements for the education of his eldest daughter. When the time came he got her admitted into the Loreto Convent School, but even before that she had been given a foundation in Bengali. He also gave Protibha a thorough training in western music, which, however, did not cause her to lose her skill in Indian music. Among the gentlemen's families of that time she had no equal in Hindustani songs.

It is one merit of western music that its scales and exercises demand diligent practice, that it makes for a sensitive ear, and that the discipline of the piano allows of no slackness in the matter of rhythm.

Meanwhile, she had learnt Indian music from her earliest years from our teacher Vishnu. In this school of music I also had to be entered. No present-day musician, whether famous or obscure, would have consented to touch the kind of songs with which Vishnu

---

1. Third elder brother.

initiated us. They were the very commonest kind of Bengali folk songs. Let me give you a few examples:

"A gypsy lass is come to town
To paint tattoos, my sister.
The painting's nothing, so they tell,
Yet she on me has cast a spell,
And, makes me weep and mocks me well,
By her tattoos, my sister."

I remember also a few fragmentary lines, such as:

"The sun and moon have owned defeat,
the firefly's lamp lights up the stage;
the Moghul and the Pathan flag,
the weaver reads the Persian page."

and:

"Your daugher-in-law is the plantain tree,
Mother of Ganesh, let her be.
For if but one flower should blossom and grow
She will have so many children you won't
know what to do."

Lines too come back to me in which one can catch a glimpse of old forgotten histories:

"There was a jungle of thorn and burr,
Fit for the dogs alone;
There did he cut for himself a throne..."

The modern custom is first to practise scales–*sā-re-ga-ma*, etc., on the harmonium, and then to teach some simple Hindu songs. But the wise supervisor who was then in charge of our studies understood that boyhood has its own childish needs, and that these simple

Bengali words would come much more easily to Bengali children than Hindi speech. Besides this, the rhythm of this folk music defied all accompaniment by *tabla.* It danced itself into our very pulses. The experiment thus made showed that just as a child learns his first enjoyment of literature from his mother's nursery rhymes, he learns his first enjoyment of music also from the same source.

The harmonium, that bane of Indian music, was not then in vogue. I practised my songs with my *tamburā* resting on my shoulder, I did not subject myself to the slavery of the keyboard.

It was no one's fault but my own, that nothing could keep me for many days together in the beaten track of learning. I strayed at will, filling my wallet with whatever gleanings of knowledge I chanced upon. If I had been disposed to give my mind to my studies, the musicians of these days would have had no cause to slight my work. For I had plenty of opportunity. As long as my brother was in charge of my education, I repeated Brahmo songs with Vishnu in an absentminded fashion. When I felt so inclined I would sometimes hang about the doorway while *Shejadādā* was practising, and pick up the song that was going on. Once he was singing to the *Behāg* air, "O thou of slow and stately tread". Unobserved I listened and fixed the tune in my mind, and astounded my mother–an easy task–by singing it to her that evening. Our family friend Srikantha Babu was absorbed in music day and night. He would sit on the verandah, rubbing *chāmeli* oil on his body before his bath, his hookāh in his hand, and the fragrance of amber-scented tobacco rising into the air. He was always humming tunes, which attracted us boys around him. He never *taught* us songs, he simply sang them to us, and we picked them up almost without knowing it. When he could no longer restrain his enthusiasm, he would stand up and dance, accompanying himself on the *sitār.* His big expressive eyes shone with enjoyment, he burst into the song, *Mai chhōrō brajaki bāsari,* and would not rest content till I joined in, too.

In matters of hospitality, people kept open house in those days. There was no need for a man to be intimately known before he was received. There was a bed to be had at any time, and a plate of rice at the regular meal times for any who chanced to come. One day, for example, one such stranger guest, who carried his *tamburā* wrapped in a quilt on his shoulder, opened his bundle, sat down, and stretched his legs at ease on one side of our reception room, and Kanai the hookāh-tender offered him the customary courtesy of the hookāh.

Pān, like tobacco, played a great part in the reception of guests. In those days the morning occupation of the women in the inner apartments consisted in preparing piles of *pān* for the use of those who visited the outer reception room. Deftly they placed the lime on the leaf, smeared *catechu* on it with a small stick, and putting in the appropriate amount of spice folded and secured it with a clove. This prepared *pān* was then piled into a brass container, and a moist piece of cloth, stained with catechu, acted as cover. Meanwhile, in the room under the staircase outside, the stir and bustle of preparing tobacco would be going on. In a big earthenware tub were balls of charcoal covered with ash, the pipes of the hookāhs hung down like snakes of *Nāgaloka*, with the scent of rosewater in their veins. This amber scent of tobacco was the first welcome extended by the household to those who climbed the steps to visit the house. Such was the invariable custom then prescribed for the fitting reception of guests. That overflowing bowl of *pān* has long since been discarded, and the caste of hookāh-tenders have thrown off their liveries and taken to the sweetmeat shops, where they knead up three-day-old *sandesh* and re-fashion it for sale.

That unknown musician stayed for a few days, just as he chose. No one asked him any questions. At dawn I used to drag him from his mosquito curtains and make him sing to me. (Those who have no fancy for regular study revel in study that is irregular). The morning melody of *Bansi hāmāri re* ... would rise on the air.

After this, when I was a little older, a very great musician called Jadu Bhatta came and stayed in the house. He made one big mistake in being determined to teach me music, and consequently no teaching took place. Nevertheless, I did casually pick up from him a certain amount of stolen knowledge. I was very fond of the song *Ruma jhuma barakhē āju bādara¯ā* ... which was set to a *Kāfi* tune, and which remains to this day in my store of rainy season songs. But unfortunately just at this time another guest arrived without warning, who had a name as a tiger-killer. A Bengali tiger-killer was a real marvel in those days, and it followed that I remained captivated in his room for the greater part of the time. I realise clearly now what I never dreamed of then, that the tiger whose fell clutches he so thrillingly described could never have bitten him at all; perhaps, he got the idea from the snarling jaws of the stuffed Museum tigers. But in those days I busied myself eagerly in the liberal provision of *pān* and tobacco for this hero, while the distant strains of *kānārā* music fell faintly on my indifferent ears.

So much for music. In other studies the foundation provided by *Shejadādā* was equally generously laid. It was the fault of my own nature that no great matter came of it. It was with people like me in view that Ramprosad Sen wrote, "O Mind, you do not understand the art of cultivation." With me, the work of cultivation never took place. But let me tell you of a few fields where the ploughing at least was done.

I got up while it was still dark and practised wrestling—on cold days I shivered and trembled with cold. In the city was a celebrated one-eyed wrestler, who gave me practice. On the north side of the outer room was an open space known as the "granary". The name clearly had survived from a time when the city had not yet completely crushed out all rural life, and a few open spaces still remained. When the life of the city was still young our granary had been filled with the whole year's store of grain, and the *ryots* who held their land on lease from us brought to it their appointed portion. It was here that the lean-to shed for wrestling was built against the compound wall. The ground had been prepared by digging and loosening the earth to a depth of about a cubit and pouring over it a maund of mustard oil. It was mere child's play for the wrestler to try a fall with me there, but I would manage to get well smeared with dust by the end of the lesson, when I put on my shirt and went indoors.

Mother did not like to see me come in every morning so covered with dust–she feared that the colour of her son's skin would be darkened and spoiled. As a result, she occupied herself on holidays in scrubbing me. (Fashionable housewives of today buy their toilet preparations in boxes from western shops; but then they used to make their unguent with their own hands. It contained almond paste, thickened cream, the rind of oranges and many other things which I forget. If only I had learnt and remembered the receipt, I might have set up a shop and sold it as "Begum Bilash" unguent, and made at least as much money as the *sandesh-wāllāhs*.) On Sunday mornings there was a great rubbing and scrubbing on the verandah, and I would begin to grow restless to get away. Incidentally, a story used to go about among our school fellows that in our house babies were bathed in wine as soon as they were born, and that was the reason for our fair European complexions.

When I came in from the wrestling ground I saw a Medical College student waiting to teach me the lore of bones. A whole skeleton hung on the wall. It used to hang at night on the wall of our bedroom, and the bones swayed in the wind and rattled together. But the fear I might otherwise have felt had been overcome by constantly handling it, and by learning by heart the long, difficult names of the bones.

The clock in the porch struck seven. Master Nilkamal was a stickler for punctuality, there was no chance of a moment's variation. He had a thin, shrunken body, but his health was as good as his pupil's, and never once, unluckily for us, was he afflicted even by a headache. Taking my book and slate I sat down before the table, and he began to write figures on the blackboard in chalk. Everything was in Bengali, arithmetic, algebra and geometry. In literature I jumped at one bound from *Sitār Banabās*[2] to *Meghnādbadh Kābya*[3]. Along with this there was natural science. From time to time Sitanath Datta would come, and we acquired some superficial knowledge of science by experiments with familiar things. Once, Heramba Tattvaratna, the Sanskrit scholar, came; and I began to learn the Mugdhabodh Sanskrit grammar by heart, though without understanding a word of it.

In this way, all through the morning, studies of all kinds were heaped upon me, but as the burden grew greater, my mind contrived to get rid of fragments of it; making a hole in the enveloping net, my parrot-learning slipped through its meshes and escaped—and the opinion that Master Nilkamal expressed of his pupil's intelligence was not of the kind to be made public.

In another part of the verandah is the old tailor, his thick-lensed spectacles on his nose, sitting bent over his sewing, and ever and anon, at the prescribed hours, going through the ritual of his Namāz[4]. I watch him and think what a lucky fellow Niāmat is. Then, with my head in a whirl from doing sums, I shade my eyes with my slate, and looking down see in front of the entrance porch Chandrabhān the *durwan* combing his long beard with a wooden comb, dividing it in two and looping it round each ear. The assistant *durwan*, a slender boy, is sitting nearby, a bracelet on his arm, and cutting tobacco. Over there the horse has already finished his morning allowance of gram, and the crows are hopping round pecking at the

---

2. "Sita in the Forest," by Iswarchandra Vidyasagar.
3. An Epic on the death of MeghnŒd (son of RŒvana in *RŒmŒyana*) by Michael Madhusudan Dutta.
4. Muslim devotional exercises.

scattered grains. Our dog Johnny's sense of duty is aroused and he drives them away barking.

I had planted a custard-apple seed in the dust which continual sweeping had collected in one corner of the verandah. All agog with excitement, I watched for the sprouting of the new leaves. As soon as Master Nilkamal had gone, I had to run and examine it, and water it. In the end my hopes went unfulfilled—the same broom that had gathered the dust together dispersed it again to the four winds.

Now ,the sun climbs higher, and the slanting shadows cover only half the courtyard. The clock strikes nine. Govinda, short and dark, with a dirty yellow towel slung over his shoulder, takes me off to bathe me. Promptly at half past nine comes our monotonous, unvarying meal—the daily ration of rice, *dāl* and fish curry—it was not much to my taste.

The clock strikes ten. From the main street is heard the hawker's cry of "Green Mangoes"—what wistful dreams it awakens! From further and further away resounds the clanging of the receding brass-peddler, striking his wares till they ring again. The lady of the neighbouring house in the lane is drying her hair on the roof, and her two little girls are playing with shells. They have plenty of leisure, for in those days girls were not obliged to go to school, and I used to think how fine it would have been to be born a girl. But as it is, the old horse draws me in the rickety carriage to my Andamans, in which from ten to four I am doomed to exile.

At half past four, I return from school. The gymnastic master has come, and for about an hour I exercise my body on the parallel bars. He has no sooner gone than the drawing master arrives.

Gradually, the rusty light of day fades away. The many blurred noises of the evening are heard as a dreamy hum resounding over the demon city of brick and mortar. In the study room an oil lamp is burning. Master Aghor has come and the English lesson begins. The black-covered reader is lying in wait for me on the table. The cover is loose; the pages are stained and a little torn; I have tried my hand at writing my name in English in it, in the wrong places, and all in capital letters. As I read I nod, then jerk myself awake again with a start, but miss far more than I read. When finally I tumble into bed I have at last a little time to call my own. And, there I listen to endless stories of the king's son travelling over an endless, trackless plain.

VIII

When I see the roofs of modern houses, uninhabited by either men or ghosts, I realise vividly the change that has taken place between those times and these. I have already mentioned how the *brahma-daitya*[1] of the *bādām* tree has fled, unable to endure the modern atmosphere of excessive learning. On the cornice where rumour had it that he had rested his foot, the crows snatch and squabble over our discarded mango stones. And, men too restrict themselves nowadays to the confined, boxed-in rooms of the lower storeys, and pass their time within four walls.

My mind goes back to the parapet-surrounded roof of the inner apartments. It is evening, and Mother has spread her mat and seated herself, with her friends gossiping round her. Their talk has no need of authentic information, it is only a means of passing the time. There was then no regular supply of valuable and varied ingredients to fill the day, which was not, as now, a closely woven mesh, but like a net of loose texture, full of holes. And therefore, stories and rumours, laughter and jokes, all in the lightest vein, filled both the social gatherings of the men and the women's assemblies. Among Mother's friends the first in importance was Braja Acharji's sister, who was called "Acharjini". She was the daily purveyor of news to the company. Almost every day she picked up, (or made up!) and brought with her, every item of fantastic, ominous news in the country. By this means expenditure on all ceremonies calculated to

1. A class of formidable ghosts believed to be the spirits of departed Brahmins.

avert impending calamity or the evil eye, was greatly increased.

Into this assembly I imported from time to time my recently acquired book-learning. I informed them that the sun is nine crore of miles distant from the earth. From the second part of my *Ṛju-Pāth* I recited a portion of Valmiki's *Rāmāyana* in the original, complete with Sanskrit terminations. Mother was no judge of the accuracy of her son's pronunciation, but the range of his learning filled her with awe, and seemed to her far to outrun the nine-crore miles journey of light. Who would have thought that any except Naradmuni himself could recite all these *slōkas?*

This inner apartment roof was entirely the women's domain, and had a close connection with the store room. The sun's rays fell full upon it, so it was used for preparing lemons for pickle. The women used to sit there with brass vessels full of *kalāi* paste, and while their hair was drying they made pulse-balls with their deft, quick fingers. The maid-servants who had washed the soiled linen came here to spread it in the sun, for the *dhoby* had little work in those days. Green mangoes were cut in slices and dried into *āmsi.* The mango juice was poured layer after layer into black stone moulds of all sizes and all patterns[2]. A pickle of young jack-fruit stood there to season in sun-warmed mustard oil. Catechu, scented with the fragrant screw-pine, would be prepared with great care.

I had a special reason for remembering this item. When my school-master informed me that he had heard the fame of my family's screw-pine catechu, it was not difficult to understand his meaning. What he had heard of, he wished to become acquainted with. So, to preserve the good name of my family, I occasionally climbed secretly to the roof containing the screw-pine catechu, and–what shall I say? "Appropriated" a piece or two sounds better than "stole". For, even kings and emperors may make "appropriations" when

2. This preparation is called *āmsatta.*

need arises, or indeed even if it does not, but vulgar "stealing" is punished by prison or impaling.

In the pleasant sunlight of the cold weather it was the family tradition for the women to sit on the roof gossiping, driving off crows and passing the time of day. I was the only younger brother-in-law in the house, the guardian of my sister-in-law's "*āmsatta*", and her friend and ally in many other trival pursuits. I used to read to them from *Bangādhipa Parājaya*[3]. From time to time the duty of cutting up betel-nut would devolve on me. I could cut betel very finely. My sister-in-law would never admit that I had any other good quality, so much so that she even made me angry with God for giving me such a faulty appearance. But she found no difficulty in speaking in exaggerated fashion of my skill in cutting betel. Therefore, the work of betel-cutting used to go on at a fine pace. But for a long time now, for want of anyone to encourage me, the hand that was so killed in fine betel-cutting has perforce busied itself in other fine work.

Around all this women's work spread on the roof there lingered the aroma of village life. These occupations belonged to the days when there was a pounding-room in the house, when confectionery balls were made, when the maid-servants sat in the evening rolling on their thighs the cotton wicks for the oil lamps, when invitations came from neighbours' houses to the ceremonies of the eighth day after birth. Modern children do not hear fairy stories from their mothers' lips, they read them for themselves in printed books. Pickles and chutney are bought from the Newmarket by the bottleful, each bottle corked and sealed with wax.

Another relic of a bygone village life was the *chandimandap*, the outer verandah where the school was held. Not only the boys of the house, but those of the neighbourhood, also, made there their first

3. "The Defeat of the King of Bengal."

attempt to search letters on palm-leaves. I suppose that I too must have traced out my first laborious letters on that verandah, but I have no clear memory of the child I then was, who seems as far removed as the farthest planet of the solar system, and I possess no telescope which can bring him into view.

The first thing I remember about reading after this is the terrible story of Ṣaṇḍāmārka Muni's school, and of the *avatār* Narasiṃha tearing the bowels of Hiraṇyakaśipu; I think also that there was a lead-plate engraving of it in the same book–and I remember also reading a few *slōkas* of Chānakya.

My chief holiday resort was the unfenced roof of the outer apartments. From my earliest childhood till I was grown up, many varied days were spent on that roof in many moods and thoughts. When my father was at home his room was on the second floor. How often I watched him at a distance, from my hiding place at the head of the staircase. The sun had not yet risen, and he sat on the roof silent as an image of white stone, his hands folded in his lap. From time to time he would leave home for long periods in the mountains, and then the journey to the roof held for me the joy of a voyage through the seven seas. Sitting on the familiar first floor verandah I had daily watched through the railings the people going about the street. But to climb to that roof was to be raised beyond the swarming habitations of men. When I went on to the roof my mind strode proudly over prostrate Calcutta to where the last blue of the sky mingled with the last green of the earth; my eye fell on the roofs of countless houses, of all shapes and sizes, high and low, with the shaggy tops of trees between.

I would go up secretly to this roof, usually at midday. The mid-day hours have always held a fascination for me. They are like the night of the daytime, the time when the *Sannyāsi* spirit in every boy makes him long to quit his familiar surroundings. I put my hand through the shutter and drew the bolt of the door. Right opposite the door was a sofa, and I sat there in perfect bliss of solitude. The servants who acted as my warders had eaten their fill and become drowsy, and yawning and stretching had betaken themselves to sleep on their mats. The afternoon sunlight deepened into gold, and the kite rose screaming into the sky. The bangle-seller went crying his wares down the opposite lane. His sudden cry would penetrate to where the housewife lay with her loosened hair falling over her pillow, a maidservant would bring him in, and the old bangle-seller dexterously kneaded the tender fingers as he fitted on the glass bangles that took her fancy. The hushed pause of that old-world mid-day is now no more, and the hawkers of the silent time are heard no longer. The girl who in those days had married status, nowadays has still not attained it, she is learning her lessons in the second class. Perhaps, the bangle-seller runs, pulling a rickshaw, down that very lane.

The roof was like what I imagined the deserts of my books to be, a sheer expanse of quivering haze. A hot wind ran panting across it, whirling up the dust, the blue of the sky paled above it. Moreover, in this roof desert there appeared an oasis. Nowadays, the pipe water does not reach the upper floors, but then it ran even up to the second floor rooms. Like some young Livingstone of Bengal, alone and unaided, I secretly sought and found a new Niagara, the private bathroom. I would turn on the tap, and the water would run all over my body. I then took a sheet from the bed and dried myself, looking the picture of innocence.

Gradually, the holiday drew towards its close, and four struck on the gateway clock. The face of the sky on Sunday evenings was always very ill-favoured. There fell across it the shadow of the coming Monday's gaping jaws, already swallowing it in dark eclipse. Below at last a search had been instituted for the boy who had given his guards the slip, for now it was tiffin time. This part of the day was a red-letter time for Brajeswar. He was in charge of buying the tiffin.

In those days the shop-keepers did not make thirty or forty per cent profit on the price of *ghee*, and in odour and flavour the tiffin was still unpoisoned. When we were lucky enough to get them, we lost no time in eating up our *kochuri*, *singārā*, or even *ālur dom*. But when the time came round and Brajeswar, with his neck still further twisted, called to us, "Look *babu*, what I have brought you today", what was usually to be found in his cone of paper was merely a handful of fried groundnuts. It was not that I did not like this, but its attractiveness lay in its price. I never made the least objection, not even on the days when only sesamum *gojā* came out of the palm-leaf wrapper.

The light of day begins to grow murky. Once more with a gloomy spirit, I make the round of the roof. I gaze down at the scene below, where a procession of geese has climbed out of the tank. People have begun to come and go again on the steps of the *ghāt*, the shadow of the banyan tree lengthens across half the tank, the driver of a carriage and pair is yelling at the pedestrians in the street.

IX

In this way the days passed monotonously on. School grabbed the best part of the day, and only fragments of time in the morning and evening slipped through its clutching fingers. As soon as I entered the classroom, the benches and tables forced themselves rudely on my attention, elbowing and jostling their way into my mind. They were always the same—stiff, cramping, and dead. In the evening I went home, and the oil lamp in our study-room, like a stern signal, summoned me to the preparation of the next day's lessons. There is a kind of grass-hopper which takes the colour of the withered leaves among which it lurks unobserved. In like manner my spirit also shrank and faded among those faded, drab-coloured days.

Now and again, there came to our courtyard a man with a dancing bear, or a snake charmer playing with his snakes. Now and again, the visit of a juggler provided some little novelty. Today, the drums of the juggler and snake-charmer no longer beat in our Chitpore Road. From afar they have salaamed to the cinema, and fled before it from the city. Games were few and of very ordinary kinds. We had marbles, we had what is called "bat-ball," a very poor distant relation of cricket, and there were also top-spinning and kite-flying. All the games of the city children were of this same lazy kind. Football, with all its running and jumping about on a big field, was still in its overseas home. And so, I was fenced in by the deadly sameness of the days, as though by an imprisoning hedge of lifeless, withered twigs.

In the midst of this monotony there played one day the flutes of festivity. A new bride came to the house, slender gold bracelets on her delicate brown hands. In the twinkling of an eye the cramping fence was broken, and a new being came into view from the magic land beyond the bounds of the familiar. I circled around her at a safe distance, but I did not dare to go near. She was enthroned at the centre of affection, and I was only a neglected, insignificant child.

The house was then divided into two suites of rooms. The men lived in the outer, and the women in the inner apartments. The ways of the *nabobs* obtained there still. I remember how my elder sister was walking on the roof with the new bride at her side, and they were exchanging intimacies freely. As soon as I tried to go near, however, I brought reprimand on my head, for these quarters were outside the boundaries laid down for boys. I saw myself obliged to go back crest-fallen to my shabby retreat of former days.

The monsoon rain, rushing down suddenly from the distant mountains, undermines the ancient banks in a moment, and that is what happened now. The new mistress brought a new régime into the house. The quarters of the bride were in the room adjoining the roof of the inner suite. That roof was under her complete control. It was there that the leaf-plates were spread for the dolls' weddings. On such feast days, boy as I was, I became the guest of honour. My new sister-in-law could cook well, and enjoyed feeding people, and I was always ready to satisfy this craving for playing the hostess. As soon as I returned from school some delicacy made with her own hands stood ready for me. One day, she gave me shrimp curry with yesterday's soaked rice, and a dash of chillies for flavouring, and I felt that I had nothing left to wish for. Sometimes, when she went to stay with relatives and I did not see her slippers outside the door of her room, I would go in a temper and steal some valuable object from her room, and lay the foundation of a quarrel. When she returned and missed it, I had only to make such a remark as "Do you expect *me* to keep an eye on your room when you go away? Am I a watchman?" She would pretend to be angry and say, "You have no need to keep an eye on the room. Watch your own hands." Modern women will smile at the naïveté of their predecessors who knew how to entertain only their own brothers-in-law, and I daresay they are right. People today are much more grown-up in every way than they were then. Then, we were all children alike, both young and old.

X

And so began a new chapter of my lonely Bedouin life on the roof, and human company and friendship entered it. Across the roof kingdom a new wind blew, and a new season began there. My brother Jyotidada played a large part in this change. At that time my father finally left our home at Jorasanko. Jyotidada settled himself into that outside second-floor room, and I claimed a little corner of it for my own.

No *purdah* was observed in my sister-in-law's apartments. That will strike no one as strange today, but it then sounded an unimaginable depth of novelty. A long time even before that, when I was a baby, my second brother had returned from England to enter the Civil Service. When he went to Bombay to take up his first post he astonished the neighbourhood by taking off his wife with him before their very eyes. And, as if it was not enough to take her away to a distant province, instead of leaving her in the family home, he made no provision for proper privacy on the journey. That was a terrible breach of propriety. Even the relatives felt as if the sky had fallen on their heads.

A style of dress suitable for going out was still not in vogue among women. It was this sister-in-law who first introduced the manner of wearing the sari and blouse which is now customary. Little girls had not then begun to wear frocks or let their hair hang in plaits—at least not in our family. The little ones used to wear the tight Rajput pyjamas instead of the traditional sari. When the Bethune School was first opened, my eldest sister was quite young.

She was one of the pioneers who made the road to education easy for girls. She was very fair, uniquely so for this country. I have heard that once when she was going to school in her palanquin the police detained her, thinking her in her Rajput dress to be an English girl who had been kidnapped.

I said before that in those days there was no bridge of intimacy between adults and children. Into the tangle of these old customs Jyotidada brought a vigorously original mind. I was twelve years younger than he, and that I should come to his notice in spite of such a difference in age is in itself surprising. What was more surprising is that in my talks with him he never called me impudent or snubbed me. Thanks to this, I never lacked courage to think for myself. Today, I live with children, I try all kind of subjects of conversation, but I find them dumb. They hesitate to ask questions. They seem to me to belong to those old times when the grown-ups talked and the children remained silent. The self-confidence that doubts and questions is the mark of the children of the new age; those of the former age are known by a meek and docile acceptance of what they are told.

A piano appeared in the terrace room. There came also modern varnished furniture from Bowbazar. My breast swelled with pride, as the cheap grandeur of modern times was displayed before eyes inured to poverty. At this time the fountain of my song was unloosed. Jyotidada's hands would stray about the piano as he composed and rattled off tunes in various new styles, and he would keep me by his side as he did so. It was my work to fix the tunes which he composed so rapidly by setting words to them then and there.

At the end of the day a mat and pillow were spread on the terrace. Nearby was a thick garland of *bel* flowers on a silver plate, in a wet handkerchief, a glass of iced water on a saucer, and some *chhānchi pān* in a bowl. My sister-in-law would bathe, dress her hair and come and sit with us. Jyotidada would come out with a silk *chaddar* thrown over his shoulders, and draw the bow across his violin, and I would sing in my clear treble voice. For, providence had not yet taken away the gift of voice it had given me, and under the sunset sky my song rang out across the house-tops. The south wind came in great gusts from the distant sea, the sky filled with stars.

My sister-in-law turned the whole roof into a garden. She arranged rows of tall palms in barrels and beside and around them *chāmeli, gandharāj, rajanigandhā, karabi* and *dolan-champā*. She considered not at all the possible damage to the roof—we were all alike unpractical visionaries.

Akshay Chaudhuri used to come almost everyday. He himself knew that he had no voice, other people knew it even better. In spite of that nothing could stop the flow of his song. His special favourite was the *Behāg* mode. He sang with his eyes shut, so he did not see the expression on the faces of his hearers. As soon as anything capable of making a noise came to hand, he took it and turned it into a drum, beating it in happy absorption, biting his lips with his teeth in his earnestness. Even a book with a stiff binding would do very well. He was by nature a dreamy kind of man, one could see no difference between his working days and his holidays.

The evening party broke up, but I was a boy of nocturnal habits. All went to lie down, I alone would wander about all night with the *Brahma-daitya*. The whole district was steeped in silence. On moonlight nights the shadows of the lines of palm-trees on the terrace lay in dream-patterns on the floor. Beyond the terrace the top of the *sishu* tree swayed and tossed in the breeze, and its leaves gleamed as they caught the light. But for some reason, what caught my eye more than anything was a squat room with a sloping roof built over the staircase of the sleeping house on the opposite side of the lane. It stood like a finger pointing for ever towards I knew not what.

It may have been one or two in the morning, when in the main street in front a wailing chant arose—*Bolō-Hari Hari-bōl.*[1]

1. Funeral chant of the Hindus.

XI

It was the fashion then in every house to keep caged birds. I hated this, and the worst thing of all to me was the call of a *koel* imprisoned in a cage in some house in the neighbourhood. *Bouthākrun*[1] had acquired a Chinese *shyama.* From under its covering of cloth its sweet whistling rose continuously, a fountain of song. Besides this, there were other birds of all kinds, and their cages hung in the west verandah. Every morning a bird-seed and insect hawker provided the birds' food. Grass-hoppers came from his basket, and gram-flour for the grain-eating birds.

Jyotidada gave me proper answers in my difficulties, but as much could not be expected from the women. Once, *Bouthākrun* took a fancy for keeping pet squirrels in cages. I said it wasn't right, and she told me not to set myself up to be her teacher. That could hardly be called a reasoned reply, and consequently, instead of wasting time in bickering, I privately set two of the little creatures free. After that too, I had to listen to a certain amount of scolding, but I made no retort.

There was a permanent quarrel between us which was never made up, which was as follows.

There was a smart fellow called Umesh. He used to go the rounds of the English tailoring shops and buy up for an old song all their scraps, remnants and strips of many coloured silk, and make up women's garments from them with the addition of a bit

---

1. Sister-in-law.

of net and cheap lace. He would open his paper parcel and spread them carefully out before the eyes of the women, extolling them as "the very latest fashion". The women could not resist the attraction of such a *mantra,* but I disliked it all intensely. Again and again, unable to contain myself, I made known my objections, but all the answer I got was "Don't be cheeky". I used to tell *Bouthākrun* that the old-fashioned black-bordered white sarees, and the Dacca ones, were far better and more tasteful than these. I sometimes wonder, do modern brothers-in-law never open their mouths when they see their *Boudidis* robed in these modern georgette sarees, with their faces painted like dolls? Even *Bouthākrun* decked out in Umesh's handiwork was not as bad as they are. Ladies then were at least not so guilty of forgery in dress or complexion.

I was, however, always beaten by *Bouthākrun* in argument, because she would never deign to give a logical answer; and I was beaten too in chess, in which she was an expert.

As I have referred to Jyotidada I ought to give a little more information about him, to make him better known. To do that I must go back to rather earlier days.

He had to go very often to Shelidah to see after the business of the zemindari. Once, when he was travelling for this purpose he took me also with him. This was quite contrary to custom in those days, in fact it was what people would have called "altogether *too* much". He certainly considered that this travelling away from home was a kind of peripatetic schooling. He realised that my nature was attuned to ramblings in the open air, that in such surroundings it nourished itself spontaneously. A little later, when I was more mature, it was in Shelidah that my nature developed.

The old indigo factory was still standing, with the river Padma in the distance. The zemindari office was on the ground floor, and our living quarters on the upper floor. In front of them was a very large terrace. Beyond were tall casuarina trees, which had grown in stature with the growing prosperity of the indigo-trading *sahebs*. Today, the blustering shouts of the sahebs are completely silent. Where is now the indigo factory's steward, that "messenger of death"? Where the troop of bailiffs, loins girded up and *lāthis* on shoulder? Where is the dining hall with its long tables, where the sahebs rode back from their business in the town and turned night into day? The feasting reached its height, the dancing couples whirled round the room, the blood coursed madly through the veins in the swelling intoxication of champagne–and the authorities never heard the appealing cries of the wretched *ryots*, whose weary journey took them only to the District Jail. All traces of those days have vanished, save one record alone–the two graves of two of the sahebs. The high casuarina trees bend and sway in the wind, and sometimes at midnight the grandsons and grand-daughters of the former *ryots* see the ghosts of the sahebs wandering in the deserted waste of garden.

Here, I revelled in my solitude. I had a little corner room, and my days of ample leisure were spacious as the wide-spreading terrace. It was the leisure of a strange and unknown region, unfathomable as the dark waters of some ancient tank. The *bou-kathā-kao*[2] calls incessantly, my fancy unweariedly takes wing. Meantime, my note-book is gradually filled with verses. They were like the blossoms of the mango-tree's first flowering in the month of *Māgh*, destined like them to wither forgotten.

In those days if a young boy, or still more a young girl, laboriously counted out the fourteen syllables and wrote two lines of verse, the wise critics of the country used to hail it as a unique and unparalleled achievement.

I saw in the papers and magazines the names of these girl-poets, and their verses also were published. Nowadays, these carefully

2. Also called "makwa-pāko", an Indian species of cuckoo. Both names are imitations of the call.

constructed metres and crude rhyming platitudes have vanished along with the names of their authors, and the names of countless modern girls have appeared in their stead.

Boys are less bold and far more self-conscious than girls. I do not remember any young boy-poet writing verse in those days, except myself. My sister's son, who was older than I, explained to me one day that if one poured words into a fourteen-syllable mould, they would condense into verse. I soon tried this magic formula for myself. The lotus of poetry blossomed in no time in this fourteen-syllabled form and even the bees found a foothold on it. The gulf between me and the poets was bridged, and from that time on I have struggled to overtake them.

I remember how, when I was in the lowest class of the *chhātra britti*[3] our superintendent Govinda Babu heard a rumour that I wrote poetry. He thereupon ordered me to write, thinking that it would redound to the credit of the Normal School. There was nothing for it but to write, to read my work before my classmates, and to hear the verdict—"this verse is assuredly stolen goods". The cynics of that day did not know that when I increased in worldly wisdom I should grow shrewd in stealing, not words but thoughts. Yet, it is these stolen goods which are valuable.

I remember once composing a poem in the *Payār* and *Tripadi* metres, in which I lamented that as one swims to pluck the lotus it floats further and further away on the waves raised by one's own arms, and remains always out of reach. Akshay Babu took me round to the houses of his relatives and made me recite it to them. "The boy has certainly a gift for writing", they said.

Bouthākrun's attitude was just the opposite. She would never admit that I should ever make a success of writing. She would say mockingly that I should never be able to write like Bihari

3. This corresponds roughly to the modern transition from "primary" to "secondary" education.

Chakravarti. I used to think despondently that even if I were placed in a far lower class than he, she would then be prevented from so disregarding her little poet – brother-in-law's disapprobation of women's fashions.

Jyotidada was very fond of riding. He actually took even *Bouthākrun* riding along Chitpore Road to the Eden Gardens. In Shelidah he gave me a pony, a beast that was no mean runner. He sent me to give the pony a run on the open *rath-talā* field.[4] I did as I was bidden, in continual imminent danger of a fall on that uneven ground. That I did not fall was solely because he was so determined that I should *not* do so. Shortly afterwards Jyotidada sent me out riding on the roads of Calcutta also. Not on the pony, but on a high-spirited thoroughbred. One day, it galloped straight in through the porch, with me on its back, to the courtyard where it was accustomed to be fed. From that day on, I had nothing more to do with it.

I have referred elsewhere to the fact that Jyotidada was a practised shot. He was always eager for a tiger-hunt. One day, the *shikāri* Visvanath brought news that a tiger was living in the Shelidah jungle, and Jyotidada at once furbished up his gun and prepared for sport. Surprising to say, he took me with him. It never seemed to occur to him that there could be any danger.

Visvanath was indeed, an expert *shikāri*. He knew that there was nothing manly about hunting from a *māchān*. He would call the tiger out and shoot face-to-face, and he never missed his aim.

The jungle was dense, and in its lights and shadows the tiger refused to show himself. A rough kind of ladder was made by cutting footholds in a stout bamboo, and Jyotidada climbed up with his gun ready to hand. As for me, I was not even wearing slippers, I had not even that poor instrument with which to beat

---

4. The field reserved in a Bengali village for the celebration of the car-festival.

and humiliate the tiger. Visvanath signed to us to be on the alert, but for some time Jyotidada could not even see the tiger. After long straining of his bespectacled eyes he at last caught a glimpse of one of its markings in the thicket. He fired. By a lucky chance the shot pierced the animal's backbone, and it was unable to rise. It roared furiously, biting at all the sticks and twigs within reach, and lashing its tail. Thinking it over, I know that it is not in the nature of tigers to wait so long and patiently to be killed. I wonder if some-one had had the forethought to mix a little opium with its feed on the previous night? Otherwise, why such sound sleep?

There was another occasion when a tiger came to the jungles of Shelidah. My brother and I set out on elephants to look for him. My elephant lurched majestically on, uprooting cane from the sugar cane fields and munching as he went, so that it was like riding on an earthquake. The jungle lay ahead of us. He crushed the trees with his knees, pulled them up with his trunk and cast them to the ground. I had previously heard tales of terrible possibilities from Visvanath's brother Chamru, how sometimes the tiger leaps on to the elephant's back and clings there, digging in his claws. Then, the elephant trumpeting with pain, rushes madly through the forest, and whoever is on his back is dashed against the trees till arms, legs and head are crushed out of all recognition. That day, as I sat my elephant, the image of myself thus being pounded to a jelly filled my imagination from first to last. For very shame I concealed my fear, and glanced from side-to-side in nonchalant fashion, as though to say, "Let me but catch a glimpse of the tiger, and then!..." The elephant entered the densest part of the jungle, and coming to a certain place, suddenly stood stock-still. The māhout made no attempt to urge it forward. He had clearly more respect for the tiger's powers as a *shikāri* than for my brother's. His great anxiety was undoubtedly that Jyotidada should so wound the tiger as to drive it to desperation. Suddenly, the tiger leaped from the jungle, swift as the thunder-charged storm from the cloud. We are accustomed to the sight of a cat, dog, or jackal, but here were shoulders of terrific bulk and power, yet no sense of heaviness in that perfectly proportioned strength. It crossed the open fields at a canter in the full blaze of the mid-day sun. What loveliness, ease and speed of motion! The land was empty of crops; here indeed, was a setting in which to feast one's eyes on the running tiger, this wide stretch of golden stubble drenched in the noonday sunlight.

There is one more story that may prove amusing. In Shelidah the gardener used to pluck flowers and arrange them in the vases. I took a fancy to write poetry with a pen dipped in the coloured essences of flowers. But the moisture that I could obtain by squeezing was not sufficient to wet the tip of my pen. I decided that it must be done by machinery. It would do, I thought, if I had a cup-shaped wooden sieve and a pestle revolving in it. It could be turned by an arrangement of ropes and pulleys. I made known my wants to Jyotidada. It may be that he smiled to himself, but he gave no outward sign. He issued instructions, and the carpenter brought wood. The machine was ready. I filled the wooden cup with flowers, but turn the ropes of the pestle as I would the flowers, merely turned to mud and not a drop of essence ran out. Jyotidada saw that the essence of flowers was incompatible with the grinding of machinery, yet he never laughed at me.

This was the only occasion in my life on which I tried my hand at engineering. It is said in the *sāstras* that there is a god who compasses the humiliation of those who ignore their own limitations. That god cast a mocking glance that day upon my engineering, and from that time I have not so much as laid hands on any kind of instrument, not even on a *sitār* or an *esrāj*.

I described in my *Reminiscences* how Jyotidada went bankrupt in his attempt to run a *swadeshi* steamer company on the rivers of Bengal in competition with the Flotilla Company. *Bouthākrun's* death had taken place before then. Jyotidada gave up his rooms on the third storey and finally built himself a house on a hill at Ranchi.

XII

A new chapter in the life of the third-storey room now opened, as I took up my abode there. Up to that time it had been merely one of my gypsy haunts, like the palanquin and the granary, and I roamed from one to another. But when *Bouthākrun* came a garden appeared on the roof, and in the room a piano was established. Its flow of new tunes symbolised the changed tenor of my life.

Jyotidada used to arrange to have his coffee in the mornings in the shade of the staircase room on the eastern side of the terrace. At such times, he would read to us the first draft of some new play of his. From time to time, I also would be called upon to add a few lines with my unpractised hand. The sun's rays gradually invaded the shade, the crows cried hoarsely to each other as they sat on the roof keeping an eye upon the bread-crumbs. By ten o'clock the patch of shade had dwindled away and the terrace grew hot.

At mid-day Jyotidada used to go down to the office on the ground floor. *Bouthākrun* peeled and cut fruit and arranged it carefully on a silver plate, along with a few sweetmeats made with her own hands, and strewed a few rose petals over it. In a tumbler was coconut milk or fruit-juice or *tāl shāns* (fresh palmyra kernels), cooled in ice. Then, she covered it with a silk kerchief embroidered with flowers, put it on a Moradabad tray, and despatched it to the office at tiffin time, about one or two o'clock.

Just then *Bangadarśan*[1] was at the height of its fame, and

1. A famous Bengali magazine edited by the well-known Bengali novelist, Bankim Chandra Chatterji.

Suryamukhi and *Kundanandini*[2] were familiar figures in every house. The whole country thought of nothing else but what had happened and what was gong to happen to the heroines.

When *Bangadarśan* came there was no mid-day nap for anyone in the neighbourhood. It was my good fortune not to have to snatch for it, for I had the gift of being an acceptable reader. *Bouthākrun* would rather listen to my reading aloud than read for herself. There were no electric fans then, but as I read I shared the benefits of *Bouthākrun's* hand fan.

2. Characters in Bankim Chandra's novel.

XIII

Now and again, Jyotidada used to go for change of air to a garden house on the bank of the Ganges. The Ganges shores had then not yet lost caste at the defiling touch of English commerce. Both shores alike were still the undisturbed haunt of birds, and the mechanised dragons of industry did not darken the light of heaven with the black breath of their upreared snouts.

My earliest memory of our life by the Ganges is of a small two-storey house. The first rains had just fallen. Cloud shadows danced on the ripples of the stream, cloud shadows lay dark upon the jungles of the further shore. I had often composed songs of my own on such days, but that day I did not do so. The lines of Vidyapati came to my mind, *e bharā bādara māha bhādara śūnya mandira mōr.*[1] Moulding them to my own melody and stamping them with my own musical mood, I made them my own. The memory of that monsoon day, jewelled with that music on the Ganges shore, is still preserved in my treasury of rainy season songs. I see in memory the tree-tops struck ever and again by great gusts of wind, till their boughs and branches were tangled together in an ecstasy of play. The boats and dinghies raised their white sails and scudded before the gale, the waves leaped against the *ghāt* with sharp, slapping sounds. *Bouthākrun* came back and I sang my song to her. She listened in silence and said no word of praise. I must then have been sixteen or seventeen years old. We used to have arguments even then

1. Brimmed with rain is the month of Bhadra (August–September), empty my spirit's dwelling stands.

about various matters, but no longer in the old spirit of childish wrangling.

A little while after we removed to Moran's Garden. That was a regular palace. The rooms, of varying heights, had coloured glass in their windows, the floors were of marble, and steps led down from the long verandah to the very edge of the Ganges. Here, a fit of wakefulness by night came upon me, and I used to pace to and fro, as I did later on the banks of the Sabarmati. That garden is no longer in existence, the iron jaws of the Dundee Mills have crushed and swallowed it.

At the mention of Moran's Garden there comes back the memory of our occasional picnics under the *bakul* tree. The food owed its flavour not to spices but to the hands that prepared it. How I remember our sacred-thread ceremony, when we two boys were fed by *Bouthākrun* with the ceremonial rice and fresh *ghee*! For those three days we had our fill of tasty and savoury dishes.

It was a great annoyance to me that it was so difficult for me to fall ill. All the other boys in the house could manage it, and then they would enjoy *Bouthākrun's* personal care. Not only did they enjoy her care, but they took up all her time, and my own share of it was correspondingly diminished.

So came to an end that page of the history of the third storey, and with it *Bouthākrun* also passed away. After that the second floor became my own domain, but it was no longer as in the old days.

I have wandered in my story up to the very gateway of my young manhood. I must return to the territory of my boyhood once more.

Now, I must give some account of my sixteenth year. At its very entrance stands *Bhārati*.[2] Nowadays the whole country seethes with

---

2. Monthly magazine founded by Jyotidada (Jyotirindranath Tagore) and first edited by the Poet's eldest brother Dwijendranath Tagore, referred to here as Ba¶adada. It ran for about half a century.

the excitement of bringing out papers, and I can well understand the strength of that passion when I look back on my own madcap escapades. That a boy like me, with neither learning nor talents, should succeed in establishing himself in that *salon*, or at least in escaping reprimand there, shows what a youthful spirit was abroad everywhere. *Bangadarśan* was then the only magazine in the country controlled by a mature hand. As for ours, it was a medley of the mature and the crude. Baḍadada's contributions were as difficult to understand as they were to write; and side-by-side with them stood a story of mine, the raw verbosity of whose style I was too young to appraise, nor did others apparently possess the critical judgement to do so.

The time has come to say something of Baḍadada. Jyotidada held court in that third-storey room, and Baḍadada in our south verandah. At one time he plunged into the deepest problems of metaphysics, far outside the range of our comprehension. There were few to listen to what he wrote and thought, and he would not lightly let any man go who showed himself willing to be audience. Nor, would the man himself soon relinquish Baḍadada, but what he claimed from him was not alone the privilege of listening to metaphysics. One such man attached himself whose name I do not remember, but everyone called him "The Philosopher". My other brothers made great fun of him, not only about his love for mutton chops, but about his endless stream of varied and urgent necessities. Besides philosophy, Baḍadada then began to take great interest in the construction of mathematical problems. The verandah would be full of papers, covered with figures, flying about in the south wind. Baḍadada could not sing, but he used to play an English flute, not for the sake of the music, but in order to measure mathematically the notes of each scale. After that he occupied himself for a time in writing *Svapna-Prayāna*. To start with, he began to experiment in verse-making, weighing the sound-values of Sanskrit words in the scales of Bengali rhythm, and so creating new forms. Many of these attempts he retained, but many he threw away, and torn pages were scattered everywhere. After that he started to write his book of poems, but he rejected far more than he kept, for he was not easily satisfied with his work. We had not the sense to pick up and keep all these discarded lines. As he wrote he would read his work, and people would gather round him to listen. Our whole household was intoxicated with this wine of poetry. Sometimes, in the midst of his reading he would burst into a great shout of laughter. His laughter was ample and generous as the skies, but woe betide the man who sat within reach when the fit took him; he received slaps on the back to shake his very soul. The south verandah was the living fountain of the life of Jorasanko, but the fountain dried up when Baḍadada went to live at the Santiniketan *asrama.* I remember, however, times spent in the garden opposite that south verandah, when with mind made listless by the touch of the autumn sun I composed and sang a new song: "Today, in the autumn sun, in my dreams of dawn, a nameless yearning fills my soul." I remember also a song made in the quivering heat of one blazing noon: "In this listless abandon of spirit, I know not what games I kept on playing with my own self."

Another striking thing about Baḍadada was his swimming. He would swim backwards and forwards across our tank at least fifty times. When he lived at Panihati Garden he used to swim far out into the Ganges. With his example before us we also learned to swim as boys. We started to learn by ourselves. We would wet our pyjamas and then pull them up tight so as to fill them with air. In the water they swelled out round our waists like balloons, and we could not possibly sink. When I was older and stayed on the riverlands[3] of Shelidah, I once swam across the Padma. This was not as wonderful an achievement as it sounds. The Padma was full of alluvial islands which broke the force of its current, so that the feat was not worthy of any great respect. Still, it was certainly a story with which to impress others, and I have used it so many times. When I went as a boy to Dalhousie, my father never forbade me to wander about by myself. With an alpenstock in my hand I traversed the footpaths, climbing one hill after another. It was most amusing to scare myself with my own make-believe. Once, while going steeply downhill I stepped on a heap of withered leaves at the foot of a tree. My foot slipped a little and I saved myself with my stick. But perhaps, I might not have been able to stop myself! I wondered how long it would have taken to roll down the steep slope and fall into the waterfall far below. I described to Mother with picturesque inventiveness all that might have happened. Then, wandering in the deep pinewoods, I might suddenly have come upon a bear that also was certainly something worth talking about. As nothing ever really happened I stored up all these imaginary adventures in my mind. The story of my swimming across the Padma was much of a piece with this class of romances.

When I was seventeen I had to leave the editorial board of *Bhārati*, for it was then decided that I should go to England. Further, it was considered that before sailing I should live with *Mejadādā*[4] for a time to get some grounding in English manners. He was then a judge at Ahmedabad, and *Meja-Bouthākrun* and her children were in England, waiting for *Mejadādā* to get a furlough and join them.

I was torn up by the roots and transplanted from one soil to another, and had to get acclimatised to a new mental atmosphere. At first, my shyness was a stumbling-block at every turn. I wondered how I should keep my self-respect among all these new acquaintances. It was not easy to habituate myself to strange surroundings, yet there was no means of escape from them; in such a situation a boy of my temperament was bound to find his path a rough one.

---

3. Tracts of rich alluvial land often found as islands in the great rivers (Beng. *Char*).
4. Second brother, Satyendranath Tagore.

My fancy, free to wander, conjured up pictures of the history of Ahmedabad in the Moghul period. The judge's quarters were in Shahibag, the former palace grounds of the Muslim kings. During the daytime *Mejadādā* was away at his work, the vast house seemed one cavernous emptiness, and I wandered about all day like one possessed. In front was a wide terrace, which commanded a view of the Sabarmati river, whose knee-deep waters meandered along through the sands. I felt as though the stone-built tanks, scattered here and there along the terrace, held locked in their masonry wonderful secrets of the luxurious bathing-halls of the Begums.

We are Calcutta people, and history nowhere gives us any evidence of its past grandeur there. Our vision had been confined to the narrow boundaries of these stunted times. In Ahmedabad I felt for the first time that history had paused, and was standing with her face turned towards the aristocratic past. Her former days were buried in the earth like the treasure of the *yakshas*.[5] My mind received the first suggestion for the story of *Hungry Stones*.

How many hundred years have passed since those times! Then, in the *nahabat-khānā*, the minstrel's gallery, an orchestra played day and night, choosing tunes appropriate to the eight periods of the day. The rhythmic beat of horses' hoofs echoed on the streets, and great parades were held of the mounted Turkish cavalry, the sun glittering on the points of their spears. In the court of the Pādshāh whispered conspiracies were ominously rife. Abyssinian eunuchs, with drawn swords, kept guard in the inner apartments. Rose-water fountains played in the *hamāms* of the Begums, the bangles tinkled on their arms. Today, Shahibag stands silent, like a forgotten tale; all its colour has faded, and its varied sounds have died away; the splendours of the day are withered and the nights have lost their savour.

---

5. Demons who guard treasure.

Only the bare skeleton of those old days remained, its head a naked skull whose crown was gone. It was like a mummy in a museum, but it would be too much to say that my mind was able fully to re-clothe those dry bones with flesh and blood and restore the original form. Both the first rough model, and the background against which it stood, were largely a creation of the fancy. Such patch-work is easy when little is known and the rest has been forgotten. After these eighty years even the picture of myself that comes before me does not correspond line for line with the reality, but is largely a product of the imagination.

After I had stayed there for some time *Mejadādā* decided that perhaps I should be less homesick if I could mix with women who could familiarise me with conditions abroad. It would also be an easy way to learn English. So, for a while I lived with a Bombay family. One of the daughters of the house was a modern educated girl who had just returned with all the polish of a visit to England. My own attainments were only ordinary, and she could not have been blamed if she had ignored me. But she did not do so. Not having any store of book-learning to offer her, I took the first opportunity to tell her that I could write poetry. This was the only capital I had with which to gain attention. When I told her of my poetical gift, she did not receive it in any carping or dubious spirit, but accepted it without question. She asked the poet to give her a special name, and I chose one for her which she thought very beautiful. I wanted that name to be entwined with the music of my verse, and I enshrined it in a poem which I made for her. She listened as I sang it in the *Bhairavi* mode of early dawn, and then said, "Poet, I think that even if I were on my death-bed your songs would call me back to life." There is an example of how well girls know how to show their appreciation by some pleasant exaggeration. They simply do it for the pleasure of pleasing. I remember that it was from her that I first heard praise of my personal appearance, –

praise that was often very delicately given.

For example, she asked me once very particularly to remember one thing: "You must never wear a beard. Don't let anything hide the outline of your face." Everyone knows that I have not followed that advice. But she herself did not live to see my disobedience proclaimed upon my face.

In some years, birds strange to Calcutta used to come and build nests in that banyan tree of ours. They would be off again almost before I had learnt to recognize the dance of their wings, but they brought with them a strangely lovely music from their distant jungle homes. So, in the course of our life's journey, some angel from a strange and unexpected quarter may cross our path, speaking the language of our own soul, and enlarging the boundaries of the heart's possessions. She comes unbidden, and when at last we call for her she is no longer there. But as she goes, she leaves on the drab web of our lives a border of embroidered flowers, and for ever and ever the night and day are for us enriched.

XIV

The Master-Workman, who made me, fashioned his first model from the native clay of Bengal. I have described this first model, which is what I call my boyhood, and in it there is little admixture of other elements. Most of its ingredients were gathered from within, though the atmosphere of the home and the home people counted for something, too. Very often the work of moulding goes no further than this stage. Some people get hammered into shape in the book-learning factories, and these are considered in the market to be goods of a superior stamp.

It was my fortune to escape almost entirely the impress of these mills of learning. The masters and pundits who were charged with my education soon abandoned the thankless task. There was Jnanachandra Bhattacharya, the son of Anandachandra Vedāntabāgish, who was a B.A. He realised that this boy could never be driven along the beaten tract of learning. The teachers of those days, alas! were not so strongly convinced that boys should all be poured into the mould of degree-holding respectability. There was then no demand that rich and poor alike should all be confined within the fenced-off regions of college studies. Our family had no wealth then, but it had a reputation, so the old traditions held good, and they were indifferent to conventional academic success. From the lower classes of the Normal School we were transferred to De Cruz's Bengal Academy. It was the hope of my guardians that even if I got nothing else, I should get enough mastery of spoken English to save my face. In the Latin class I was deaf and dumb, and my exercise books of all kinds kept from beginning to end the unrelieved whiteness of a widow's cloth. Confronted by such unprecedented determination not to study, my class teacher complained to Mr. De Cruz, who explained that we were not born for study, but for the purpose of paying our monthly fees. Jnana Babu was of a similar opinion, but found means of keeping me occupied nevertheless. He gave me the whole of *Kumārasambhava*[1] to learn by heart. He shut me in a room and gave me *Macbeth* to translate. Then, Pundit Ramsarbaswa read *Sakuntalā* with me. By setting me free in this way from the fixed curriculum, they reaped some reward for their labours. These then were the materials that formed my boyish mind, together with what other Bengali books I picked up at random.

I landed in England, and foreign workmanship began to play a part in the fashioning of my life. The result is what is known in chemistry as a compound. How capricious is Fortune!–I went to England for a regular course of study, and a desultory start was made, but it came to nothing. *Meja-Bouthān* was there, and her children, and my own family circle absorbed nearly all my interest. I hung about around the school-room, a master taught me at the house, but I did not give my mind to it.

However, gradually the atmosphere of England made its impression on my mind, and what little I brought back from that country was from the people I came in contact with. Mr. Palit finally succeeded in getting me away from my own family. I went to live with a doctor's family, where they made me forget that I was in a foreign land. Mrs Scott lavished on me a genuine affection, and cared for me like a mother. I had then been admitted to London University, and Henry Morley was teaching English literature. His teaching was no dry-as-dust exposition of dead books. Literature came to life in

---

1. A work of Kalidasa.

his mind and in the sound of his voice, it reached to our inner being where the soul seeks its nourishment, and nothing of its essential nature was lost. With his guidance, I found the study of the Clarendon Press books at home to be an easy matter and I took upon myself to be my own teacher. For no reason at all Mrs Scott would sometimes fancy that I did not look well, and would become very worried about me. She did not know that the portals of sickness had been barred against me from childhood. I used to bathe every morning in ice-cold water–in fact, in the opinion of the doctors, it was almost a sacrilege that I should survive such flagrant disregard of the accepted rules!

I was able to study in the University for three months only, but I obtained almost all my understanding of English culture from personal contacts. The Artist who fashions us takes every opportunity to mingle new elements in his creation. Three months of close intimacy with English hearts sufficed for this development. Mrs Scott made it my duty each evening till eleven o'clock to read aloud from poetic drama and history by turn. In this way I did a great deal of reading in a short space of time. It was not prescribed class study, and my understanding of human nature developed side-by-side with my knowledge of literature. I went to England but I did not become a barrister. I received no shock calculated to shatter the original framework of my life–rather East and West met in friendship in my own person. Thus, it has been given me to realise in my own life the meaning of my name.[2]

---

2. The poet's name *Rabi* means the sun, which does not distinguish between East and West.

LOVER'S GIFT

LOVER'S GIFT

1

You allowed your kingly power to vanish, Shahjahan, but your wish was to make imperishable a tear-drop of love.

Time has no pity for the human heart, he laughs at its sad struggle to remember.

You allured him with beauty, made him captive, and crowned the formless death with fadeless form.

The secret whispered in the hush of night to the ear of your love is wrought in the perpetual silence of stone.

Though empires crumble to dust, and centuries are lost in shadows, the marble still sighs to the stars, 'I remember.'

'I remember.'—But life forgets, for she has her call to the Endless: and she goes on her voyage unburdened, leaving her memories to the forlorn forms of beauty.

2

Come to my garden walk, my love. Pass by the fervid flowers that press themselves on your sight. Pass them by, stopping at some chance joy, that like a sudden wonder of sunset illumines, yet eludes.

For love's gift is shy, it never tells its name, it flits across the shade, spreading a shiver of joy along the dust. Overtake it or miss it for ever. But a gift that can be grasped is merely a frail flower, or a lamp with a flame that will flicker.

3

The fruits come in crowds into my orchard, they jostle each other.

They surge up in the light in an anguish of fullness.

Proudly step into my orchard, my queen, sit there in the shade, pluck the ripe fruits from their stems, and let them yield, to the utmost, their burden of sweetness at your lips.

In my orchard the butterflies shake their wings in the sun, the leaves tremble, the fruits clamour to come to completion.

4

She is near to my heart as the meadow-flower to the earth; she is sweet to me as sleep is to tired limbs. My love for her is my life flowing in its fullness, like a river in autumn flood, running with serene abandonment. My songs are one with my love, like the murmur of a stream, that sings with all its waves and currents.

5

I would ask for still more, if I had the sky with all its stars, and the world with its endless riches; but I would be content with the smallest corner of this earth if only she were mine.

6

In the light of this thriftless day of spring, my poet, sing of those who pass by and do not linger, who laugh as they run and never look back, who blossom in an hour of unreasoning delight, and fade in a moment without regret.

Do not sit down silently, to tell the beads of your past tears and smiles,—do not stop to pick up the dropped petals from the flowers of overnight, do not go to seek things that evade you, to know the meaning that is not plain,—leave the gaps in your life where they are, for the music to come out of their depths.

7

It is little that remains now, the rest was spent in one careless summer. It is just enough to put in a song and sing to you; to weave in a flower-chain gently clasping your wrist; to hang in your ear like a round pink pearl, like a blushing whisper; to risk in a game one evening and utterly lose.

My boat is a frail small thing, not fit for crossing wild waves in the rain. If you but lightly step on it I shall gently row you by the shelter of the shore, where the dark water in ripples are like a dream-ruffled sleep; where the dove's cooing from the drooping branches makes the noonday shadows plaintive. At the day's end, when you are tired, I shall pluck a dripping lily to put in your hair and take my leave.

8

There is room for you. You are alone with your few sheaves of rice. My boat is crowded, it is heavily laden, but how can I turn you away? Your young body is slim and swaying; there is a twinkling smile in the edge of your eyes, and your robe is coloured like the rain-cloud.

The travellers will land for different roads and homes. You will sit for a while on the prow of my boat, and at the journey's end none will keep you back.

Where do you go, and to what home, to garner your sheaves? I will not question you, but when I fold my sails and moor my boat, I shall sit and wonder in the evening,—Where do you go, and to what home, to garner your sheaves?

9

Woman, your basket is heavy, your limbs are tired. For what distance have you set out, with what hunger of profit? The way is long and the dust is hot in the sun.

See, the lake is deep and full, its water dark like a crow's eye. The banks are sloping and tender with grass.

Dip your tired feet into the water. The noon-tide wind will pass its fingers through your hair; the pigeons will croon their sleep songs, the leaves will murmur the secrets that nestle in the shadows.

What matters it if the hours pass and the sun sets; if the way through the desolate land be lost in the waning light.

Yonder is my house, by the hedge of flowering *henna*; I will guide you. I will make a bed for you, and light a lamp. In the morning when the birds are roused by the stir of milking the cows, I will waken you.

10

What is it that drives these bees from their home; these followers of unseen trails? What cry is this in their eager wings? How can they hear the music that sleeps in the flower soul? How can they find their way to the chamber where the honey lies shy and silent?

11

It was only the budding of leaves in the summer, the summer that came into the garden by the sea. It was only a stir and rustle in the south wind, a few lazy snatches of songs, and then the day was done.

But let there be flowering of love in the summer to come in the garden by the sea. Let my joy take its birth and clap its hands and dance with the surging songs, and make the morning open its eyes wide in sweet amazement.

12

Ages ago when you opened the south gate of the garden of gods, and came down upon the first youth of the earth, O Spring; men and women rushed out of their houses, laughing and dancing, and pelting each other with flower-dust in a sudden madness of mirth.

Year after year you bring the same flowers that you scattered in your path in that earliest April. Therefore, today, in their pervading perfume, they breathe the sigh of the days that are now dreams—the clinging sadness of vanished worlds. Your breeze is laden with love-legends that have faded from all human language.

One day, with fresh wonder, you came into my life that was fluttered with its first love. Since then the tender timidness of that inexperienced joy comes hidden every year in the early green buds of your lemon flowers; your red roses carry in their burning silence all that was unutterable in me: the memory of lyric hours, those days of May, rustles in the thrill of your new leaves born again and again.

13

Last night in the garden I offered you my youth's foaming wine. You lifted the cup to your lips, you shut your eyes and smiled while I raised your veil, unbound your tresses, drawing down upon my breast your face sweet with its silence; last night when the moon's dream overflowed the world of slumber.

Today, in the dew-cooled calm of the dawn you are walking to God's temple, bathed and robed white, with a basketful of flowers in your hand. I stand aside in the shade under the tree, with my head bent, in the calm of the dawn by the lonely road to the temple.

14

If I am impatient today, forgive me, my love. It is the first summer rain, and the riverside forest is aflutter, and the blossoming *kadam* trees, are tempting the passing winds with wine-cups of perfume. See, from all corners of the sky lightnings are darting their glances, and winds are rampant in your hair.

If today, I bring my homage to you, forgive me, my love. The everyday world is hidden in the dimness of the rain, all work has stopped in the village, the meadows are desolate. In your dark eyes the coming of the rain finds its music, and it is at your door that

July waits with jasmines for your hair in its blue skirt.

15

Her neighbours call her dark in the village—but she is a lily to my heart, yes, a lily though not fair. Light came muffled with clouds, when first I saw her in the field; her head was bare, her veil was off, her braided hair hanging loose on her neck. She may be dark as they say in the village, but I have seen her black eyes and am glad.

The pulse of the air boded storm. She rushed out of the hut, when she heard her dappled cow low in dismay. For a moment, she turned her large eyes to the clouds, and felt a stir of the coming rain in the sky. I stood at the corner of the ricefield,—if she noticed me, it was known only to her (and perhaps, I know it). She is dark as the message of shower in summer, dark as the shade of flowering woodland; she is dark as the longing for unknown love in the wistful night of May.

16

She dwelt here by the pool with its landing-stairs in ruins. Many an evening she had watched the moon made dizzy by the shaking of bamboo leaves, and on many a rainy day the smell of the wet earth had come to her over the young shoots of rice.

Her pet name is known here among those date-palm groves, and in the courtyards where girls sit and talk, while stitching their winter quilts. The water in this pool keeps in its depth the memory of her swimming limbs, and her wet feet had left their marks, day after day, on the footpath leading to the village.

The women who come today with their vessels to the water, have all seen her smile over simple jests, and the old peasant, taking his bullocks to their bath, used to stop at her door everyday to greet her.

Many a sailing boat passes by this village; many a traveller takes rest beneath that banyan tree; the ferry boat crosses to yonder ford carrying crowds to the market; but they never notice this spot by the village road, near the pool with its ruined landing-stairs,—where dwelt she whom I love.

17

While ages passed and the bees haunted the summer gardens, the moon smiled to the lilies of the night, the lightnings flashed their fiery kisses to the clouds and fled laughing, the poet stood in a corner, one with the trees and clouds. He kept his heart silent, like a flower, watched through his dreams as does the crescent moon; and wandered like the summer breeze for no purpose.

One April evening, when the moon rose up like a bubble from the depth of the sunset; and one maiden was busy watering the plants; and one feeding her doe, and one making her peacock dance, the poet broke out singing,—'O listen to the secrets of the world. I know that the lily is pale for the moon's love. The lotus draws her veil aside before the morning sun, and the reason is simple if you think. The meaning of the bee's hum in the ear of the early jasmine has escaped the learned, but the poet knows.'

The sun went down in a blaze of blush, the moon loitered behind the trees, and the south wind whispered to the lotus, that the poet was not as simple as he seemed. The maidens and youth clapped their hands and cried,—'The world's secret is out.' They looked into each other's eyes and sang—'Let our secret as well be flung into the winds.'

18

Your days will be full of cares, if you must give me your heart. My house by the cross-roads has its doors open and my mind is absent,—for I sing.

I shall never be made to answer for it, if you must give me your heart. If I pledge my word to you in tunes now, and am too much in earnest to keep it when music is silent, you must forgive me; for the law laid in May is best broken in December.

Do not always keep remembering it, if you must give me your heart. When your eyes sing with love, and your voice ripples with laughter, my answers to your questions will be wild, and not miserly accurate in facts,—they are to be believed for ever and then forgotten for good.

19

It is written in the book, that Man, when fifty, must leave the noisy world, to go to the forest seclusion. But the poet proclaims that only for the young is the forest hermitage. For, it is the birth-place of flowers, and the haunt of birds and bees; and hidden nooks are waiting there for the thrill of lover's whispers. There the moonlight, that is all one kiss for the *malati* flowers, has its deep message, but those who understand it are far below fifty.

And alas, youth is inexperienced and wilful, therefore, it is but meet, that the old should take charge of the household, and the young take to the seclusion of forest shades, and the severe discipline of courting.

20

Where is the market for you, my song? Is it there where the learned muddle the summer breeze with their snuff; where dispute is unending if the oil depend upon the cask, or the cask upon the oil; where yellow manuscripts frown upon the fleet-footed frivolousness of life? My song cries out, Ah, no, no, no.

Where is the market for you, my song? Is it there where the man of fortune grows enormous in pride and flesh in his marble palace, with his books on the shelves, dressed in leather, painted in gold, dusted by slaves, their virgin pages dedicated to the god obscure? My song gasped and said, Ah, no, no, no.

Where is the market for you, my song? Is it there where the young student sits, with his head bent upon his books, and his mind straying in youth's dream-land; where prose is prowling on the desk, and poetry hiding in the heart? There, among that dusty disorder would you care to play hide-and-seek? My song remains silent in shy hesitation.

Where is the market for you, my song? Is it there where the bride is busy in the house, where she runs to her bedroom the moment she is free, and snatches, from under her pillows, the book of romance so roughly handled by the baby, so full of the scent of her hair? My song heaves a sigh and trembles with uncertain desire.

Where is the market for you, my song? Is it there where the least of a bird's notes is never missed, where the stream's babbling finds its full wisdom, where all the lute-strings of the world shower their music upon two fluttering hearts? My song bursts out and cries, Yes, yes.

21

Methinks, my love, before the daybreak of life you stood under some waterfall of happy dreams, filling your blood with its liquid turbulence. Or, perhaps, your path was through the garden of the gods, where the merry multitude of jasmine, lilies, and oleanders fell in your arms in heaps, and entering your heart became boisterous.

Your laughter is a song whose words are drowned in the clamour of tune, a rapture of odour of flowers that are not seen; it is like the moonlight breaking through your lips' window when the moon is hiding in your heart. I ask for no reason, I forget the cause, I only know that your laughter is the tumult of insurgent life.

22

I shall gladly suffer the pride of culture to die out in my house, if only in some fortunate future I am born a herd boy in the Brinda forest.

The herd boy who grazes his cattle sitting under the banyan tree, and idly weaves *gunja* flowers into garlands, who loves to splash and plunge in the Jamuna's cool deep stream.

He calls his companions to wake up when morning dawns, and all the houses in the lane hum with the sound of the churn, clouds of dust are raised by the cattle, the maidens come out in the courtyard to milk the kine.

As the shadows deepen under the *tomal* trees, and the dusk gathers on the river-banks; when the milkmaids, while crossing the turbulent water tremble with fear; and loud peacocks, with tails outspread, dance in the forest, he watches the summer clouds.

When the April night is sweet as a fresh-blown flower, he disappears in the forest with a peacock's plume in his hair; the swing ropes are twined with flowers on the branches; the south wind throbs with music, and the merry shepherd boys crowd on the banks of the blue river.

No, I will never be the leader, brothers, of this new age of new Bengal; I shall not trouble to light the lamp of culture for the benighted. If only I could be born, under the shady Ashoka groves, in some village of Brinda, where milk is churned by the maidens.

23

I loved the sandy bank where, in the lonely pools, ducks clamoured and turtles basked in the sun; where, with evening, stray fishing boats took shelter in the shadow by the tall grass.

You loved the wooded bank where shadows were gathered in the arms of the bamboo thickets; where women came with their vessels through the winding lane.

The same river flowed between us, singing the same song to both its banks. I listened to it, lying alone on the sand under the stars; and you listened sitting by the edge of the slope in the early morning light. Only the words I heard from it you did not know and the secret it spoke to you was a mystery forever to me.

24

Your window half-opened and veil half-raised you stand there waiting for the bangle-seller to come with his tinsel. You idly watch the heavy cart creak on in the dusty road, and the boat-mast crawling along the horizon across the far-off river.

The world to you is like an old woman's chant at her spinning wheel, unmeaning rhymes crowded with random images.

But who knows if he is on his way this lazy sultry noon, the Stranger, carrying his basket of strange wares. He will pass by your door with his clear cry, and you shall fling open your window, cast off your veil, come out of the dusk of your dreams and meet your destiny.

25

I clasp your hands, and my heart plunges into the dark of your eyes, seeking you, who ever evade me behind words and silence.

Yet, I know that I must be content in my love, with what is fitful and fugitive. For, we have met for a moment in the crossing of the roads. Have I the power to carry you through this crowd of worlds, through this maze of paths? Have I the food that can sustain you, across the dark passage gaping with arches of death?

26

If, by chance you think of me, I shall sing to you when the rainy evening loosens her shadows upon the river, slowly trailing her dim light towards the west,–when the day's remnant is too narrow for work or for play.

You will sit alone in the balcony of the south, and I shall sing from the darkened room. In the growing dusk, the smell of the wet leaves will come through the window; and the stormy winds will become clamorous in the coconut grove.

When the lighted lamp is brought into the room I shall go. And then, perhaps, you will listen to the night, and hear my song when I am silent.

27

I filled my tray with whatever I had, and gave it to you. What shall I bring to your feet tomorrow, I wonder. I am like the tree that, at the end of the flowering summer, gazes at the sky with its lifted branches bare of their blossoms.

But in all my past offerings is there not a single flower made fadeless by the eternity of tears?

Will you remember it and thank me with your eyes when I stand before you with empty hands at the leave-taking of my summer days?

28

I dreamt that she sat by my head, tenderly ruffling my hair with her fingers, playing the melody of her touch. I looked at her face and struggled with my tears, till the agony of unspoken words burst my sleep like a bubble.

I sat up and saw the glow of the milky way above my window, like a world of silence on fire, and I wondered if at this moment she had a dream that rhymed with mine.

29

I thought I had something to say to her when our eyes met across the hedge. But she passed away. And it rocks day and night, like a boat, on every wave of the hours the word that I had to say to her. It seems to sail in the autumn clouds in an endless quest and to bloom into evening flowers seeking its lost moment in the sunset. It twinkles like fireflies in my heart to find its meaning in the dusk of despair the word that I had to say to her.

30

The spring flowers break out like the passionate pain of unspoken love. With their breath comes the memory of my old day songs. My heart of a sudden has put on green leaves of desire. My love came not but her touch is in my limbs, and her voice comes across the fragrant fields. Her gaze is in the sad depth of the sky, but where are her eyes? Her kisses flit in the air, but where are her lips?

A POSY

31

My flowers were like milk and honey and wine; I bound them into a posy with a golden ribbon, but they escaped my watchful care and fled away and only the ribbon remains.

My songs were like milk and honey and wine, they were held in the rhythm of my beating heart, but they spread their wings and fled away, the darlings of the idle hours, and my heart beats in silence.

The beauty I loved was like milk and honey and wine, her lips like the rose of the dawn, her eyes bee-black. I kept my heart silent, lest it should startle her, but she eluded me like my flowers and like my songs, and my love remains alone.

32

Many a time when the spring day knocked at our door I kept busy with my work and you did not answer. Now, when I am left alone and heartsick the spring day comes once again, but I know not how to turn him away from the door. When he came to crown us with joy the gate was shut, but now when he comes with his gift of sorrow his path must be open.

33

The boisterous spring, who once came into my life with its lavish laughter, burdening her hours with improvident roses, setting skies aflame with the red kisses of new-born a*shoka* leaves, now comes stealing into my solitude through the lonely lanes along the brooding shadows heavy with silence, and sits still in my balcony gazing across the fields, where the green of the earth swoons exhausted in the utter paleness of the sky.

34

When our farewell moment came, like a low-hanging rain cloud, I had only time to tie a red ribbon on your wrist, while my hands trembled. Today, I sit alone on the grass in the season of *mahua* flowers, with one quivering question in my mind, 'Do you still keep the little red ribbon tied on your wrist?'

You went by the narrow road that skirted the blossoming field of flax. I saw that my garland of overnight was still hanging loose from your hair. But why did you not wait till I could gather, in the morning, new flowers for my final gift? I wonder if unaware it dropped on your way,–the garland hanging loose from your hair.

Many a song I had sung to you, morning and evening, and the last one you carried in your voice when you went away. You never tarried to hear the one song unsung I had for you alone and forever. I wonder if, at last, you are tired of my song that you hummed to yourself while walking through the field.

35

Last night clouds were threatening and *amlak* branches struggled in the grips of the gusty wind. I hoped, if dreams came to me, they would come in the shape of my beloved, in the lonely night loud with rain.

The winds still moan through the fields, and the tear-stained cheeks of dawn are pale. My dreams have been in vain, for truth is hard, and dreams, too, have their own ways.

Last night when the darkness was drunken with storm, and the rain, like night's veil, was torn by the winds into shreds, would it make truth jealous, if untruth came to me in the shape of my beloved, in the starless night loud with rain?

36

MY FETTERS, you made music in my heart. I played with you all day long and made you my ornament. We were the best of friends, my fetters. There were times when I was afraid of you, but my fear made me love you the more. You were companions of my long dark night, and I make my bow to you, before I bid you good-bye, my fetters.

37

You had your rudder broken many a time, my boat, and your sails torn to tatters. Often, had you drifted towards the sea, dragging anchor and heeded not. But now, there has spread a crack in your hull and your hold is heavy. Now, is the time for you to end your voyage, to be rocked into sleep by the lapping of the water by the beach.

Alas, I know all warning is vain. The veiled face of dark doom lures you. The madness of the storm and the waves is upon you. The music of the tide is rising high. You are shaken by the fever of that dance.

Then break your chain, my boat, and be free, and fearlessly rush to your wreck.

38

The current in which I drifted ran rapid and strong when I was young. The spring breeze was spendthrift of itself, the trees were on fire with flowers; and the birds never slept from singing. I sailed with giddy speed, carried away by the flood of passion; I had no time to see and feel and take the world into my being. Now, that youth has ebbed and I am stranded on the bank, I can hear the deep music of all things, and the sky opens to me its heart of stars.

39

There is a looker-on who sits behind my eyes. It seems he has seen things in ages and worlds beyond memory's shore, and those forgotten sights glisten on the grass, and shiver on the leaves. He has seen under new veils the face of the one beloved, in twilight hours of many a nameless star. Therefore, his sky seems to ache with the pain of countless meetings and partings, and a longing pervades this spring breeze,—the longing that is full of the whisper of ages without beginning.

40

A message came from my youth of vanished days, saying, 'I wait for you among the quiverings of unborn May, where smiles ripen for tears and hours ache with songs unsung.'

It says, 'Come to me across the worn-out track of age, through the gates of death. For, dreams fade, hopes fail, the gathered fruits of the year decay, but I am the eternal truth, and you shall meet me again and again in your voyage of life from shore to shore.'

41

The girls are out to fetch water from the river—their laughter comes through the trees, I long to join them in the lane, where goats graze in the shade, and squirrels flit from sun to shadow, across the fallen leaves.

But my day's task is already done, my jars are filled. I stand at my door to watch the glistening green of the *areca* leaves, and hear the laughing women going to fetch water from the river.

It has ever been dear to me to carry the burden of my full vessel day after day, in the dew-dipped morning freshness and in the tired glimmer of the dayfall.

Its gurgling water babbled to me when my mind was idle, it

laughed with the silent laughter of my joyous thoughts–it spoke to my heart with tearful sobs when I was sad. I have carried it in stormy days, when the loud rain drowned the anxious cooing of doves.

My day's task is done, my jars are filled, the light wanes in the west, and shadows gather beneath the trees; a sigh comes from the flowering linseed field, and my wistful eyes follow the lane, that runs through the village to the bank of the dark water.

42

Are you a mere picture, and not as true as those stars, true as this dust? They throb with the pulse of things, but you are immensely aloof in your stillness, painted form.

The day was when you walked with me, your breath warm, your limbs singing of life. My world found its speech in your voice, and touched my heart with your face. You suddenly stopped in your walk, in the shadow-side of the Forever, and I went on alone.

Life, like a child, laughs, shaking its rattle of death as it runs; it beckons me on, I follow the unseen; but you stand there, where you stopped behind that dust and those stars; and you are a mere picture.

No, it cannot be. Had the lifeflood utterly stopped in you, it would stop the river in its flow, and the footfall of dawn in her cadence of colours. Had the glimmering dusk of your hair vanished in the hopeless dark, the woodland shade of summer would die with its dreams.

Can it be true that I forgot you? We haste on without heed, forgetting the flowers on the roadside hedge. Yet, they breathe unaware into our forgetfulness, filling it with music. You have moved from my world, to take seat at the root of my life, and therefore, is this forgetting–remembrance lost in its own depth.

You are no longer before my songs, but one with them. You

came to me with the first ray of dawn. I lost you with the last gold of evening. Ever since I am always finding you through the dark. No, you are no mere picture.

43

Dying, you have left behind you the great sadness of the Eternal in my life. You have painted my thought's horizon with the sunset colours of your departure, leaving a track of tears across the earth to love's heaven. Clasped in your dear arms, life and death united in me in a marriage bond.

I think I can see you watching there in the balcony with your lamp lighted, where the end and the beginning of all things meet. My world went hence through the doors that you opened–you holding the cup of death to my lips, filling it with life from your own.

44

When in your death you died to all that was outside me, vanishing from the thousand things of the world, to be fully reborn in my sorrow, I felt that my life had grown perfect, the man and the woman becoming one in me forever.

45

Bring beauty and order into my forlorn life, woman, as you brought them into my house when you lived. Sweep away the dusty fragments of the hours, fill the empty jars and mend all neglects. Then, open the inner door of the shrine, light the candle, and let us meet there in silence before our God.

46

The sky gazes on its own endless blue and dreams. We clouds are its whims, we have no home. The stars shine on the crown of

Eternity. Their records are permanent, while ours are pencilled, to be rubbed off the next moment. Our part is to appear on the stage of the air to sound our tambourines and fling flashes of laughter. But from our laughter comes the rain, which is real enough, and thunder which is no jest. Yet, we have no claim upon Time for wages, and the breath that blew us into being blows us away before we are given a name.

47

The road is my wedded companion. She speaks to me under my feet all day, she sings to my dreams all night.

My meeting with her had no beginning, it begins endlessly at each daybreak, renewing its summer in fresh flowers and songs, and her every new kiss is the first kiss to me.

The road and I are lovers. I change my dress for her night after night, leaving the tattered cumber of the old in the wayside inns when the day dawns.

48

I travelled the old road everyday, I took my fruits to the market, my cattle to the meadows, I ferried my boat across the stream and all the ways were well known to me.

One morning, my basket was heavy with wares. Men were busy in the fields, the pastures crowded with cattle; the breast of earth heaved with the mirth of ripening rice.

Suddenly, there was a tremor in the air, and the sky seemed to kiss me on my forehead. My mind started up like the morning out of mist.

I forgot to follow the track. I stepped a few paces from the path, and my familiar world appeared strange to me, like a flower I had only known in bud.

My everyday wisdom was ashamed. I went astray in the fairyland of things. It was the best luck of my life, that I lost my path that morning, and found my eternal childhood.

49

Where is heaven? you ask me, my child,—the sages tell us it is beyond the limits of birth and death, unswayed by the rhythm of day and night; it is not of this earth.

But your poet knows that its eternal hunger is for time and space, and it strives evermore to be born in the fruitful dust. Heaven is fulfilled in your sweet body, my child, in your palpitating heart.

The sea is beating its drums in joy, the flowers are a-tiptoe to kiss you. For heaven is born in you, in the arms of the mother dust.

THE CHILD

50

Come, moon, come down, kiss my darling on the forehead,' cries the mother as she holds the baby girl in her lap while the moon smiles as it dreams. There come stealing in the dark the vague fragrance of the summer and the night-bird's songs from the shadow-laden solitude of the mango grove. At a far-away village rises from a peasant's flute a fountain of plaintive notes, and the young mother, sitting on the terrace, baby in her lap, croons sweetly, 'Come, moon, come down, kiss my darling on the forehead.' Once, she looks up at the light of the sky, and then at the light of the earth in her arms, and I wonder at the placid silence of the moon.

The baby laughs and repeats her mother's call, 'Come, moon, come down.' The mother smiles, and smiles the moonlit night, and I, the poet, the husband of the baby's mother, watch this picture from behind, unseen.

51

The early autumn day is cloudless. The river is full to the brim, washing the naked roots of the tottering tree by the ford. The long narrow path, like the thirsty tongue of the village, dips down into the stream.

My heart is full, as I look around me and see the silent sky and the flowing water, and feel that happiness is spread abroad, as simply as a smile on a child's face.

52

Tired of waiting, you burst your bonds, impatient flowers, before the winter had gone. Glimpses of the unseen comer reached your wayside watch, and you rushed out running and panting, impulsive jasmines, troops of riotous roses.

You were the first to march to the breach of death, your clamour of colour and perfume troubled the air. You laughed and pressed and pushed each other, bared your breast and dropped in heaps.

The Summer will come in its time, sailing in the floodtide of the south wind. But you never counted slow moments to be sure of him. You recklessly spent your all in the road, in the terrible joy of faith.

You heard his footsteps from afar, and flung your mantle of death for him to tread upon. Your bonds break even before the rescuer is seen, you make him your own ere he can come and claim you.

CHAMPA

53

I opened my bud when April breathed her last and the summer scorched with kisses the unwilling earth. I came half-afraid and half-curious, like a mischievous imp peeping at a hermit's cell.

I heard the frightened whispers of the despoiled woodland, and the *Kokil* gave voice to the languor of the summer; through the fluttering leaf curtain of my birth-chamber I saw the world grim, grey, and haggard.

Yet, boldly I came out strong with the faith of youth, quaffed the fiery wine from the glowing bowl of the sky, and proudly saluted the morning, I, the *champa* flower, who carry the perfume of the sun in my heart.

54

In the beginning of time, there rose from the churning of God's dream two women. One is the dancer at the court of paradise, the desired of men, she who laughs and plucks the minds of the wise from their cold meditations and of fools from their emptiness; and scatters them like seeds with careless hands in the extravagant winds of March, in the flowering frenzy of May.

The other is the crowned queen of heaven, the mother, throned on the fullness of golden autumn; she who in the harvest-time brings straying hearts to the smile sweet as tears, the beauty deep as the sea of silence,—brings them to the temple of the Unknown, at the holy confluence of Life and Death.

55

The noonday air is quivering, like gauzy wings of a dragon-fly. Roofs of the village huts brood birdlike over the drowsy households, while a *Kokil* sings unseen from its leafy loneliness.

The fresh liquid notes drop upon the tuneless toil of the human crowd, adding music to lovers' whispers, to mothers' kisses, to children's laughter. They flow over our thoughts, like a stream over pebbles, rounding them in beauty every unconscious moment.

56

The evening was lonely for me, and I was reading a book till my heart became dry, and it seemed to me that beauty was a thing fashioned by the traders in words. Tired, I shut the book and snuffed the candle. In a moment the room was flooded with moonlight.

Spirit of Beauty, how could you, whose radiance overbrims the sky, stand hidden behind a candle's tiny flame? How could a few vain words from a book rise like a mist, and veil her whose voice has hushed the heart of earth into ineffable calm?

57

This autumn is mine, for she was rocked in my heart. The glistening bells of her anklets rang in my blood, and her misty veil fluttered in my breath. I know the touch of her blown hair in all my dreams. She is abroad in the trembling leaves that danced in my life-throbs, and her eyes that smile from the blue sky drank their light from me.

58

Things throng and laugh loud in the sky; the sands and dust dance and whirl like children. Man's mind is aroused by their shouts; his thoughts long to be the playmates of things.

Our dreams, drifting in the stream of the vague, stretch their arms to clutch the earth,—their efforts stiffen into bricks and stones, and thus the city of man is built.

Voices come swarming from the past,—seeking answers from the living moments. Beats of their wings fill the air with tremulous shadows, and sleepless thoughts in our minds leave their nests to take flight across the desert of dimness, in the passionate thirst for forms. They are lampless pilgrims, seeking the shore of light, to find themselves in things. They will be lured into poet's rhymes, they will be housed in the towers of the town not yet planned, they have their call to arms from the battlefields of the future, they are bidden to join hands in the strifes of peace yet to come.

59

They do not build high towers in the Land of All-I-Have-Found. A grassy lawn runs by the road, with a stream of fugitive water at its side. The bees haunt the cottage porches abloom with passion flowers. The men set out on their errands with a smile, and in the evening they come home with a song, with no wages, in the Land of All-I-Have-Found.

In the mid-day, sitting in the cool of their courtyards, the women hum and spin at their wheels, while over the waving harvest comes wafted the music of shepherds' flutes. It rejoices the wayfarers' hearts who walk singing through the shimmering shadows of the fragrant forest in the Land of All-I-Have-Found.

The traders sail with their merchandise down the river, but they do not moor their boats in this land; soldiers march with banners flying, but the king never stops his chariot. Travellers who come from afar to rest here awhile, go away without knowing what there is in the Land of All-I-Have-Found.

Here, crowds do not jostle each other in the roads. O poet, set up your house in this land. Wash from your feet the dust of distant wanderings, tune your lute, and at the day's end stretch yourself on the cool grass under the evening star in the Land of All-I-Have-Found.

60

Take back your coins, King's Councillor. I am of those women you sent to the forest shrine to decoy the young ascetic who had never seen a woman. I failed in your bidding.

Dimly day was breaking when the hermit boy came to bathe in the stream, his tawny locks crowded on his shoulders, like a cluster of morning clouds, and his limbs shining like a streak of sunbeam. We laughed and sang as we rowed in our boat; we jumped into the river in a mad frolic, and danced around him, when the sun rose staring at us from the water's edge in a flush of divine anger.

Like a child-god, the boy opened his eyes and watched our movements, the wonder deepening till his eyes shone like morning stars. He lifted his clasped hands and chanted a hymn of praise in his bird-like young voice, thrilling every leaf of the forest. Never such words were sung to a mortal woman before; they were like the silent hymn to the dawn which rises from the hushed hills. The women hid their mouths with their hands, their bodies swaying with laughter, and a spasm of doubt ran across his face. Quickly came I to his side, sorely pained, and, bowing to his feet, I said, 'Lord, accept my service.'

I led him to the grassy bank, wiped his body with the end of my silken mantle, and, kneeling on the ground, I dried his feet with my trailing hair. When I raised my face and looked into his eyes, I thought I felt the world's first kiss to the first woman,—Blessed am I, blessed is God, who made me a woman. I heard him say to me, 'What God unknown are you? Your touch is the touch of the Immortal, your eyes have the mystery of the midnight.'

Ah, no, not that smile, King's Councillor,—the dust of worldly wisdom has covered your sight, old man. But this boy's innocence pierced the mist and saw the shining truth, the woman divine.

Ah, how the goddess wakened in me, at the awful light of that first adoration. Tears filled my eyes, the morning ray caressed my hair like a sister, and the woodland breeze kissed my forehead as it kisses the flowers.

The women clapped their hands, and laughed their obscene laugh, and with veils dragging on the dust and hair hanging loose, they began to pelt him with flowers.

Alas, my spotless sun, could not my shame weave fiery mist to cover you in its folds? I fell at his feet and cried, 'Forgive me.' I fled like a stricken deer through shade and sun, and cried as I fled, 'Forgive me.' The women's foul laughter pressed me like a crackling fire, but the words ever rang in my ears, 'What God unknown are you?'

THE POST OFFICE

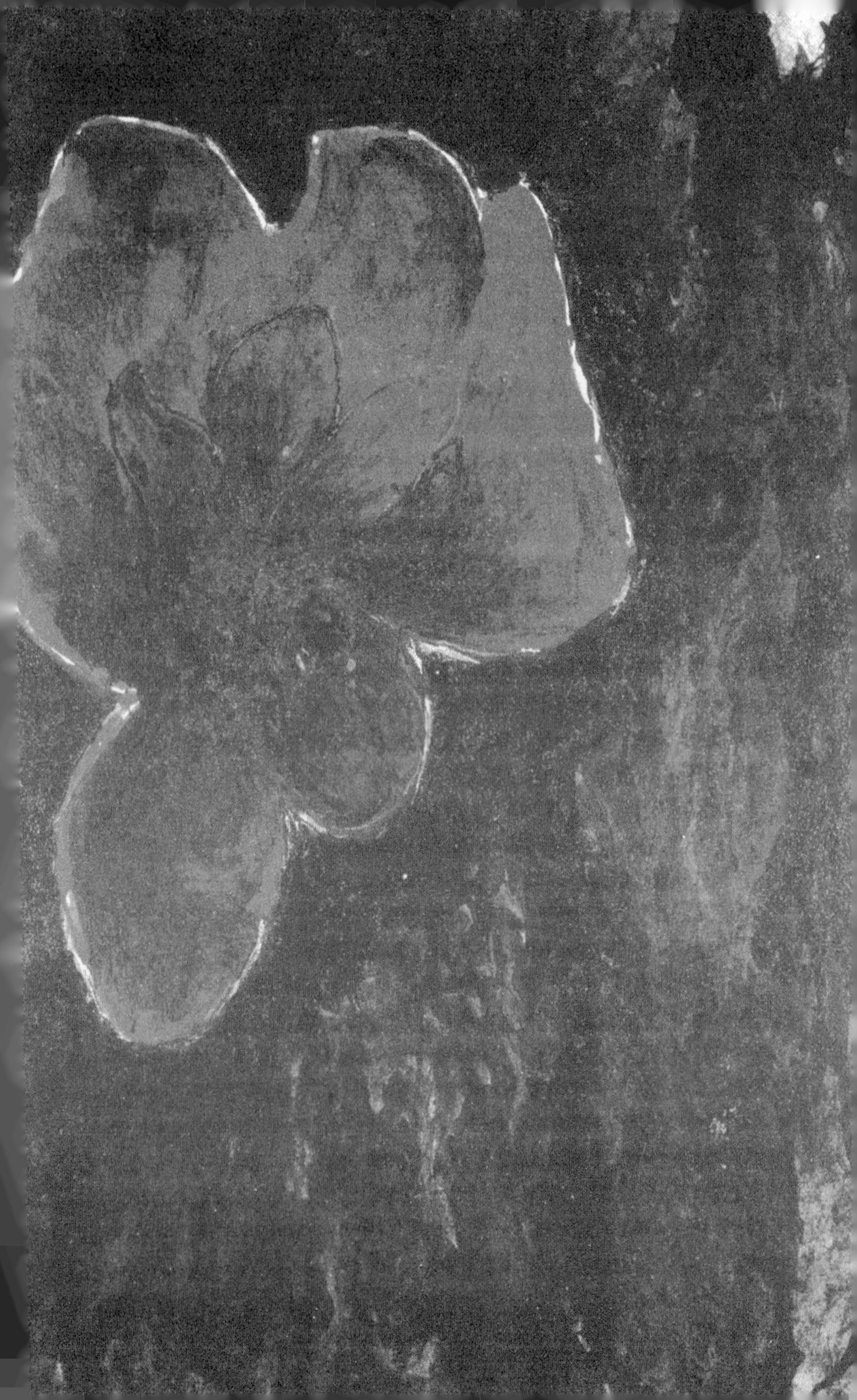

The Characters

MADHAV

AMAL, his adopted child

SUDHA, a little flower-girl

THE DOCTOR

DAIRYMAN

WATCHMAN

GAFFER

VILLAGE HEADMAN, a bully

KING'S HERALD

ROYAL PHYSICIAN

ACT I

(Madhav's House)

Madhav. What a state I am in! Before he came, nothing mattered; I felt so free. But now that he has come, goodness knows from where, my heart is filled with his dear self, and my home will be no home to me when he leaves. Doctor, do you think he –

Physician. If there's life in his fate, then he will live long. But what the medical scriptures say, it seems –

Madhav. Great heavens, what?

Physician. The scriptures have it: "Bile or palsy, cold or gout spring all alike."

Madhav. Oh, get along, don't fling your scriptures at me; you only make me more anxious; tell me what I can do.

Physician (taking snuff). The patient needs the most scrupulous care.

Madhav. That's true; but tell me how.

Physician. I have already mentioned, on no account must he be let out of doors.

Madhav. Poor child, it is very hard to keep him indoors all day long.

Physician. What else can you do? The autumn sun and the damp are both very bad for the little fellow – for the scriptures have it:

"In wheezing, swooning, or in nervous fret,

In jaundice or leaden eyes –"

Madhav. Never mind the scriptures, please. Eh, then we must shut the poor thing up. Is there no other method?

Physician. None at all: for "In the wind and in the sun –"

Madhav. What will your "in this and in that" do for me now? Why don't you let them alone and come straight to the point? What's to be done, then? Your system is very, very hard for the poor boy; and he is so quiet too with all his pain and sickness. It tears my heart to see him wince, as he takes your medicine.

Physician. The more he winces, the surer is the effect. That's why the sage Chyabana observes: "In medicine as in good advice, the least palatable is the truest." Ah, well! I must be trotting now.

[Exit

(*Gaffer enters*)

Madhav. Well, I'm jiggered, there's Gaffer now.

Gaffer. Why, why, I won't bite you.

Madhav. No, but you are a devil to send children off their heads.

Gaffer. But you aren't a child, and you've no child in the house; why worry, then?

Madhav. Oh, but I have brought a child into the house.

Gaffer. Indeed, how so?

Madhav. You remember how my wife was dying to adopt a child?

Gaffer. Yes, but that's an old story; you didn't like the idea.

Madhav. You know, brother, how hard all this getting money in has been. That somebody else's child would sail in and waste all this money earned with so much trouble – Oh, I hated the idea. But this boy clings to my heart in such a queer sort of way –

Gaffer. So, that's the trouble! And your money goes all for him and feels jolly lucky it does go at all.

Madhav. Formerly, earning was a sort of passion with me; I simply couldn't help working for money. Now, I make money, and as I know it is all for this dear boy, earning becomes a joy to me.

Gaffer. Ah, well, and where did you pick him up?

Madhav. He is the son of a man who was a brother to my wife by village ties. He has had no mother since infancy; and now the other day he lost his father as well.

Gaffer. Poor thing: and so he needs me all the more.

Madhav. The doctor says all the organs of his little body are at loggerheads with each other, and there isn't much hope for his life. There is only one way to save him and that is to keep him out of this autumn wind and sun. But you are such a terror! What with this game of yours at your age, too, to get children out of doors!

Gaffer. God bless my soul! So, I'm already as bad as autumn wind and sun, eh! But, friend, I know something, too, of the game of keeping them indoors. When my day's work is over I am coming in to make friends with this child of yours. *[Exit*

(Amal enters)

Amal. Uncle, I say, Uncle!

Madhav. Hullo! Is that you, Amal?

Amal. Mayn't I be out of the courtyard at all?

Madhav. No, my dear, no.

Amal. See there, where Auntie grinds lentils in the quern, the squirrel is sitting with his tail up and with his wee hands he's picking up the broken grains of lentils and crunching them. Can't I run up there?

Madhav. No, my darling, no.

Amal. Wish I were a squirrel!–it would be lovely. Uncle, why won't you let me go about?

Madhav. Doctor says it's bad for you to be out.

Amal. How can the doctor know?

Madhav. What a thing to say! The doctor can't know and he reads such huge books!

Amal. Does his book-learning tell him everything?

Madhav. Of course, don't you know!

Amal (with a sigh). Ah, I am so stupid! I don't read books.

Madhav. Now, think of it; very, very learned people are all like you; they are never out of doors.

Amal. Aren't they really?

Madhav. No, how can they? Early and late they toil and moil at their books, and they've eyes for nothing else. Now, my little man, you are going to be learned when you grow up; and then you will stay at home and read such big books, and people will notice you and say, "He's a wonder."

Amal. No, no, Uncle; I beg of you, by your dear feet—I don't want to be learned; I won't.

Madhav. Dear, dear; it would have been my saving if I could have been learned.

Amal. No, I would rather go about and see everything that there is.

Madhav. Listen to that! See! What will you see, what is there so much to see?

Amal. See that far-away hill from our window—I often long to go beyond those hills and right away.

Madhav. Oh, you silly! As if there's nothing more to be done but just get up to the top of that hill and away! Eh! You don't talk sense, my boy. Now listen, since that hill stands there upright as a barrier, it means you can't get beyond it. Else, what was the use in heaping up so many large stones to make such a big affair of it, eh!

Amal. Uncle, do you think it is meant to prevent us crossing over? It seems to me because the earth can't speak it raises its hands into the sky and beckons. And, those who live far off and sit alone by their windows can see the signal. But I suppose the learned people–

Madhav. No, they don't have time for that sort of nonsense. They are not crazy like you.

Amal. Do you know, yesterday I met someone quite as crazy as I am.

Madhav. Gracious me, really, how so?

Amal. He had a bamboo staff on his shoulder with a small bundle at the top, and a brass pot in his left hand, and an old pair of shoes on; he was making for those hills straight across that meadow there. I called out to him and asked, "Where are you going?" He answered, "I don't know; anywhere!" I asked again, "Why are you going?" He said, "I'm going out to seek work." Say, Uncle, have you to seek work?

Madhav. Of course, I have to. There's many about looking for jobs.

Amal. How lovely! I'll go about like them, too, finding things to do.

Madhav. Suppose you seek and don't find. Then –

Amal. Wouldn't that be jolly? Then I should go farther! I watched that man slowly walking on with his pair of worn-out shoes. And when he got to where the water flows under the fig tree, he stopped and washed his feet in the stream. Then he took out from his bundle some gram-flour, moistened it with water and began to eat. Then he tied up his bundle and shouldered it again; tucked up his cloth above his knees and crossed the stream. I've asked Auntie to let me go up to the stream, and eat my gram-flour just like him.

Madhav. And what did your Auntie say to that?

Amal. Auntie said, "Get well and then I'll take you over there." Please, Uncle, when shall I get well?

Madhav. It won't be long, dear.

Amal. Really, but then I shall go right away the moment I'm well again.

Madhav. And where will you go?

Amal. Oh, I will walk on, crossing so many streams, wading through water. Everybody will be asleep with their doors shut in the heat of the day and I will tramp on and on seeking work far, very far.

Madhav. I see! I think you had better be getting well first; then–

Amal. But then you won't want me to be learned, will you, Uncle?

Madhav. What would you rather be, then?

Amal. I can't think of anything just now; but I'll tell you later on.

Madhav. Very well. But mind you, you aren't to call out and talk to strangers again.

Amal. But I love to talk to strangers!

Madhav. Suppose they had kidnapped you?

Amal. That would have been splendid! But no one ever takes me away. They all want me to stay in here.

Madhav. I am off to my work–but, darling, you won't go out, will you?

Amal. No, I won't. But, Uncle, you'll let me be in this room by the roadside. *[Exit Madhav*

'*Dairyman*. Curds, curds, good nice curds.

Amal. Curdseller, I say, Curdseller.

Dairyman. Why do you call me? Will you buy some curds?

Amal. How can I buy? I have no money.

Dairyman. What a boy! Why call out then? Ugh! What a waste of time!

Amal. I would go with you if I could.

Dairyman. With me?

Amal. Yes, I seem to feel homesick when I hear you call from far down the road.

Dairyman (lowering his yoke-pole). Whatever are you doing here, my child?

Amal. The doctor says I'm not to be out, so I sit here all day long.

Dairyman. My poor child, whatever has happened to you?

Amal. I can't tell. You see, I am not learned, so I don't know what's the matter with me. Say, Dairyman, where do you come from?

Dairyman. From our village.

Amal. Your village? Is it very far?

Dairyman. Our village lies on the river Shamli at the foot of the Panch-mura hills.

Amal. Panch-mura hills! Shamli river! I wonder. I may have seen your village. I can't think when, though!

Dairyman. Have you seen it? Been to the foot of those hills?

Amal. Never. But I seem to remember having seen it. Your village is under some very old big trees, just by the side of the red road–isn't that so?

Dairyman. That's right, child.

Amal. And on the slope of the hill cattle grazing.

Dairyman. How wonderful! Cattle grazing in our village! Indeed there are!

Amal. And your women with red sarees fill their pitchers from the river and carry them on their heads.

Dairyman. Good, that's right! Women from our dairy village do come and draw their water from the river; but then it isn't everyone who has a red saree to put on. But, my dear child, surely you must have been there for a walk some time.

Amal. Really, Dairyman, never been there at all. But the first day doctor lets me go out, you are going to take me to your village.

Dairyman. I will, my child, with pleasure.

Amal. And you'll teach me to cry curds and shoulder the yoke like you and walk the long, long road?

Dairyman. Dear, dear, did you ever? Why should you sell curds? No, you will read big books and be learned.

Amal. No, I never want to be learned–I'll be like you and take my curds from the village by the red road near the old banyan tree, and I will hawk it from cottage to cottage. Oh, how do you cry – "Curds, curds, fine curds"? Teach me the tune, will you?

Dairyman. Dear, dear, teach you the tune; what a notion!

Amal. Please do. I love to hear it. I can't tell you how queer I feel when I hear you cry out from the bend of that road through the line of those trees! Do you know I feel like that when I hear the shrill cry of kites from almost the end of the sky?

Dairyman. Dear child, will you have some curds? Yes, do.

Amal. But I have no money.

Dairyman. No, no, no, don't talk of money! You'll make me so happy if you take some curds from me.

Amal. Say, have I kept you too long?

Dairyman. Not a bit; it has been no loss to me at all; you have taught me how to be happy selling curds. *[Exit*

Amal (intoning). Curds, curds, fine curds–from the dairy village – from the country of the Panch-mura hills by the Shamli bank. Curds, good curds; in the early morning the women make the cows stand in a row under the trees and milk them, and in the evening they turn the milk into curds. Curds, good curds. Hello, there's the watchman on his rounds. Watchman, I say, come and have a word with me.

Watchman. What's all this row about? Aren't you afraid of the likes of me?

Amal. No, why should I be?

Watchman. Suppose I march you off, then?

Amal. Where will you take me to? Is it very far, right beyond the hills?

Watchman. Suppose I march you straight to the King?

Amal. To the King! Do, will you? But the doctor won't let me go out. No one can ever take me away. I've got to stay here all day long.

Watchman. Doctor won't let you, poor fellow! So I see! Your face is pale and there are dark rings round your eyes. Your veins stick out from your poor thin hands.

Amal. Won't you sound the gong, Watchman?

Watchman. Time has not yet come.

Amal. How curious! Some say time has not yet come, and some say time has gone by! But surely your time will come the moment you strike the gong!

Watchman. That's not possible; I strike up the gong only when it is time.

Amal. Yes, I love to hear your gong. When it is mid-day and our meal is over, Uncle goes off to his work and Auntie falls asleep reading her *Ramayana*, and in the courtyard under the shadow of the wall our doggie sleeps with his nose in his curled-up tail; then your gong strikes out, "Dong, dong, dong!" Tell me, why does your gong sound?

Watchman. My gong sounds to tell the people, Time waits for none, but goes on forever.

Amal. Where, to what land?

Watchman. That none knows.

Amal. Then I suppose no one has ever been there! Oh, I do wish to fly with the time to that land of which no one knows anything.

Watchman. All of us have to get there one day, my child.

Amal. Have I too?

Watchman. Yes, you too!

Amal. But doctor won't let me out.

Watchman. One day the doctor himself may take you there by the hand.

Amal. He won't; you don't know him. He only keeps me in.

Watchman. One greater than he comes and lets us free.

Amal. When will this great doctor come for me? I can't stick in here anymore.

Watchman. Shouldn't talk like that, my child.

Amal. No. I am here where they have left me–I never move a bit. But, when your gong goes off, dong, dong, dong, it goes to my heart. Say, Watchman?

Watchman. Yes, my dear.

Amal. Say, what's going on there in that big house on the other side, where there is a flag flying high up and the people are always going in and out?

Watchman. Oh, there? That's our new Post Office.

Amal. Post Office? Whose?

Watchman. Whose? Why, the King's, surely!

Amal. Do letters come from the King to his office here?

Watchman. Of course. One fine day there may be a letter for you in there.

Amal. A letter for me? But I am only a little boy.

Watchman. The King sends tiny notes to little boys.

Amal. Oh, how splendid! When shall I have my letter? How do you know he'll write to me?

Watchman. Otherwise why should he set his Post Office here right in front of your open window, with the golden flag flying?

Amal. But who will fetch me my King's letter when it comes?

Watchman. The King has many postmen. Don't you see them run about with round gilt badges on their chests?

Amal. Well, where do they go?

Watchman. Oh, from door to door, all through the country.

Amal. I'll be the King's postman when I grow up.

Watchman. Ha! ha! Postman, indeed! Rain or shine, rich or poor, from house to house delivering letters–that's very great work!

Amal. That's what I'd like best. What makes you smile so? Oh, yes, your work is great too. When it is silent everywhere in the heat of the noonday, your gong sounds, Dong, dong, dong,–and sometimes when I wake up at night all of a sudden and find our lamp blown out, I can hear through the darkness your gong slowly sounding, Dong, dong, dong!

Watchman. There's the village headman! I must be off. If he catches me gossiping there'll be a great to-do.

Amal. The headman? Whereabouts is he?

Watchman. Right down the road there; see that huge palm-leaf umbrella hopping along? That's him!

Amal. I suppose the King's made him our headman here?

Watchman. Made him? Oh, no! A fussy busybody!

He knows so many ways of making himself unpleasant that everybody is afraid of him. It's just a game for the likes of him, making trouble for everybody. I must be off now! Mustn't keep work waiting, you know! I'll drop in again tomorrow morning and tell you all the news of the town. *[Exit*

Amal. It would be splendid to have a letter from the King

everyday. I'll read them at the window. But, oh! I can't read writing. Who'll read them out to me, I wonder! Auntie reads her *Ramayana*; she may know the King's writing. If no one will, then I must keep them carefully and read them when I'm grown up. But if the postman can't find me? Headman, Mr. Headman, may I have a word with you?

Headman. Who is yelling after me on the highway? Oh, it's you, is it, you wretched monkey?

Amal. You're the headman. Everybody minds you.

Headman (looking pleased). Yes, oh yes, they do! They must!

Amal. Do the King's postmen listen to you?

Headman. They've got to. By Jove, I'd like to see—

Amal. Will you tell the postman it's Amal who sits by the window here?

Headman. What's the good of that?

Amal. In case there's a letter for me.

Headman. A letter for you! Whoever's going to write to you?

Amal. If the King does.

Headman. Ha! ha! What an uncommon little fellow you are! Ha! ha! the King, indeed; aren't you his bosom friend, eh! You haven't met for a long while and the King is pining for you, I am sure. Wait till tomorrow and you'll have your letter.

Amal. Say, Headman, why do you speak to me in that tone of voice? Are you cross?

Headman. Upon my word! Cross, indeed! You write to the King! Madhav is a devilish swell nowadays. He's made a little pile; and so kings and padishahs are everyday talk with his people. Let me find him once and I'll make him dance. Oh, you,—you snipper-snapper! I'll get the King's letter sent to your house—indeed I will!

Amal. No, no, please don't trouble yourself about it.

Headman. And why not, pray! I'll tell the King about you and he won't be long. One of his footmen will come presently for news of you. Madhav's impudence staggers me. If the King hears of this, that'll take some of his nonsense out of him. *[Exit*

Amal. Who are you walking there? How your anklets tinkle! Do stop a while, won't you? (*A girl enters*)

Girl. I haven't a moment to spare; it is already late!

Amal. I see, you don't wish to stop; I don't care to stay on here either.

Girl. You make me think of some late star of the morning! Whatever's the matter with you?

Amal. I don't know; the doctor won't let me out.

Girl. Ah me! Don't go, then! Should listen to the doctor. People will be cross with you if you're naughty. I know, always looking out and watching must make you feel tired. Let me close the window a bit for you.

Amal. No, don't, only this one's open! All the others are shut. But will you tell me who you are? Don't seem to know you.

Girl. I am Sudha.

Amal. What Sudha?

Sudha. Don't you know? Daughter of the flower-seller here.

Amal. What do *you* do?

Sudha. I gather flowers in my basket.

Amal. Oh, flower-gathering! That is why your feet seem so glad and your anklets jingle so merrily as you walk. Wish I could be out too. Then I would pick some flowers for you from the very topmost branches right out of sight.

Sudha. Would you really? Do you know as much about flowers as I?

Amal. Yes, I do, quite as much. I know all about Champa of the fairy tale and his six brothers. If only they let me, I'll go right into the dense forest where you can't find your way. And where the honey-sipping humming-bird rocks himself on the end of the thinnest branch, I will blossom into a *champa*. Would you be my sister Parul?

Sudha. You are silly! How can I be sister Parul when I am Sudha and my mother is Sasi, the flower-seller? I have to weave so many garlands a day. It would be jolly if I could lounge here like you!

Amal. What would you do then, all the day long?

Sudha. I could have great times with my doll Benay the bride, and Meni the pussy-cat, and–but I say, it is getting late and I mustn't stop, or I won't find a single flower.

Amal. Oh, wait a little longer; I do like it so!

Sudha. Ah, well–now don't you be naughty. Be good and sit still, and on my way back home with the flowers I'll come and talk with you.

Amal. And you'll let me have a flower, then?

Sudha. No, how can I? It has to be paid for.

Amal. I'll pay when I grow up–before I leave to look for work out on the other side of that stream there.

Sudha. Very well, then.

Amal. And you'll come back when you have your flowers?

Sudha. I will.

Amal. You will, really?

Sudha. Yes, I will.

Amal. You won't forget me? I am Amal, remember that.

Sudha. I won't forget you, you'll see. *[Exit*

(A Troop of Boys enter)

Amal. Say, brothers, where are you all off to? Stop here a little.

A Boy. We're off to play.

Amal. What will you play at, brothers?

A Boy. We'll play at being ploughmen.

Another Boy (showing a stick). This is our ploughshare.

Another Boy. We two are the pair of oxen.

Amal. And you're going to play the whole day?

A Boy. Yes, all day long.

Amal. And you will come home in the evening by the road along the river bank?

A Boy. Yes.

Amal. Do you pass our house on your way home?

A Boy. Come out and play with us; yes, do.

Amal. Doctor won't let me out.

A Boy. Doctor! Do you mean to say you mind what the doctor says? Let's be off; it is getting late.

Amal. Don't go. Play on the road near this window. I could watch you, then.

A Boy. What can we play at here?

Amal. With all these toys of mine that are lying about. Here you are; have them. I can't play alone. They are getting dirty and are of no use to me.

Boys. How jolly! What fine toys! Look, here's a ship. There's old mother Jatai. Isn't this a gorgeous sepoy? And you'll let us have them all? You don't really mind?

Amal. No, not a bit; have them by all means.

A Boy. You don't want them back?

Amal. Oh, no, I shan't want them.

A Boy. Say, won't you get a scolding for this?

Amal. No one will scold me. But will you play with them in front of our door for a while every morning? I'll get you new ones when these are old.

A Boy. Oh, yes, we will. I say, put these sepoys into a line. We'll play at war; where can we get a musket? Oh, look here, this bit of reed will do nicely. Say, but you're off to sleep already.

Amal. I'm afraid I'm sleepy. I don't know, I feel like it at times. I have been sitting a long while and I'm tired; my back aches.

A Boy. It's hardly mid day now. How is it you're sleepy? Listen! The gong's sounding the first watch.

Amal. Yes, Dong, dong, dong; it tolls me to sleep.

A Boy. We had better go, then. We'll come in again to-morrow morning.

Amal. I want to ask you something before you go. You are always out—do you know of the King's postmen?

Boys. Yes, quite well.

Amal. Who are they? Tell me their names.

A Boy. One's Badal.

Another Boy. Another's Sarat.

Another Boy. There's so many of them.

Amal. Do you think they will know me if there's a letter for me?

A Boy. Surely, if your name's on the letter they will find you out.

Amal. When you call in to-morrow morning, will you bring one of them along so that he'll know me?

A Boy. Yes, if you like.

CURTAIN

ACT II

(*Amal in Bed*)

Amal. Can't I go near the window to-day, Uncle? Would the doctor mind that too?

Madhav. Yes, darling; you see you've made yourself worse squatting there day after day.

Amal. Oh, no, I don't know if it's made me more ill, but I always feel well when I'm there.

Madhav. No, you don't; you squat there and make friends with the whole lot of people round here, old and young, as if they are holding a fair right under my eaves—flesh and blood won't stand that strain. Just see—your face is quite pale.

Amal. Uncle, I fear my *fakir* 'll pass and not see me by the window.

Madhav. Your *fakir*; whoever's that?

Amal. He comes and chats to me of the many lands where he's been. I love to hear him.

Madhav. How's that? I don't know of any fakirs.

Amal. This is about the time he comes in. I beg of you, by your dear feet, ask him in for a moment to talk to me here.

(*Gaffer enters in a Fakir's guise*)

Amal. There you are. Come here, Fakir, by my bed-side.

Madhav. Upon my word, but this is—

Gaffer (winking hard). I am the Fakir.

Madhav. It beats my reckoning what you're not.

Amal. Where have you been this time, Fakir?

Gaffer. To the Isle of Parrots. I am just back.

Madhav. The Parrots' Isle!

Gaffer. Is it so very astonishing? I am not like you. A journey doesn't cost a thing. I tramp just where I like.

Amal (clapping). How jolly for you! Remember your promise to take me with you as your follower when I'm well.

Gaffer. Of course, and I'll teach you so many travellers' secrets that nothing in sea or forest or mountain can bar your way.

Madhav. What's all this rigmarole?

Gaffer. Amal, my dear, I bow to nothing in sea or mountain; but if the doctor joins in with this uncle of yours, then I with all my magic must own myself beaten.

Amal. No. Uncle won't tell the doctor. And I promise to lie quiet; but the day I am well, off I go with the Fakir, and nothing in sea or mountain or torrent shall stand in my way.

Madhav. Fie, dear child, don't keep on harping upon going! It makes me so sad to hear you talk so.

Amal. Tell me, Fakir, what the Parrots' Isle is like.

Gaffer. It's a land of wonders; it's a haunt of birds. No men are there; and they neither speak nor walk, they simply sing and they fly.

Amal. How glorious! And it's by some sea?

Gaffer. Of course. It's on the sea.

Amal. And green hills are there?

Gaffer. Indeed, they live among the green hills; and in the time of the sunset when there is a red glow on the hillside, all the birds with their green wings go flocking to their nests.

Amal. And there are waterfalls!

Gaffer. Dear me, of course; you don't have a hill without its waterfalls. Oh, it's like molten diamonds; and, my dear, what dances they have! Don't they make the pebbles sing as they rush over them to the sea! No devil of a doctor can stop them for a moment. The birds looked upon me as nothing but a man, merely a trifling creature without wings—and they would have nothing to do with me. Were it not so I would build a small cabin for myself among their crowd of nests and pass my days counting the sea-waves.

Amal. How I wish I were a bird! Then—

Gaffer. But that would have been a bit of a job; I hear you've fixed up with the dairyman to be a hawker of curds when you grow up; I'm afraid such business won't flourish among birds; you might land yourself into serious loss.

Madhav. Really this is too much. Between you two I shall turn crazy. Now, I'm off.

Amal. Has the dairyman been, Uncle?

Madhav. And why shouldn't he? He won't bother his head running errands for your pet fakir, in and out among the nests in his Parrots' Isle. But he has left a jar of curds for you saying that he is busy with his niece's wedding in the village, and has to order a band at Kamlipara.

Amal. But he is going to marry me to his little niece.

Gaffer. Dear me, we are in a fix now.

Amal. He said she would be my lovely little bride with a pair of pearl drops in her ears and dressed in a lovely red saree; and in the morning she would milk with her own hands the black cow and feed me with warm milk with foam on it from a brand-new earthen cruse; and in the evenings she would carry the lamp round the cow-house, and then come and sit by me to tell me tales of Champa and his six brothers.

Gaffer. How charming! It would even tempt me, a hermit! But never mind, dear, about this wedding. Let it be. I tell you that when you marry there'll be no lack of nieces in his household.

Madhav. Shut up! This is more than I can stand. [*Exit*

Amal. Fakir, now that Uncle's off, just tell me, has the King sent me a letter to the Post Office?

Gaffer. I gather that his letter has already started; it is on the way here.

Amal. On the way? Where is it? Is it on that road winding through the trees which you can follow to the end of the forest when the sky is quite clear after rain?

Gaffer. That is where it is. You know all about it already.

Amal. I do, everything.

Gaffer. So I see, but how?

Amal. I can't say; but it's quite clear to me. I fancy I've seen it often in days long gone by. How long ago I can't tell. Do you know when? I can see it all: there, the King's postman coming down the hillside alone, a lantern in his left hand and on his back a bag of letters; climbing down for ever so long, for days and nights, and where at the foot of the mountain the waterfall becomes a stream he takes to the footpath on the bank and walks on through the rye; then comes the sugar cane field and he disappears into the narrow lane cutting through the tall stems of sugar canes; then he reaches the open meadow where the cricket chirps and where there is not a single man to be seen, only the snipe wagging their tails and poking at the mud with their bills. I can feel him coming nearer and nearer and my heart becomes glad.

Gaffer. My eyes are not young; but you make me see all the same.

Amal. Say, Fakir, do you know the King who has this Post Office?

Gaffer. I do; I go to him for my alms everyday.

Amal. Good! When I get well I must have my alms too from him, mayn't I?

Gaffer. You won't need to ask, my dear; he'll give it to you of his own accord.

Amal. No, I will go to his gate and cry, "Victory to thee, O King!" and dancing to the tabor's sound, ask for alms. Won't it be nice?

Gaffer. It will be splendid, and if you're with me I shall have my full share. But what will you ask?

Amal. I shall say, "Make me your postman, that I may go about, lantern in hand, delivering your letters from door to door. Don't let me stay at home all day!"

Gaffer. What is there to be sad for, my child, even were you to stay at home?

Amal. It isn't sad. When they shut me in here first I felt the day was so long. Since the King's Post Office was put there I like more and more being indoors, and as I think I shall get a letter one day, I feel quite happy and then I don't mind being quiet and alone. I wonder if I shall make out what'll be in the King's letter?

Gaffer. Even if you didn't wouldn't it be enough if it just bore your name?

(*Madhav enters*)

Madhav. Have you any idea of the trouble you've got me into, between you two?

Gaffer. What's the matter?

Madhav. I hear you've let it get rumoured about that the King has planted his office here to send messages to both of you,

Gaffer. Well, what about it?

Madhav. Our headman Panchanan has had it told to the King anonymously,

Gaffer. Aren't we aware that everything reaches the King's ears?

Madhav. Then why don't you look out? Why take the King's

name in vain? You'll bring me to ruin if you do.

Amal. Say, Fakir, will the King be cross?

Gaffer. Cross, nonsense! And with a child like you and a fakir such as I am? Let's see if the King be angry, and then won't I give him a piece of my mind!

Amal. Say, Fakir, I've been feeling a sort of darkness coming over my eyes since the morning. Everything seems like a dream. I long to be quiet. I don't feel like talking at all. Won't the King's letter come? Suppose this room melts away all of a sudden, suppose—

Gaffer (fanning Amal). The letter's sure to come today, my boy.

(Doctor enters)

Doctor. And how do you feel to-day?

Amal. Feel awfully well to-day, Doctor. All pain seems to have left me.

Doctor (aside to Madhav). Don't quite like the look of that smile. Bad sign that, his feeling well! Chakradhan has observed—

Madhav. For goodness' sake, Doctor, leave Chakradhan alone. Tell me what's going to happen?

Doctor. Can't hold him in much longer, I fear! I warned you before—this looks like a fresh exposure.

Madhav. No, I've used the utmost care, never let him out of doors; and the windows have been shut almost all the time.

Doctor. There's a peculiar quality in the air to-day. As I came in I found a fearful draught through your front door. That's most hurtful. Better lock it at once. Would it matter if this kept your visitors off for two or three days? If someone happens to call unexpectedly—there's the back door. You had better shut this window as well, it's letting in the sunset rays only to keep the patient awake.

Madhav. Amal has shut his eyes. I expect he is sleeping. His face tells me–Oh, Doctor, I bring in a child who is a stranger and love him as my own, and now I suppose I must lose him!

Doctor. What's that? There's your headman sailing in!–What a bother! I must be going, brother. You had better stir about and see to the doors being properly fastened. I will send on a strong dose directly I get home. Try it on him–it may save him at last, if he can be saved at all. *[Exeunt Madhav and Doctor*

(The Headman enters)

Headman. Hello, urchin!–

Gaffer (rising hastily). 'Sh, be quiet.

Amal. No, Fakir, did you think I was asleep? I wasn't. I can hear everything; yes, and voices far away. I feel that mother and father are sitting by my pillow and speaking to me.

(Madhav enters)

Headman. I say, Madhav, I hear you hobnob with bigwigs nowadays.

Madhav. Spare me your jokes, Headman; we are but common people.

Headman. But your child here is expecting a letter from the King.

Madhav. Don't you take any notice of him, a mere foolish boy!

Headman. Indeed, why not! It'll beat the King hard to find a better family! Don't you see why the King plants his new Post Office right before your window? Why, there's a letter for you from the King, urchin.

Amal (starting up). Indeed, really!

Headman. How can it be false? You're the King's chum. Here's your letter (*showing a blank slip of paper*). Ha, ha, ha! This is the letter.

Amal. Please don't mock me. Say, Fakir, is it so?

Gaffer. Yes, my dear. I as Fakir tell you it is his letter.

Amal. How is it I can't see? It all looks so blank to me. What is there in the letter, Mr. Headman?

Headman. The King says, "I am calling on you shortly; you had better have puffed rice for me.–Palace fare is quite tasteless to me now." Ha! ha! ha!

Madhav (with folded palms). I beseech you, Headman, don't you joke about these things–

Gaffer. Joking indeed! He would not dare.

Madkav. Are you out of your mind too, Gaffer?

Gaffer. Out of my mind; well then, I am; I can read plainly that the King writes he will come himself to see Amal, with the State Physician.

Amal. Fakir, Fakir, 'sh, his trumpet! Can't you hear?

Headman. Ha! ha! ha! I fear he won't until he's a bit more off his head.

Amal. Mr. Headman, I thought you were cross with me and didn't love me. I never could have believed you would fetch me the King's letter. Let me wipe the dust off your feet.

Headman. This little child does have an instinct of reverence. Though a little silly, he has a good heart.

Amal. It's hard on the fourth watch now, I suppose. Hark, the gong, "Dong, dong, ding–Dong, dong, ding." Is the evening star up? How is it I can't see–

Gaffer. Oh, the windows are all shut; I'll open them.

(A knocking outside)

Madhav. What's that?–Who is it?–What a bother!

Voice (from outside). Open the door.

Madhav. Headman–I hope they're not robbers.

Headman. Who's there?–It is Panchanan, the headman, who calls.–Aren't you afraid to make that noise? Fancy! The noise has ceased! Panchanan's voice carries far.–Yes, show me the biggest robbers!–

Madhav (peering out of the window). No wonder the noise has ceased. They've smashed the outer door. (*The King's Herald enters*)

Herald. Our Sovereign King comes to-night!

Headman. My God!

Amal. At what hour of the night, Herald?

Herald. On the second watch.

Amal. When my friend the watchman will strike his gong from the city gates, "Ding dong ding, ding dong ding"–then?

Herald. Yes, then. The King sends his greatest physician to attend on his young friend. (*State Physician enters*)

State Physician. What's this? How close it is here! Open wide all the doors and windows. (*Feeling Amal's body*.) How do you feel, my child?

Amal. I feel very well, Doctor, very well. All pain is gone. How fresh and open! I can see all the stars now twinkling from the other side of the dark.

Physician. Will you feel well enough to leave your bed when the King comes in the middle watches of the night?

Amal. Of course, I'm dying to be about for ever so long. I'll ask the King to find me the polar star.–I must have seen it often, but I don't know exactly which it is.

Physician. He will tell you everything. (*To Madhav*.) Arrange flowers through the room for the King's visit. (*Indicating the Headman*.) We can't have that person in here.

Amal. No, let him be, Doctor. He is a friend. It was he who brought me the King's letter.

Physician. Very well, my child. He may remain if he is a friend of yours.

Madhav (whispering into Amal's ear). My child, the King loves you. He is coming himself. Beg for a gift from him. You know our humble circumstances.

Amal. Don't you worry, Uncle.–I've made up my mind about it.

Madhav. What is it, my child?

Amal. I shall ask him to make me one of his postmen that I may wander far and wide, delivering his message from door to door.

Madhav (slapping his forehead). Alas, is that all?

Amal. What'll be our offerings to the King, Uncle, when he comes?

Herald. He has commanded puffed rice.

Amal. Puffed rice. Say, Headman, you're right. You said so. You knew all we didn't.

Headman. If you would send word to my house I could manage for the King's advent really nice–

Physician. No need at all. Now be quiet, all of you. Sleep is coming over him. I'll sit by his pillow; he's dropping asleep. Blow out the oil-lamp. Only let the star-light stream in. Hush, he sleeps.

Madhav (addressing Gaffer). What are you standing there for like a statue, folding your palms?–I am nervous.–Say, are there good omens? Why are they darkening the room? How will star-light help?

Gaffer. Silence, unbeliever!

(*Sudha enters*)

Sudha. Amal!

Physician. He's asleep.

Sudha. I have some flowers for him. Mayn't I give them into his own hand?

Physician. Yes, you may.
Sudha. When will he be awake?
Physician. Directly the King comes and calls him.
Sudha. Will you whisper a word for me in his ear?
Physician. What shall I say?
Sudha. Tell him Sudha has not forgotten him.

CURTAIN

CHITRA

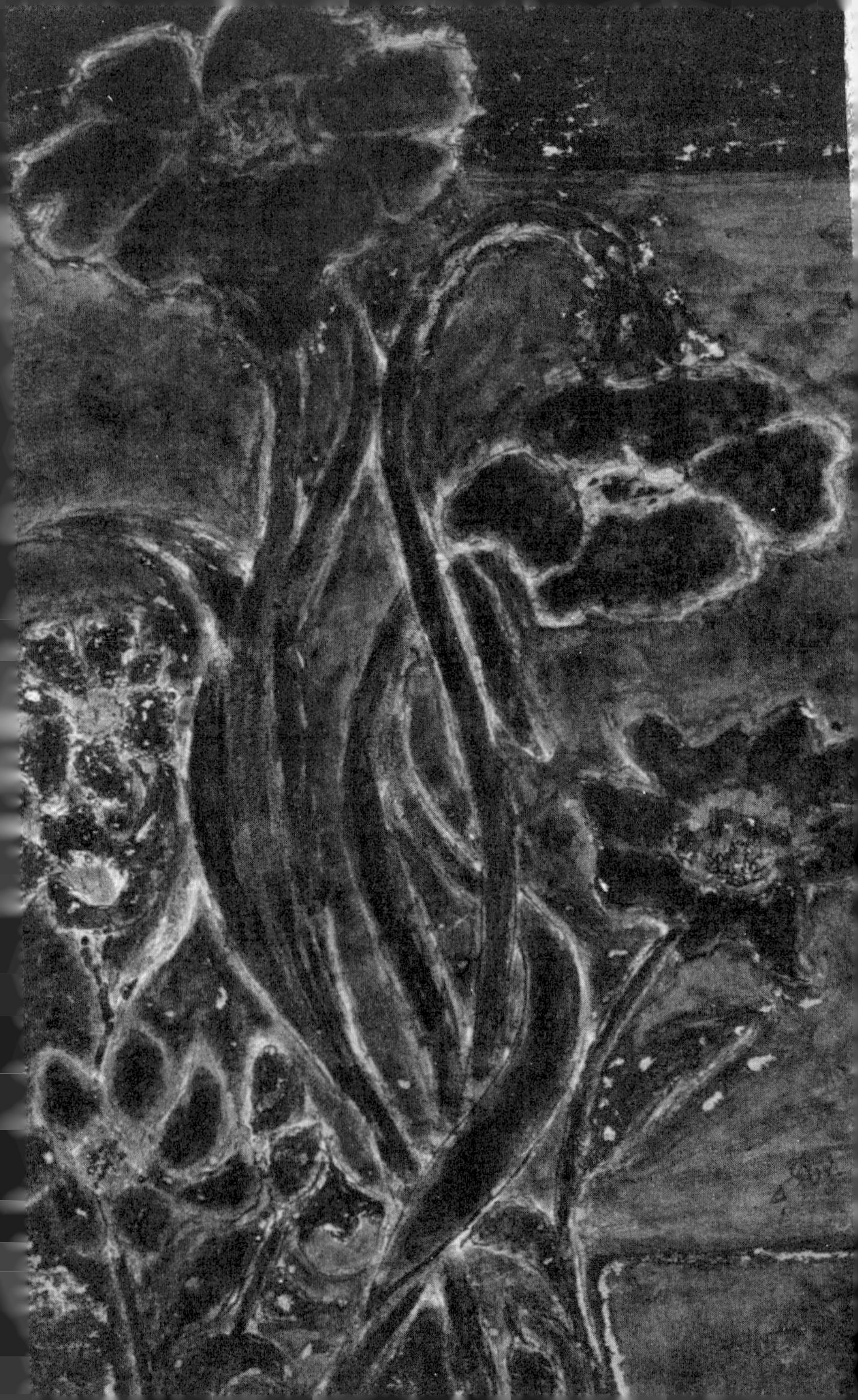

SCENE I

CHITRA: Art thou the god with the five darts, the Lord of Love?

MADANA: I am he who was the first born in the heart of the Creator. I bind in bonds of pain and bliss the lives of men and women!

CHITRA: I know, I know what that pain is and those bonds.—And who art thou, my lord?

VASANTA: I am his friend—Vasanta—the King of the Seasons. Death and decrepitude would wear the world to the bone but that I follow them and constantly attack them. I am Eternal Youth.

CHITRA: I bow to thee, Lord Vasanta.

MADANA: But what stern vow is thine, fair stranger? Why dost thou wither thy fresh youth with penance and mortification? Such a sacrifice is not fit for the worship of love. Who art thou and what is thy prayer?

CHITRA: I am Chitra, the daughter of the kingly house of Manipur. With god-like grace Lord Shiva promised to my royal grandsire an unbroken line of male descent. Nevertheless, the divine word proved powerless to change the spark of life in my mother's womb—so invincible was my nature, woman though I be.

MADANA: I know, that is why thy father brings thee up as his son. He has taught thee the use of the bow and all the duties of a king.

CHITRA: Yes, that is why I am dressed in man's attire and have left the seclusion of a woman's chamber. I know no feminine wiles for winning hearts. My hands are strong to bend the bow, but

I have never learnt Cupid's archery, the play of eyes.

MADANA: That requires no schooling, fair one. The eye does its work untaught, and he knows how well, who is struck in the heart.

CHITRA: One day, in search of game I roved alone to the forest on the bank of the Purna river. Tying my horse to a tree trunk I entered a dense thicket on the track of a deer. I found a narrow sinuous path meandering through the dusk of the entangled boughs, the foliage vibrated with the chirping of crickets, when all of a sudden I came upon a man lying on a bed of dried leaves, across my path. I asked him haughtily to move aside, but he heeded not. Then, with the sharp end of my bow I pricked him in contempt. Instantly, he leapt up with straight, tall limbs, like a sudden tongue of fire from a heap of ashes. An amused smile flickered round the corners of his mouth, perhaps at the sight of my boyish countenance. Then, for the first time in my life I felt myself a woman, and knew that a man was before me.

MADANA: At the auspicious hour I teach the man and the woman this supreme lesson to know themselves. What happened after that?

CHITRA. With fear and wonder I asked him 'Who are you?' 'I am Arjuna,' he said, 'of the great Kuru clan.' I stood petrified like a statue, and forgot to do him obeisance. Was this indeed, Arjuna, the one great idol of my dreams! Yes, I had long ago heard how he had vowed a twelve-years' celibacy. Many a day my young ambition had spurred me on to break my lance with him, to challenge him in disguise to single combat, and prove my skill in arms against him. Ah, foolish heart, whither fled thy presumption? Could I but exchange my youth with all its aspirations for the clod of earth under his feet? I should deem it a most precious grace. I know not in what whirlpool of thought I was lost, when suddenly I saw him vanish through the trees.

O foolish woman, neither didst thou greet him, nor speak a word, nor beg forgiveness, but stoodest like a barbarian boor while he contemptuously walked away!... Next morning, I laid aside my man's clothing. I donned bracelets, anklets, waist-chain, and a gown of purple red silk. The unaccustomed dress clung about my shrinking shame; but I hastened on my quest, and found Arjuna in the forest temple of Shiva.

MADANA: Tell me the story to the end. I am the heart-born god, and I understand the mystery of these impulses.

CHITRA: Only vaguely can I remember what things I said, and what answer I got. Do not ask me to tell you all. Shame fell on me like a thunderbolt, yet could not break me to pieces, so utterly hard, so like a man am I. His last words as I walked home pricked my ears like red hot needles. 'I have taken the vow of celibacy. I am not fit to be thy husband!' Oh, the vow of a man! Surely, thou knowest, thou god of love, the unnumbered saints and sages have surrendered the merits of their life-long penance at the feet of a woman. I broke my bow in two and burnt my arrows in the fire. I hated my strong, lithe arm, scored by drawing the bowstring. O Love, god Love, thou hast laid low in the dust the vain pride of my man-like strength; and all my man's training lies crushed under thy feet. Now, teach me thy lessons; give me the power of the weak and the weapon of the unarmed hand.

MADANA: I will be thy friend. I will bring the world-conquering Arjuna a captive before thee, to accept his rebellion's sentence at thy hand.

CHITRA: Had I but the time needed, I could win his heart by slow degrees, and ask no help of the gods. I would stand by his side as a comrade, drive the fierce horses of his war-chariot, attend him in the pleasures of the chase, keep guard at night at the entrance of his tent, and help him in all the great duties of a Kshatriya, rescuing the weak, and meting out justice where it is due. Surely at last, the day would have come for him to look at me and wonder, 'What boy is this? Has one of my slaves in a former life followed me like my good deeds into this?' I am not the woman who nourishes her despair in lonely silence, feeding it with nightly tears and covering it with the daily patient smile, a widow from her birth. The flower of my desire shall never drop into the dust before it has ripened to fruit. But it is the labour of a life-time to make one's true self known and honoured. Therefore, I have come to thy door, thou world-vanquishing Love, and thou, *Vasanta*, youthful Lord of the Seasons, take from my young body this primal injustice, an unattractive plainness. For a single day make me superbly beautiful, even as beautiful as was the sudden blooming of love in my heart. Give me but one brief day of perfect beauty, and I will answer for the days that follow.

MADANA: Lady, I grant thy prayer.

VASANTA: Not for the short span of a day, but for one whole year the charm of spring blossoms shall nestle round thy limbs.

SCENE II

ARJUNA: Was I dreaming or was what I saw by the lake truly there? Sitting on the mossy turf, I mused over bygone years in the sloping shadows of the evening, when slowly there came out from the folding darkness of foliage an apparition of beauty in the perfect form of a woman, and stood on a white slab of stone at the water's brink. It seemed that the heart of the earth must heave in joy under her bare white feet. Methought the vague veilings of her body should melt in ecstasy into air as the golden mist of dawn melts from off the snowy peak of the eastern hill. She bowed herself above the shining mirror of the lake and saw the reflection of her face. She started up in awe and stood still; then smiled, and with a careless sweep of her left arm unloosed her hair and let it trail on the earth at her feet. She bared her bosom and looked at her arms, so flawlessly modelled, and instinct with an exquisite caress. Bending her head she saw the sweet blossoming of her youth and the tender bloom and blush of her skin. She beamed with a glad surprise. So, if the white lotus bud on opening her eyes in the morning were to arch her neck and see her shadow in the water, would she wonder at herself the live-long day. But a moment after the smile passed from her face and a shade of sadness crept into her eyes. She bound up her tresses, drew her veil over her arms, and sighing slowly, walked away like a beauteous evening fading into the night. To me the supreme fulfilment of desire seemed to have been revealed in a flash and then to have vanished.... But who is it that pushes the door?

[*Enter* CHITRA, *dressed as a woman.*]

Ah! it is she. Quiet, my heart!.... Fear me not, lady! I am a Kshatriya.

CHITRA: Honoured sir, you are my guest. I live in this temple. I know not in what way I can show you hospitality.

ARJUNA: Fair lady, the very sight of you is indeed, the highest hospitality. If you will not take it amiss I would ask you a question.

CHITRA: You have permission.

ARJUNA: What stern vow keeps you immured in this solitary temple, depriving all mortals of a vision of so much loveliness?

CHITRA: I harbour a secret desire in my heart, for the fulfilment of which I offer daily prayers to Lord Shiva.

ARJUNA: Alas, what can you desire, you who are the desire of the whole world! From the eastern-most hill on whose summit the morning sun first prints his fiery foot to the end of the sunset land have I travelled. I have seen whatever is most precious, beautiful and great on the earth. My knowledge shall be yours, only say for what or for whom you seek.

CHITRA: He whom I seek is known to all.

ARJUNA: Indeed! Who may this favourite of the gods be, whose fame has captured your heart?

CHITRA: Sprung from the highest of all royal houses, the greatest of all heroes is he.

ARJUNA: Lady, offer not such a wealth of beauty as is yours on the altar of false reputation. Spurious fame spreads from tongue to tongue like the fog of the early dawn before the sun rises. Tell me who in the highest of kingly lines is the supreme hero?

CHITRA: Hermit, you are jealous of other men's fame. Do you not know that all over the world the royal house of the Kurus is the most famous?

ARJUNA: The house of the Kurus!

CHITRA: And have you never heard of the greatest name of that far-famed house?

ARJUNA: From your own lips let me hear it.

CHITRA: Arjuna, the conqueror of world. I have culled from the mouths of the multitude that imperishable name and hidden it with care in my maiden heart. Hermit, why do you look perturbed? Has that name only a deceitful glitter? Say so, and I will not hesitate to break this casket of my heart and throw the false gem to the dust.

ARJUNA: Be his name and fame, his bravery and prowess false or true, for mercy's sake do not banish him from your heart—for he kneels at your feet even now.

CHITRA: You, Arjuna!

ARJUNA: Yes, I am he, the love-hungered guest at your door.

CHITRA: Then, it is not true that Arjuna has taken a vow of chastity for twelve long years?

ARJUNA: But you have dissolved my vow even as the moon dissolves the night's vow of obscurity.

CHITRA: Oh, shame upon you! What have you seen in me that makes you false to yourself? Whom do you seek in these dark eyes, in these milk-white arms, if you are ready to pay for her the price of your probity? Not my true self, I know. Surely, this cannot be love, this is not man's highest homage to woman! Alas, that this frail disguise, the body, should make one blind to the light of the deathless spirit! Yes, now indeed, I know, Arjuna, the fame of your heroic manhood is false.

ARJUNA: Ah, I feel how vain is fame, the pride of prowess! Everything seems to me a dream. You alone are perfect; you are the wealth of the world, the end of all poverty, the goal of all efforts, the one woman! Others there are who can be but slowly known.

While to see you for a moment is to see perfect completeness once and forever.

CHITRA: Alas, it is not I, not I Arjuna! It is the deceit of a god. Go, go, my hero, go. Woo not falsehood, offer not your great heart to an illusion! Go.

SCENE III

CHITRA: No, impossible. To face that fervent gaze that almost grasps you like clutching hands of the hungry spirit within; to feel his heart struggling to break its bounds urging its passionate cry through the entire body—and then to send him away like a beggar—no, impossible.

[*Enter* MADANA *and* VASANTA.]

Ah, god of love, what fearful flame is this with which thou hast enveloped me! I burn, and I burn whatever I touch.

MADANA: I desire to know what happened last night.

CHITRA: At evening, I lay down on a grassy bed strewn with the petals of spring flowers, and recollected the wonderful praise of my beauty I had heard from Arjuna;—drinking drop-by-drop the honey that I had stored during the long day. The history of my past life like that of my former existences was forgotten. I felt like a flower, which has but a few fleeting hours to listen to all the humming flatteries and whispered murmurs of the woodlands and then must lower its eyes from the sky, bend its head and at a breath give itself up to the dust without a cry, thus ending the short story of a perfect moment that has neither past nor future.

VASANTA: A limitless life of glory can bloom and spend itself in a morning.

MADANA: Like an endless meaning in the narrow span of a song.

CHITRA: The southern breeze caressed me to sleep. From the flowering *Malati* bower overhead silent kisses dropped over my body. On my hair, my breast, my feet, each flower chose a bed to die on. I slept. And suddenly, in the depth of my sleep, I felt as if some intense eager look, like tapering fingers of flame, touched my slumbering body. I started up and saw the Hermit standing before me. The moon had moved to the west, peering through the leaves to espy this wonder of divine art wrought in a fragile human frame. The air was heavy with perfume; the silence of the night was vocal with the chirping of crickets; the reflections of the trees hung motionless in the lake; and with his staff in his hand he stood, tall and straight and still, like a forest tree. It seemed to me that I had, on opening my eyes, died to all realities of life and undergone a dream birth into a shadow land. Shame slipped to my feet like loosened clothes. I heard his call–'Beloved, my most beloved!' And all my forgotten lives united as one and responded to it. I said, 'Take me, take all I am!' And I stretched out my arms to him. The moon set behind the trees. One curtain of darkness covered all. Heaven and earth, time and space, pleasure and pain, death and life merged together in an unbearable ecstasy.... With the first gleam of light, the first twitter of birds, I rose up and sat leaning on my left arm. He lay asleep with a vague smile about his lips like the crescent moon in the morning. The rosy red glow of the dawn fell upon his noble forehead. I sighed and stood up. I drew together the leafy lianas to screen the streaming sun from his face. I looked about me and saw the same old earth. I remembered what I used to be, and ran and ran like a deer afraid of her own shadow, through the forest path strewn with *Shephali* flowers. I found a lonely nook, and sitting down covered my face with both hands, and tried to weep and cry. But no tears came to my eyes.

MADANA: Alas, thou daughter of mortals! I stole from the divine storehouse the fragrant wine of heaven, filled with it one earthly night to the brim, and placed it in thy hand to drink–

yet still I hear this cry of anguish!

CHITRA: [*bitterly*]. Who drank it? The rarest completion of life's desire, the first union of love was proffered to me, but was wrested from my grasp? This borrowed beauty, this falsehood that enwraps me, will slip from me taking with it the only monument of that sweet union, as the petals fall from an overblown flower; and the woman ashamed of her naked poverty will sit weeping day and night. Lord Love, this cursed appearance companions me like a demon robbing me of all the prizes of love—all the kisses for which my heart is athirst.

MADANA: Alas, how vain thy single night had been! The barque of joy came in sight, but the waves would not let it touch the shore.

CHITRA: Heaven came so close to my hand that I forgot for a moment that it had not reached me. But when I woke in the morning from my dream I found that my body had become my own rival. It is my hateful task to deck her everyday, to send her to my beloved and see her caressed by him. O god, take back thy boon!

MADANA: But if I take it from you, how can you stand before your lover? To snatch away the cup from his lips when he has scarcely drained his first draught of pleasure, would not that be cruel? With what resentful anger he must regard thee then?

CHITRA: That would be better far than this. I will reveal my true self to him, a nobler thing than this disguise. If he rejects it, if he spurns me and breaks my heart, I will bear even that in silence.

VASANTA: Listen to my advice. When with the advent of autumn the flowering season is over then comes the triumph of fruitage. A time will come of itself when the heat-cloyed bloom of the body will droop and Arjuna will gladly accept the abiding fruitful truth in thee. O child, go back to thy mad festival.

SCENE IV

CHITRA: Why do you watch me like that, my warrior?

ARJUNA: I watch how you weave that garland. Skill and grace, the twin brother and sister, are dancing playfully on your finger tips. I am watching and thinking.

CHITRA: What are you thinking, sir?

ARJUNA: I am thinking that you, with this same lightness of touch and sweetness, are weaving my days of exile into an immortal wreath, to crown me when I return home.

CHITRA: Home! But this love is not for a home!

ARJUNA: Not for a home?

CHITRA: No. Never talk of that. Take to your home what is abiding and strong. Leave the little wild flower where it was born; leave it beautifully to die at the day's end among all fading blossoms and decaying leaves. Do not take it to your palace hall to fling it on the stony floor which knows no pity for things that fade and are forgotten.

ARJUNA: Is ours that kind of love?

CHITRA: Yes, no other! Why regret it? That which was meant for idle days should never outlive them. Joy turns into pain when the door by which it should depart is shut against it. Take it and keep it as long as it lasts. Let not the satiety of your evening claim more than the desire of your morning could earn.... The day is done. Put this garland on. I am tired. Take me in your arms, my love. Let all vain bickerings of discontent die away at the sweet meeting of our lips.

ARJUNA: Hush! Listen, my beloved, the sound of prayer bells from the distant village temple steals upon the evening air across the silent trees!

SCENE V

VASANTA: I cannot keep pace with thee, my friend! I am tired. It is a hard task to keep alive the fire thou hast kindled. Sleep overtakes me, the fan drops from my hand, and cold ashes cover the glow of the fire. I start up again from my slumber and with all my might rescue the weary flame. But this can go on no longer.

MADANA: I know, thou art as fickle as a child. Ever restless is thy play in heaven and on earth. Things that thou for days buildest up with endless detail thou dost shatter in a moment without regret. But this work of ours is nearly finished. Pleasure-winged days fly fast, and the year, almost at its end, swoons in rapturous bliss.

SCENE VI

ARJUNA: I woke in the morning and found that my dreams had distilled a gem. I have no casket to inclose it, no king's crown whereon to fix it, no chain from which to hang it, and yet have not the heart to throw it away. My Kshatriya's right arm, idly occupied in holding it, forgets its duties.

[*Enter* CHITRA.]

CHITRA: Tell me your thoughts, sir!

ARJUNA: My mind is busy with thoughts of hunting today. See, how the rain pours in torrents and fiercely beats upon the hillside. The dark shadow of the clouds hangs heavily over the forest, and the swollen stream, like reckless youth, overleaps all barriers with mocking laughter. On such rainy days we five brothers would go to the Chitraka forest to chase wild beasts. Those were glad times. Our hearts danced to the drumbeat of rumbling clouds. The woods resounded with the screams of peacocks. Timid deer could not hear our approaching steps for the patter of rain and the noise of waterfalls; the leopards would leave their tracks on the wet earth, betraying their lairs. Our sport over, we dared each other to swim across turbulent streams on our way back home. The restless spirit is on me. I long to go hunting.

CHITRA: First, run down the quarry you are now following. Are you quite certain that the enchanted deer your pursue must needs be caught? No, not yet. Like a dream the wild creature eludes you when it seems most nearly yours. Look how the wind is chased by the mad rain that discharges a thousand arrows after it. Yet, it goes free and unconquered. Our sport is like that, my love! You give chase to the fleet-footed spirit of beauty, aiming at her every dart you have in your hands. Yet, this magic deer runs ever free and untouched.

ARJUNA: My love, have you no home where kind hearts are waiting for your return? A home which you once made sweet with your gentle service and whose light went out when you left it for this wilderness?

CHITRA: Why these questions? Are the hours of unthinking pleasure over? Do you not know that I am no more than what you see before you? For me there is no vista beyond. The dew that hangs on the tip of a *Kinsuka* petal has neither name nor destination. It offers no answer to any question. She whom you love is like that perfect bead of dew.

ARJUNA: Has she no tie with the world? Can she be merely like a fragment of heaven dropped on the earth through the carelessness of a wanton god?

CHITRA: Yes.

ARJUNA: Ah, that is why I always seem about to lose you. My heart is unsatisfied, my mind knows no peace. Come closer to me, unattainable one! Surrender yourself to the bonds of name and home and parentage. Let my heart feel you on all sides and live with you in the peaceful security of love.

CHITRA: Why this vain effort to catch and keep the tints of the clouds, the dance of the waves, the smell of the flowers?

ARJUNA: Mistress mine, do not hope to pacify love with airy nothings. Give me something to clasp, something that can last longer than pleasure, that can endure even through suffering.

CHITRA: Hero mine, the year is not yet full, and you are tired already! Now, I know that it is Heaven's blessing that has made the flower's term of life short. Could this body of mine have drooped and died with the flowers of last spring it surely would have died with honour. Yet, its days are numbered, my love. Spare it not, press it dry of honey, for fear your beggar's heart come back to it again and again with unsated desire, like a thirsty bee when summer blossoms lie dead in the dust.

SCENE VII

MADANA: Tonight is thy last night.

VASANTA: The loveliness of your body will return tomorrow to the inexhaustible stores of the spring. The ruddy tint of thy lips freed from the memory of Arjuna's kisses, will bud anew as a pair of fresh *Asoka* leaves, and the soft, white glow of thy skin will be born again in a hundred fragrant jasmine flowers.

CHITRA: O gods, grant me this my prayer! Tonight, in its last hour let my beauty flash its brightest, like the final flicker of a dying flame.

MADANA: Thou shalt have thy wish.

SCENE VIII

VILLAGERS: Who will protect us now?

ARJUNA: Why, by what danger are you threatened?

VILLAGERS: The robbers are pouring from the northern hills like a mountain flood to devastate our village.

ARJUNA: Have you in this kingdom no warden?

VILLAGERS: Princess Chitra was the terror of all evildoers. While she was in this happy land we feared natural deaths, but had no other fears. Now, she has gone on a pilgrimage, and none knows where to find her.

ARJUNA: Is the warden of this country a woman?

VILLAGERS: Yes, she is our father and mother in one.

[*Exeunt.*]

[*Enter* CHITRA.]

CHITRA: Why are you sitting all alone?

ARJUNA: I am trying to imagine what kind of woman Princess Chitra may be. I hear so many stories of her from all sorts of men.

CHITRA: Ah, but she is not beautiful. She has no such lovely eyes as mine, dark as death. She can pierce any target she will, but not our hero's heart.

ARJUNA: They say that in valour she is a man, and a woman in tenderness.

CHITRA: That, indeed, is her greatest misfortune. When a woman is merely a woman; when she winds herself round and round men's hearts with her smiles and sobs and services and caressing endearments; then she is happy. Of what use to her are learning and great achievements? Could you have seen her only yesterday in the court of the Lord Shiva's temple by the forest path, you would have passed by without deigning to look at her. But have you grown so weary of woman's beauty that you seek in her for a man's strength?

With green leaves wet from the spray of the foaming waterfall, I have made our noonday bed in a cavern dark as night. There the cool of the soft green mosses thick on the black and dripping stone, kisses your eyes to sleep. Let me guide you thither.

ARJUNA: Not today, beloved.

CHITRA: Why not today?

ARJUNA: I have heard that a horde of robbers has neared the plains. Needs must I go and prepare my weapons to protect the frightened villagers.

CHITRA: You need have no fear for them. Before she started on her pilgrimage, Princess Chitra had set strong guards at all the frontier passes.

ARJUNA: Yet, permit me for a short while to set about a Kshatriya's work. With new glory will I ennoble this idle arm, and make of it a pillow more worthy of your head.

CHITRA: What, if I refuse to let you go, if I keep you entwined in my arms? Would you rudely snatch yourself free and leave me? Go then! But you must know that the liana, once broken in two, never joins again. Go, if your thirst is quenched. But, if not, then remember that the goddess of pleasure is fickle, and waits for no man. Sit for a while, my Lord! Tell me what uneasy thoughts tease you. Who occupied your mind today? Is it Chitra?

ARJUNA: Yes, it is Chitra. I wonder in fulfilment of what vow she has gone on her pilgrimage. Of what could she stand in need?

CHITRA: Her needs? Why, what has she ever had, the unfortunate creature? Her very qualities are as prison walls, shutting her woman's heart in a bare cell. She is obscured, she is unfulfilled. Her womanly love must content itself dressed in rags; beauty is denied her. She is like the spirit of a cheerless morning, sitting upon the stony mountain peak, all her light blotted out by dark clouds. Do not ask me of her life. It will never sound sweet to man's ear.

ARJUNA: I am eager to learn all about her. I am like a traveller come to a strange city at midnight. Domes and towers and garden-trees look vague and shadowy, and the dull moan of the sea comes fitfully through the silence of sleep. Wistfully, he waits for the morning to reveal to him all the strange wonders. Oh, tell me her story.

CHITRA: What more is there to tell?

ARJUNA: I seem to see her, in my mind's eye, riding on a white horse, proudly holding the reins in her left hand, and in her right a bow, and like the Goddess of Victory dispensing glad hope all round her. Like a watchful lioness she protects the litter at her dugs with a fierce love. Woman's arms, though adorned with naught but unfettered strength, are beautiful! My heart is restless, fair one, like a serpent reviving from his long winter's sleep. Come, let us both race on swift horses side-by-side, like twin orbs of light sweeping through space. Out from this slumbrous prison of green gloom, this dank, dense cover of perfumed intoxication, choking breath.

CHITRA: Arjuna, tell me true, if, now at once, by some magic I could shake myself free from this voluptuous softness, this timid bloom of beauty shrinking from the rude and healthy touch of the world, and fling it from my body like borrowed clothes, would you be able to bear it? If I stand up straight and strong with the strength of a daring heart spurning the wiles and arts of twining weakness, if I hold my head high like a tall young mountain fir, no longer trailing in the dust like a liana, shall I then appeal to man's eye? No, no, you could not endure it. It is better that I should keep spread about me all the dainty playthings of fugitive youth, and wait for you in patience. When it pleases you to return, I will smilingly pour out for you the wine of pleasure in the cup of this beauteous body. When you are tired and satiated with this wine, you can go to work or play; and when I grow old I will accept humbly and gratefully whatever corner is left for me. Would it please your heroic soul if the playmate of the night aspired to be the helpmate of the day, if the left arm learnt to share the burden of the proud right arm.

ARJUNA: I never seem to know you aright. You seem to me like a goddess hidden within a golden image. I cannot touch you, I cannot pay you my dues in return for your priceless gifts. Thus, my love is incomplete. Sometimes, in the enigmatic depth of your sad look, in your playful words mocking at their own meaning, I gain glimpses of being trying to rend asunder the languorous grace of her body, to emerge in a chaste fire of pain through a vaporous veil of smiles. Illusion is the first appearance of Truth. She advances towards her lover in disguise. But a time comes when she throws off her ornaments and veils and stands clothed in naked dignity. I grope for that ultimate *you*, that bare simplicity of truth.

Why these tears, my love? Why cover your face with your hands? Have I pained you, my darling? Forget what I said. I will be content with the present. Let each separate moment of beauty come to me like a bird of mystery from its unseen nest in the dark bearing a message of music. Let me forever sit with my hope on the brink of its realisation, and thus end my days.

SCENE IX

CHITRA [*cloaked*]: My lord, has the cup been drained to the last drop? Is this, indeed, the end? No, when all is done something still remains, and that is my last sacrifice at your feet.

I brought from the garden of heaven flowers of incomparable beauty with which to worship you, god of my heart. If the rites are over, if the flowers have faded, let me throw them out of the temple. [*Unveiling in her original male attire*] Now, look at your worshipper with gracious eyes.

I am not beautifully perfect as the flowers with which I worshipped. I have many flaws and blemishes. I am a traveller in the great world-path, my garments are dirty, and my feet are bleeding with thorns. Where should I achieve flower-beauty, the unsullied loveliness of a moment's life? The gift that I proudly bring you is the heart of a woman. Here, have all pains and joys gathered, the hopes and fears and shames of a daughter of the dust; here love springs up struggling toward immortal life. Herein lies an imperfection which yet is noble and grand. If the flower-service is finished, my master, accept *this* as your servant for the days to come!

I am Chitra, the king's daughter. Perhaps, you will remember the day when a woman came to you in the temple of Shiva, her body loaded with ornaments and finery. That shameless woman came to court you as though she were a man. You rejected her; you did well. My Lord, I am that woman. She was my disguise. Then, by the boon of gods I obtained for a year the most radiant form that a mortal ever wore, and wearied my hero's heart with the burden of that deceit. Most surely, I am not that woman.

I am Chitra. No goddess to be worshipped, nor yet the object of common pity to be brushed aside like a moth with indifference. If you deign to keep me by your side in the path of danger and daring, if you allow me to share the great duties of your life, then you will know my true self. If your babe, whom I am nourishing in my womb be born a son, I shall myself teach him to be a second Arjuna, and send him to you when the time comes, and then at last you will truly know me. Today, I can only offer you Chitra, the daughter of a king.

ARJUNA: Beloved, my life is full.

TWO SISTERS

SARMILA

Women are of two kinds, the mother-kind and the beloved-kind—so I have heard some learned men say. If a comparison may be drawn with the seasons, the mother is the rainy season. She brings the gift of water and of fruit, tempers the heat, and dissolving from the heights drives away the drought. She fills with plenty. The beloved, on the other hand, is the Spring. Deep its mystery, sweet its enchantment. Its restlessness rocks the blood into waves and swings over into the jewel-chamber of the mind where the solitary string of the golden *veena* is lying mute, waiting for the vibration to set the body and the mind ringing in some wordless melody.

Sasanka's wife Sarmila was the mother-kind. Her large, gentle eyes had a deep, steady look. The dark, well-rounded limbs had the comely grace of the first rain-laden clouds. The vermilion mark at the parting of her hair, the broad black border of her sari, the thick *makar*-shaped bangles on her wrists bespoke homely grace rather than elegance of style.

There was no outlying region in the territory of her husband's life over which her empire was not actively exercised. The extreme solicitude with which she had surrounded his life had made him careless. If by any chance the fountain pen was so misplaced on the table as not to be readily at hand the moment he needed it, his wife would have to discover it for him. If he could not remember where he had left his wrist-watch before going to bathe, his wife was sure to know where it was. So, too, she must be there to repair his error when, having put on socks of different shades, he was ready to go out. He mixed up English dates with Bengali months and sent out invitations to friends accordingly, and when the unexpected guests made their untimely appearance, it was his wife who had to bear the brunt of it. He knew full well that any negligence in the day's routine would be set right by her. To perpetrate negligences, therefore, had become second nature with him.

"It's the limit," his wife would complain, half, derisively, half lovingly. "Will you never learn?"

If he had learnt, Sarmila's days would have lain idle as untilled land.

One day, Sasanka was at some friend's, playing bridge. It was getting rather late at night. Suddenly, his friends burst out laughing. "Ah! here comes your bearer with the summons! Your time is up." Sure enough, there was the inevitable Mahesh, with his moustache gone grey and the hair still black on his head, wearing a vest, with a coloured duster on his shoulder, and a bamboo rod in his hand.

"The mistress has sent me to inquire if the master is here. She is afraid of some mishap to the master on his way back in the dark night. She has sent a lantern as well."

Irritated, Sasanka threw down the cards and got up. The friends taunted, "Ah, the lonely, unguarded male!"

On reaching home Sasanka addressed his wife in no gentle terms or peaceful manner. Sarmila quietly accepted the scolding. What was she to do? She simply could not get rid of her fear that when her husband was not with her, all sorts of impossible perils were conspiring to waylay him.

Another day, some stranger had called on business. Every now and then a chit would be handed in. "You know you were indisposed yesterday. Do come in early to dinner." Sasanka lost his temper, but yielded, nevertheless.

Once in extreme exasperation he had told his wife. "For goodness' sake, get hold of some god or deity like that Chakravarty wife. It's too much for me to withstand your attentions all by myself. Sharing them with a god would make it easier. The gods can stand excesses, but man is frail."

"Indeed!" retorted Sarmila. "Have you forgotten your condition that time when I went to Hardwar with my uncle?"

He had himself related to his wife, adding embellishment for effect, how very pathetic his condition had been in her absence. He knew that such exaggeration would make her feel at once penitent and happy. How could he now go back on his own immoderate version! And so, he swallowed the retort and kept quiet. Nor did it end there. Fancying that in the morning he had a slight touch of cold, she made him swallow ten grains of quinine as well, with juice of *tulsi* leaves in tea. He dared not object, for, having refused to take quinine on a previous occasion, he had developed fever—which incident had remained ineffaceably engraved in the domestic annals.

As she was solicitous of her husband's well-being and comfort at home, so was Sarmila jealously mindful of his dignity abroad. Let me recall an incident.

Once, they were going to Nainital on holiday and had their compartment reserved "through". At a junction where they changed trains, they went out to dine. Returning they found a villainous looking figure in livery actively occupied in dispossessing them of their berths. The station-master came and explained that the compartment had been actually reserved for a certain celebrated general, though through inadvertence their name had been affixed to it. Opening his eyes wide, flabbergasted, Sasanka made ready to shift, when up jumped Sarmila into the compartment and standing against the door challenged:

"Let me see who dares pull me down! Call your General here!"

Sasanka, who was a government servant, and was well accustomed to keeping a safe distance from the path of the superior official tribe, grew nervous and began to protest: "But what's the use?

There are plenty of other carriages–"

But Sarmila would not heed. In the end the General who had returned from the refreshment room, cigar in mouth, and was witnessing this spectacle of feminine wrath, himself retired to another compartment. Sasanka turned to his wife: "Do you know how big that man is?"

"Don't care to know. In a compartment reserved for us, he is no bigger than you."

"What if he had insulted us?" ventured Sasanka

"What are you for then?" retorted Sarmila.

Sasanka was a graduate of the Sibpur Engineering College. However irresponsible he might be in the other walks of his life, he was careful enough in his official duties; the main reason being that the planet presiding over his official world was not his wife but the ruthless eye of the "Bara Sahib".

When he was acting as the district engineer his newly won promotion was suddenly reversed and he was superseded, despite his superior claim, by an inexperienced English youth, with the mere down of a moustache–an unsuspected proof of what right connections in high quarters can achieve. Sasanka knew that he would still have to carry on the real work, while that white booby would be installed in the chair. The big boss patted him on the back and said consolingly:

"Very sorry, Mazumdar. As soon as feasible, we'll push you up."

Both of them were Freemasons.

But despite this hope and consolation, the whole affair was exceedingly unpleasant for Mazumdar. At home he found cause for quarrel with every little thing. Suddenly, he noticed soot in a corner of his office room; suddenly, he felt that he couldn't bear the sight of the green cover of his sofa. He thundered at the office-boy who was sweeping the verandah for blowing dust in his direction. The inevitable specks of dust blew daily, but the master's thunder was something new.

He kept the news of his humiliation from his wife, afraid she would only add one more complication to the already complicated affairs of his service. She might even go and pick a quarrel with his boss, in no pleasant language, specially as she already nursed a grudge against Donaldson. Once, while engaged in suppressing the monkey pest in the garden of the circuit house, he had instead marked holes in Sasanka's sola hat. Fortunately, there was no accident, but an accident there might easily have been. People blamed Sasanka, which only added to Sarmila's wrath against Donaldson. What inflamed her wrath most was that Sasanka's enemies made much of the joke that a bullet aimed at a monkey had landed on Sasanka.

However, she herself found out all about the reverse in her husband's official status. She had suspected from his manner that somewhere a thorn was pricking. It did not take long to discover the cause. Rejecting the way of 'constitutional agitation', she went straight for 'self-determination'. She told her husband:

"Have done with it. Hand in your resignation immediately."

Resignation would no doubt remove the leech of humiliation from his breast. But then, there stretched before his mind's eye the rich field of regular monthly income and beyond that the golden prospect of a pension.

In the very year in which Sasankamauli had topped the pinnacle of the M.Sc. degree, his father-in-law, unwilling to delay the auspicious event, married him off to Sarmila. With the wealthy father-in-law's help he passed the engineering course. Seeing his speedy rise in service, Rajaram Babu had felt assured of his son-in-law's steady progress in prosperity. The daughter, too, never suspected till now that the contrary could happen. Not that any want was actually felt in the house; the ways of her father's house had been maintained here, too, the reason being that in the domestic dyarchy all management was in Sarmila's control. She had no child, nor any longer the hope of one. Whatever her husband earned was delivered into her hands to the last copper. If any special need arose he had no alternative but to go and beg from the *Annapurna* of his home. If the demand was unreasonable, it was refused; he accepted the decision, scratching his head. But there was always some other sweet compensation to make up for this disappointment.

"To give up the job," said Sasanka, "matters little to me. It's for your sake that I hesitate. You'll be put to hardship."

"It's a worse hardship to try to swallow injustice which sticks in the throat."

"But," remonstrated Sasanka, "one must work. If I give up the certain, where shall I go about looking for the uncertain?"

"Where you don't care to look now. You jokingly call your government service your *luchi-sthan*–beyond the arid wastes of *beluchisthan*, and you are so obsessed with it that you ignore the whole wide world outside it."

"Good Heavens! The whole world is too big for me. Who is going to survey all its highways and byways? Where am I to find a telescope big enough for that?"

"No big telescope is needed. My cousin Mathurdada is a big contractor in Calcutta. If you join him as a partner, we'll manage to make both ends meet."

"It would be an unfair sharing, for the weight on this side of the scale would not be enough. To hobble in such partnership seems too undignified."

"The weight on this side of the scale would be not one whit too light. You know the amount father had deposited in the bank in my name–well, it's there, only bloated with interest. You would not have to feel small before your partner."

"How can I take that? That money is yours." Saying which Sasanka got up. There were visitors waiting outside. Sarmila caught hold of his dress and pulled him back into the seat.

"I too am yours," she said. And added: "Pull out that fountain-pen from your pocket, here's the paper, write out your resignation. I can have no peace till I have posted that letter."

"Nor can I have any peace either, it seems." He wrote the letter of resignation.

The very next day, Sarmila went to Calcutta and straight to Mathurdada's house. Petulantly she greeted him:

"Not once have you cared to inquire after your sister."

One of her own sex would have retorted: "Nor have you." But the male brain could think of no such retort. Mathurdada admitted his fault:

"Have I even the time to breathe? Sometimes, I even forget whether or not I exist. Besides, you two are always on tour."

"I read in the papers," said Sarmila, "that you have secured the contract for building a bridge at Mayurbhanj or Mathurganj or some such place. I was so delighted that I thought, let me go and congratulate Mathurdada in person."

"Wait a little, *Khuki*. It's not time yet."

The trouble was that liquid capital was needed for which he had offered to enter into partnership with a wealthy Marwari. In the end it turned out that the Marwari's conditions were such that while the Marwari would have all the juice, he would be left only the refuse. So, he was trying to back out.

"Impossible," cried Sarmila excitedly. "It can't be allowed. If you needs must enter into partnership, then let it be with us. It would be too bad to let such business slip from your hands. I simply will not allow it, say what you will."

It did not take long to render all this into a written deed. Mathurdada's heart too was touched.

The business went ahead. Formerly, Sasanka's work had been

'service', it limits were well defined. Working under a boss, his responsibility ended with the demand made on it. Now, however, he was his own boss, subject to no will but his own. The claim of duty and his response to it were now merged in one. The days were no longer woven in a network of work-days and holiday, but became one compact whole. Because he was now free to ignore his responsibility, its hold on his mind became all the more tenacious. If nothing else, he must at least pay back his debt to his wife; after that there would be time enough to set the pace slow and easy. And so, in khaki pants, his leather belt fastened tight, wearing thick-soled shoes, a sola hat on his head, his sleeves rolled up, a watch strapped to his left wrist, and sun-glasses to protect his eyes, Sasanka plunged headlong into his work. Nor, was the pressure of the steam relaxed, even when the debt had been wellnigh liquidated; the mind was still in full heat.

Formerly, his income and expenditure had flowed through one single channel; now they branched into two, one flowing bankwards, the other homewards. Sarmila continued to receive her old portion and dispensed it as before, Sasanka remaining a stranger to its mysteries. On the other hand, Sasanka's leather-bound ledger of business accounts was to her inaccessible, incomprehensible. There was no harm in that. But the fact that this path of her husband's business life ran outside her domestic orbit did, however, mean that her jurisdiction to that extent had suffered.

"Don't overdo it please," she pleaded, "your health will break down."

To no avail. Strangely enough, his health did not break down. Impetuously ignoring all pleadings of conjugal solicitude, her anxiety for his health, her complaints at his lack of rest, her fussy concern over the details of his comfort, *et cetera*, Sasanka left the house early in the morning, blowing the horn of his second-hand Ford, himself at the wheel; returned at about two or half-past two, received a scolding and then his food which he gulped down.

One day, his car ran into another. He was unhurt, but the car was damaged and had to be sent to the garage for repairs. Sarmila was greatly upset.

"You must not drive anymore," she beseeched, her voice hoarse.

"An accident at another's hands can be equally fatal," replied Sasanka, laughingly dismissing her concern.

One day, while he was supervising some repair work, a packing-box nail pierced through the shoe right into his foot. At the hospital the wound was bandaged and he was given an anti-tetanus injection. That day, Sarmila was all tears.

"Stay in bed for a day or two at least," she pleaded. But Sasanka replied laconically: "Work."

It is not possible to improve on such brevity of expression.

"But," remonstrated Sarmila,–but Sasanka had left, without even a word, and with bandage on.

Sarmila dared not test her powers anymore. The man's masterfulness in his own field was now evident. Beyond all argument, entreaty, pleading, was the one phrase, "I've work to do."

For no reason Sarmila was uneasy, anxious. The slightest delay in returning home and she thought of an accident to the car. When she saw her husband's face flushed with the sun's heat, she thought it must surely be influenza. Timidly, she would suggest the doctor–and immediately stop, seeing the reaction on him. Nowadays, she was afraid even to express her anxiety fully and freely.

In no time Sasanka became sun-burnt and dry. His dress, like his leisure, was cut short to tightness; his movements became hurried; his speech abrupt like sparks. To this quick rhythm Sarmila's ministry strove to adjust its motions. Some food must always be kept ready and warm near the stove–for who knew when the husband might suddenly and untimely declare: "I'm off. Shall be late in returning." A provision of soda water and dry food-stuff in a tin was neatly stored in his car; a bottle of eau-de-cologne carefully concealed from view—in case of headache. She looked into them carefully each time the car returned home, only to find that nothing had been used. It was distressing. Every day a clean change of clothes, neatly folded, was prominently displayed in his bedroom, nevertheless, at least four days in the week he found no time to change. Domestic consultation reduced to the briefest, in the staccato style of an express telegram, had to be carried out in a most casual manner, standing, walking or calling from behind, "Just a word, dear." The little connection which Sarmila had with his business also came to an end with the repayment of her loan, interest and all. The interest, too, had been paid to the penny and a formal receipt taken.

"What a pity!" wailed Sarmila. "Even in love men cannot wholly lose themselves. A portion of themselves they needs must set apart for the exercise of their masculine ego."

From his share of the profits Sasanka built a house in Bhowanipore, after his own heart. To astound Sarmila he planned the latest devices of hygiene, comfort and order. Sarmila too, was not remiss in allowing herself to be properly astounded. There was the laundry machine installed by the engineer. Sarmila looked at it from this side and that and praised it profusely; but to herself she added: "Nevertheless, the clothes will continue to be sent to the *dhobi* as they have been till this day. I've known the donkey carry soiled clothes, but have not known science take its place yet."

Seeing the potato-peeling machine she was all amazement. "Three-fourths of the drudgery of cooking potatoes is gone now," she declared. Later on, it was rumoured that this machine had earned its liberation from toil in some limbo of oblivion, alongside many a leaking pot and broken kettle.

When the house was completed, Sarmila's repressed affection found a stable object for its exercise. The infinite patience of a brick-and-mortar body makes it a convenient object of affection. The endless pother of setting and fitting, furnishing and arranging drove the two bearers to the end of their tether; one of them gave notice. The interior decoration was for Sasanka's benefit. He hardly ever sat in the drawing room; yet cushions of various patterns were devotedly spread for his tired back-bone; tables and teapoys were there, with fringed covers embroidered with flowered patterns; and many a flower-vase. He no longer entered the bedroom during the day, the reason being that in his current calendar Sunday had been adopted as twin-brother of Monday. Even on other holidays when the office was closed he managed to find some little work or other to do and went and sat in his study with his files or with his tracing cloth. Nevertheless, in the bedroom the old order persisted. In front of the spacious, cushioned sofa were the knitted slippers; beside it the *pans* ready as of old in the betel box; on the rack a *punjabi* of fine silk and a *dhoti*, pleated and crinkled, ready for wear.

It was a risky business to meddle with Sasanka's study; despite the risk Sarmila ventured in with a duster when he was not there. With unremitting diligence she strove to bring order and harmony in the medley of things useful and useless.

Thus, Sarmila continued to be serviceable, but her service went a great deal unobserved. Her devotion which was once offered directly to its object was now directed to its symbols–in looking after the house and the garden, in knitting a cover for Sasanka's sofa, embroidering flower patterns on his pillow-case, in setting on a corner of his office-table bouquets of tuberoses in blue crystal vases. It cost her no little pain to worship her deity from so great a distance. She was still bathing with her secret tears the wound inflicted on her only the other day. It was the 29th of *Karthik*, Sasanka's birthday, the most festive day in her life. And usual, invitations had been sent out to friends and the house and the gate specially decorated with flower and leaf. Returning from work just before noon, Sasanka inquired: "What's the matter? A doll's wedding, I suppose!"

"Dear me! You have even forgotten it's your birthday today. But say what you will, you must stay in this evening."

"Business bends its head before no day, save the day of death."

"I won't ever ask you again, but today I have already sent out the invitations."

"Look here, Sarmila, don't you ever try to set me up as a plaything and call in the crowd to watch you play."

Saying which Sasanka hurriedly left. Shutting the bedroom door, Sarmila cried awhile.

In the afternoon the guests arrived. They readily acknowledged the paramount claim of 'business'. Had it been Kalidasa's birthday instead, the plea that he had to finish the third Act of *Sakuntala* would have been dismissed by them as too frivolous to be seriously entertained as an excuse for his absence. But business! However, there was enough of amusement and gaiety. Nalu Babu made everyone laugh by his caricatures of the current stage-acting; even Sarmila joined in the hilarity. Sasanka's birthday, bereft of Sasanka, prostrated itself before the business presided over by him. Even Sarmila's heart, aggrieved as it was, made its distant obeisance to the flying banner on the racing chariot of that business.

Unbending was this work, which cared for none, which ignored everything, the wife's entreaties, the invitations to friends, his own comfort even. Such faith in his work gives man faith in himself; it is the homage of self to its own power. Standing on one bank of their river–the bank of daily domestic routine–Sarmila watched with awe Sasanka's work on the other bank which made itself felt far and wide, beyond the boundaries of the household, in distant lands, on the shores of distant seas, gathering in the net of its authority men both known and unknown.

Man is at daily war with his fate; if the soft entwining arms of woman hinder him in his rugged onward march, it is but natural that he should ruthlessly break away. With loving faith Sarmila had accepted this ruthlessness. But there were times when she could not help herself, and impelled by love, her tender solicitude trespassed on forbidden ground. Rebuffed, she acknowledged the rebuff as well-merited and sorrowfully retraced her steps, praying to the Deity to watch her husband's steps where access to her was barred.

NIRAD

When the prosperity of this family, riding on bank investments, was running into six figures, Sarmila was attacked and laid prostrate by a disease which could not be diagnosed. It is necessary to explain why this fact caused so much consternation.

Sarmila's father, Rajaram Babu, had owned a considerable estate in Barisal, near the mouth of the Ganges, besides holding shares in a ship-building yard at Salimar. He was born at the junction of the old times and the new. He could wrestle, hunt, wield a *lathi* like an expert, and was also famous for his skill at *pakhwaj*. He could recite from memory passages from *The Merchant of Venice*, *Julius Caesar* and *Hamlet*, held Macaulay's English as his ideal, and was an ardent admirer of Burke's orations. His appreciation of Bengali literature extended as far as *Meghnadbadh Kabya*. In his middle age he had looked upon the taking of alcoholic drinks and proscribed food as a *sine qua non* of modern culture. In his old age, however, he gave it up. Handsome and dignified in appearance, of tall and sturdy build, he dressed with meticulous care, and was of a hearty and sociable disposition. He never could say 'No" to needy importunity. Though he himself was indifferent to religious forms, they were nevertheless, observed in his house with great pomp, for such impressive observances add to the prestige of the family. As regards the actual worship of the deity there were the ladies of the house and many others to look after it. Had he been keen, he could easily have secured the title of a Raja for himself. If anyone asked him why he was indifferent to it, Rajaram laughingly replied that his father having already conferred on him the name Raja, it would be belittling that honour to add a duplicate to it. At the Government House he was honoured with entry by the special gate. On the occasion of the customary *Jagadhatri Puja* in his house, champagne used to flow freely and high English officials had their fill of it.

After Sarmila's marriage, his widowed home was left with only his eldest son Hemanta and his youngest daughter Urmimala. "Brilliant!"–that is how the teachers had always spoken of the boy. His appearance was such that when one had passed him one turned to look at him again. There was no subject in which he did not secure the highest marks at every examination. In athletic achievements, too, he promised to live up to his father's reputation. It is superfluous to state that he was constantly besieged by eager agents of prospective brides, but he was averse to marriage as yet. For the present his heart was bent on the prospect of a degree at a European University, with which object he had even begun to study French and German. Meanwhile, for want of anything better, he began the study of law as well, though there was hardly any necessity for it.

About this time, however, Hemanta was suddenly attacked by a disease, whether of the intestines or of some other organ, the doctors failed to diagnose. The mysterious ailment was lodged in his robust body as in a citadel; it was as difficult to locate it as to attack it. Rajaram Babu had implicit faith in an English doctor, who enjoyed at that time high reputation as a surgeon. The surgeon began an exploration of his patient's body and, as is the way of surgeons, came to the conclusion that the trouble was rooted in some inaccessible organ which must therefore be uprooted. But when, accordingly, his skilful instruments cut open the outer layer of the flesh and exposed the interior, neither the alleged enemy nor any trace of its havoc was discovered. The mischief was irremediable and the boy died. The father was disconsolate with bitter grief. It was not the death so much as the picture of a strong, beautiful and palpitating body being mutilated which, like a black bird of prey, dug its piercing claws into his mind, and sucking his vitals day and night, brought him to the very verge of death.

Dr. Nirad Mukherjee, an old classmate of Hemanta's, who had recently qualified as a doctor and was helping in the nursing of his friend, had protested from the very beginning that the case was being wrongly treated. He had given his own diagnosis and had advised a change of climate and a long stay in some dry place. But the prejudices of an older generation were too firmly fixed in the mind of Rajaram, who believed that only an English doctor could effectively combat the fierce onslaught of death. But after this experience his affection for Nirad and confidence in him rose disproportionately high. His young daughter Urmi too suddenly realied that here was a man of uncommon genius and said to her father:

"So young in years, father, and yet how strong his confidence in himself! See, how boldly and without any hesitation or doubt he asserted his judgement even against that of such a big and hefty foreign doctor!"

The father replied: "A doctor does not learn from books alone. Some are endowed with a rare, God-given insight–which I find Nirad has."

Thus, under the impact of sorrow and in the pain of remorse, a slight proof of merit was sufficient to give rise to their loving admiration which, once born, went on growing without waiting for any further evidence of worth.

One day, Rajaram called his daughter and said:

"Urmi, I almost hear Hemanta calling to me,–calling upon me to alleviate the suffering of diseased humanity. I have decided to found a hospital in his name."

"Excellent!" exclaimed Urmi exultingly, carried away by her

natural enthusiasm. "Send me to Europe. Let me return as a doctor and take charge of the hospital."

The suggestion appealed to Rajaram.

"This hospital will be a *Debottar* property," he said, "and you shall be the *Shebait.* Great pain was Hemanta's portion; he loved you much; your devoted service will bring him peace in the other world. You served him day and night on his sick bed; now that service will attain a larger scope in your hands."

It did not strike him as preposterous that a girl of aristocratic family should take to medicine as a profession; for he had now deeply realised what it meant to rescue life from the clutches of disease. His own son could not survive, but the sons of others might; which would be some compensation for his loss, some lightening of the weight of his sorrow. He said to his daughter:

"Finish your science course at the University here, and then proceed to Europe."

From now on, one thought constantly recurred to Rajaram's mind, the thought of that boy Nirad. A veritable piece of gold. The more he saw him, the more he liked him. Having covered the tedious course of examinations, how smoothly he was swimming his way through the deep ocean of medical knowledge! Despite his young years, he was unmoved by the pleasures of light-hearted gaiety, deeply absorbed in the latest discoveries, discussing them, analysing them and putting them to the test, even at the risk of his professional career. He had great contempt for those who had only built up a practice, and would say: "The foolish achieve success, the worthy glory." An epigram taken from a book.

At last, Rajaram told Urmi one day: "I've been thinking that it would be best for the success of the mission if you and Nirad join hands in this work. I too, would feel reassured. It's rare to come across a boy like that."

Whatever else Rajaram could do, he could not be indifferent to

Hemanta's opinions; and Hemanta used to say that it was barbarous of parents to ignore the daughter's wishes in the matter and to force on her a marriage of their own choice. Rajaram had once argued that marriage was not a mere personal affair but involved the whole family, and that therefore, in its making not only desire but experience also should count. But argue as he might, and despite his own likes and dislikes, so great was his affection for Hemanta that in this family it was really the latter's will that prevailed.

Nirad Mukherjee had always been a frequent visitor. Hemanta had nicknamed him the Owl. When invited to explain the significance, Hemanta used to say: "This man is mythological; he has no age, only learning; hence I call him Minerva's mount." Nirad was a frequent guest at their tea-table, where he would often enter into a terrific argument with Hemanta. No doubt, Urmi was in his mind; if his behaviour gave no indication of the fact, it was because his nature had not fitted him for the ways appropriate to such expression. He could discuss, but could not converse. Even if the heat of youth was in him, he was without its glow. Hence, he took a particular delight in running down those in whom the exuberance of youth was self-evident. Naturally, therefore, no one had reckoned him as a suitor for Urmi's hand, though now it so happened that this very apparent indifference raised Urmi's respect for him to the point of veneration.

When Rajaram had made it quite clear that, provided his daughter had no objection, it would make him happy to see her wedded to Nirad, Urmi signified her consent by a nod of her head; only adding that the wedding would have to wait till she had completed her course of education, both here and in Europe.

"That's as it should be," replied the father, "as long as the engagement is accepted and made definite by both the parties."

It did not take long to get Nirad's consent, though his manner implied that for a scientist marriage was a kind of self-abnegation, almost amounting to suicide. Perhaps, as a partial alleviation of this calamity, he made it a condition that in education as in other matters Urmi would be guided entirely by him, so that he might gradually mould and fashion her as his future wife. This training would be scientific, rigidly prescribed and regulated, infallible as a laboratory process.

"The birds and beasts," explained Nirad to Urmi "come out ready-made from Nature's workshop. But human life is in a raw, unformed state. It's for man to put it into shape."

Urmi gently replied: "You may by all means experiment. I'll make no difficulties."

"The life-force in you is dispersed," went on Nirad. "It has to be mobilised and marshalled round one single object of your life. Then will your life gain a meaning. When that which is scattered is gathered and concentrated towards a single aim and becomes intense and dynamic, then alone can we call it a moral organism."

Urmi was thrilled. So many young men frequented their tea-table and their tennis court, but not one ever said anything thought-provoking or did anything but yawn, if someone else happened to say it.

Indeed, Nirad did have a way of imparting the utmost profoundity to anything he uttered. In whatever he said Urmi discovered a wonderful depth of meaning. Amazingly intellectual!

Rajaram would often invite his elder son-in-law to his house and tried to encourage intimacy between the two sons-in-law.

"What an insufferably cheeky blighter!" remarked Sasanka to Sarmila. "He thinks we are all his pupils—and that too, at the very bottom of the very lowest Form."

"That is your jealousy," replied Sarmila laughing. "Why, I rather like him."

"Why not change places with your younger sister?" asked Sasanka.

"That might mean a great relief to you," replied Sarmila, "but to me–it is different."

Nirad, too, did not seem to feel any particularly brotherly regard for Sasanka. "A mason–not a scientist!" he said to himself. "He has hands–but what of the brain?"

Sasanka would often chaff his sister-in-law about Nirad.

"It is time you changed your name."

"In the English manner?"

"No, in the pure Sanskrit way."

"Let's hear the new name."

"Vidyut-lata. Nirad will like it. He is familiar with this thing in his laboratory. Now, he will have it harnessed at home."

To himself he said: 'Indeed, the name does suit her.' A secret pang pricked him. 'Pity that such a girl should fall into the hands of so great a prig.' In whose hands it would have consoled and pleased Sasanka to see her fall, it is hard to say.

Shortly after, Rajaram died. The future rightful master of Urmi now wholeheartedly took upon himself the responsibility of guiding her mind to its full maturity.

Good looking as Urmimala was, she seemed even better looking than she was; the luminous intensity of her mind scintillated in the lively movements of her body. She was eager about everything: interested in science, even more so in literature; greatly excited at the prospect of witnessing a football match on the *maidan*; not indifferent to the cinema; must be present when the physicist from Europe lectured at the Presidency College; listened to the radio and though she might now and again ejaculate an "ugh!" was nevertheless interested; ran out to the verandah to watch a wedding party pass-by, with its bride-groom and the fanfare of trumpets; was a frequent visitor to the Zoo which she enjoyed greatly, especially when she stood watching the monkeys in their cage; would accompany her father and sit by his side when he went angling; played tennis; was particularly good at badminton. All these interests she had derived from her brother. Slender and delicate as a frail creeper, she swayed with every breath of the wind. She dressed simply but elegantly; knew how to bring out the full beauty of the figure in a *sari* by a slight turn here, a right twist there, a little tightening here and a little loosening there–in a way whose secret no one could catch. Though she could not sing well, she could play on the *sitar.* When she played, it was difficult to say whether it was a thing to hear or a sight to see–it seemed as though her wild unruly fingers were in an uproar. She was never in want of a topic for conversation, never waited for a proper excuse for laughter. She had an inexhaustible talent for creating company out of dullness and filling emptiness with her mere presence. Only in Nirad's presence she became an altogether different person, as though the wind had left the sail and the boat had to be slowly and gently towed.

Everyone said that Urmi's nature was like her brother's, full of vitality and liveliness. Urmi knew that it was her brother who had released the current of her mind. Hemanta used to say: "Our homes are like moulds for fashioning human beings of clay, which is why the foreign juggler has succeeded so long in keeping thirty-three crores of puppets dancing to his tune. When the time comes, I'll break into this puppet-dom and wreak the havoc of a Kalapahar." The time never came–but he left Urmi's mind very living, indeed.

What caused all the trouble was the extreme rigidity of Nirad's method of work. He prescribed a course of study for her, and admonished her thus: "Look here, Urmi, if you let your mind spill over in its onward march, what will be left in your pitcher at the end of the journey?" He added: "You are like a butterfly, restlessly flitting about without gathering anything. You should be like a bee. Every moment is of account. Life is not dalliance."

Of late, Nirad had been studying books on Pedagogy borrowed from the Imperial Library. All these maxims were to be found in them. His very language was of the books, for he did not know how to put things in simple and natural words of his own. Urmi was left in no doubt that she was at fault. Great was her mission and yet every now and then her mind wandered away from it, leaving her in a state of perpetual self-reproof. Before her was the example of Nirad. How amazingly steadfast, how single-minded of purpose! How sternly he had set his face against all fun and frivolity! If any work of fiction or light literature caught his eye on Urmi's table, it was immediately forfeited. One day, when he came to pay his supervisory call, he learnt that she had gone to spend the evening at an English theatre to see Gilbert and Sullivan's *Mikado*. She had never missed such chances while her brother lived. She was severely taken to task by Nirad. He spoke in English in a tone of the utmost gravity:

"Have you already begun to forget that you have dedicated your life to the mission of making your brother's death fruitful in service?"

The words stung Urmi with extreme remorse. She said to herself: "What an uncommon power of seeing through the mind this person has! Indeed, it does seem that my grief is losing its intensity–I myself couldn't realise it. Shame on this fickleness in my character!'

She began a strict watch on herself, removing every trace of attractiveness from her dress. The *sari* was now coarse, its colour all gone. The chocolates were still in the drawer, but the desire for them was gone. She leashed her unchained mind to the dry post of duty within a severely restricted orbit. Her elder sister scolded her; as for Sasanka, the bitter epithets he showered on Nirad were too strong and too foreign to be found in the dictionary–they were not exactly pleasant to hear.

Sasanka and Nirad had one thing in common: both took to English–Sasanka when in a furiously abusive temper, and Nirad when he was discoursing on something profound. Nirad disliked it most when Urmi was invited to her sister's house. It was not that she merely went–she was most eager to go. This intimacy of blood relationship seemed to cut through his own rights over her.

One day, with a grave countenance he said to Urmi:

"Please, don't mind the unpleasant words which my sense of responsibility towards you obliges me to say. I must warn you that this intimacy is injurious to the development of your character. Family attachment makes you blind–but I can see quite clearly the likelihood of degradation."

The first mortgage deed of the thing called Urmi's character being in Nirad's strong box, the loss would naturally be his if anything happened to that character. As a result of Nirad's ban, Urmi, on various pretexts, made her visits to Bhowanipore very rare. This imposition of restraint on herself she regarded as a sort of repayment of her huge debt. For, what sacrifice could be greater for a votary of science than that which Nirad had made by encumbering his work for his own ideal with this life-long charge of her life?

Though in a sense Urmi had got used to the unhappy strain of withholding herself from every enjoyment, now and again her mind was seized with a painful yearning which she could not wholly suppress as a mere frivolity. Nirad merely directed her–why did he never for a moment woo her? For such an expression of ardour on his part her heart ever waited, and for want of it, remained unfulfilled; her very acts of duty became dry and lifeless. Sometimes, when she suddenly caught a look of wistfulness in Nirad's eyes, it seemed to her that the deep secret of his heart would now be laid bare. But, God knows, even if deep yearning was in him anywhere, its language was not known to him. And because he could not express himself, he found fault with the urge for self-expression and prided himself on the very dumbness of his agitated heart, which he thought was but a proof of his strength of character. "Sentimentality is not in my grain," he declared. On such occasions Urmi felt like crying, but so hypnotised was she by her own devotion that she too thought that this indeed, was manliness. And then she would begin again ruthlessly chastising her 'weak' mind. But try as she might, she could not get away from the consciousness that the spontaneous readiness with which, under the impact of great sorrow, she had at first undertaken her arduous mission had steadily flagged until now it had to cling for support to another's will.

Nirad put it quite plainly to her: "You had better understand, Urmi, that it is no good expecting from me the kind of adulation which girls commonly hope for from men. What I give you is something far more true and valuable than all their made-up pretty talk."

With bent head Urmi silently wondered: "Can't anything ever remain hidden from him?"

She is unable to fix her mind on anything. On the roof-terrace she paces about alone. The afternoon fades into dusk. Across the uneven heights of the city mansions, the sun sinks to its rest beyond the distant masts of ships on the Ganges. The clouds with their many-coloured bars raise barricades at the day's frontier. Gradually, the barricades fade out of sight. The moon climbs above the church spire. In the misty light the city looks like a dream, like an enchanted land. She wonders, is life really so uncompromisingly severe? Can it be so niggardly as to allow no holiday, no gift of joy? And then, a maddening impulse seizes her, a desire to do something wicked, to shout at the top of her voice, 'I don't care!'

URMIMALA

Nirad finished the piece of research he had taken in hand, and sent the thesis to a scientific association in Europe. It brought him recognition as well as a scholarship. He made up his mind to cross the seas for a degree at a European university.

The moment of parting was not marked by any tender words. He merely kept on repeating "Now that I am leaving, I am afraid you will slacken in your efforts."

"Have no fear," replied Urmi.

"I am leaving detailed instructions in writing," said Nirad, "to guide your future conduct and studies."

"I shall follow them faithfully."

"I'll remove these books from your almirah," went on Nirad, "and leave them locked up in my house."

"You may take them," said Urmi handing him the key.

He glanced once at her *sitar* but hesitated and said nothing. But he felt obliged by his sense of responsibility to utter the last admonition.

"My only fear is that if you start once more frequenting Sasanka Babu's house your steadiness will again falter. There's no doubt of it. Please, don't imagine that I am out to malign Sasanka Babu. He is an excellent man. I've seen very few Bengalis with his zeal and aptitude for business. His only drawback is that he acknowledges no ideals. To tell you the truth, at times I feel very apprehensive about him."

This led to further elaboration of Sasanka's many drawbacks.

Nirad could not help giving vent to his grave concern at the several other shortcomings in Sasanka's character which, though dormant then, were bound to become more active with age. But that, nevertheless, he was an excellent man, Nirad was anxious vociferously to admit, adding in the same breath that it was imperative for Urmi to guard herself against his house. It would be a sure degradation for Urmi if her mind ever came down to their level.

"But why are you so apprehensive?" asked Urmi.

"Shall I tell you why? You won't resent it?"

"You have taught me to bear the truth. I will stand it though I know it won't be easy."

"Then, listen. I've observed a sort of likeness between your temperament and Sasanka Babu's. It's this very light-heartedness of his that appeals to you, isn't it?"

'Is this man omniscient?' Urmi wondered. Undoubtedly, she liked her brother-in-law very much—and mainly for his capacity for rollicking laughter, his pleasantries and his waggish pranks. Then, also he knew just what flower Urmi loved best and what colour pleased her most in a *sari*.

"Yes, that's true, I like it," she admitted.

"Sarmila-didi's love," proceeded Nirad, "is serene and deep; her care and devotion are like an act of religious merit; her duty knows no holiday. It's by virtue of these that Sasanka Babu is enabled to give his whole mind to his work. But the day you go to Bhowanipore the mask falls off his face—there he is with his tomfooleries, pulling out your hair-pins and letting loose your coiffure, snatching your book and hiding it on the almirah-top. His interest in tennis suddenly becomes overwhelming despite other engagements."

Urmi could not help admitting to herself that it was this very naughtiness of Sasankada's which drew her to him. Her own irresponsible girlishness surged up in her when she was with him, and he too was no less a victim of her pranks. Her Didi would smile her gentle, serene smile at their wild frolics. Sometimes, she would mildly chide, though the chiding was but a pretence.

"You should stick only to that," said Nirad, winding up, "which gives the least scope to your own nature. There was little fear so long as I was there, for my nature is the exact contrary of yours. While I was your guardian it was impossible that any of my acts should ever vitiate your mind."

"I'll always bear in mind what you have said," said Urmi, her head bent low.

"I am leaving behind some books for you," said Nirad. "Read especially the chapters I have marked. You will find them useful."

Urmi needed this tutoring. Of late she had been assailed by doubts that perhaps, she had been misled by the first fervour of her enthusiasm in selecting medicine as her line, that perhaps she had no aptitude for it. The books marked by Nirad would act like a rope tied to her, towing her upstream.

After Nirad's departure, Urmi subjected herself to even harder severities. Except that she went to college, she practically shut herself up as if in a zenana. Returning home at the end of the day, she would again ruthlessly chain her mind to study, however much the tired mind yearned for rest. She made no progress whatsoever, her listless wandering mind vainly lingering over the same page. But she would not admit defeat. Because Nirad was not there, his will from its distance began to work all the more effectively on her.

She particularly despised herself when in the midst of work she was haunted by memories of the past. Many were her admirers among the young men; to some she had been indifferent, towards some she had felt drawn. Though in no case had it yet matured into love, the longing to love, like the sweet and gentle breeze of spring, played about her mind; so that now she would be humming a tune all by herself, now copying a poem that had caught her fancy, now playing on the *sitar*, if the mind were stirred a little too deeply. Nowadays, it was not uncommon that as she sat in the evening, her eyes fixed on the pages of her book, she was suddenly startled to discover that her mind was haunted by the memory of a face and of a day which had moved her but little at the time. Sometimes, the face would be of one whose persistent wooing had actually irritated her, though today that very memory seemed to stir in her mind a pang of discontent, as the light, fleeting wings of the butterfly leave on the flower a touch of spring.

The more fiercely she tried to fling these thoughts away from her mind, the more surely they boomeranged back into it. She had placed a photograph of Nirad on her desk at which she would look long and steadily. The light of intellect was in that face, but no trace of the heart's ardour. If that face did not call, to what was her spirit to respond? All she could do was to work up her mind into a state of exalted contemplation of his genius, his heroic striving, his unblemished character and her own undreamt-of good fortune.

We might as well state here that in one respect Nirad had triumphed. At the time of his engagement to Urmi, Sasanka, as well as several other skeptics, had laughed and had mockingly declared: "The simple-minded Rajaram Babu has convinced himself that Nirad is an idealist. An idealist, indeed! No pious platitudes can hide the fact that his idealism is secretly worming its way into Urmi's purse. True, he has 'sacrificed' himself—but to the deity enthroned in the Imperial Bank. Where we would plainly and bluntly tell our father-in-law that we need money, which won't be wasted but will, on the contrary, be used for his daughter's benefit, this great man condescends to marry only for the sake of a great mission! And then, he will daily translate that mission into figures in his father-in-law's cheque book."

Knowing that such comments were inevitable, Nirad had told Urmi that the one condition of his marriage was that he would not touch a penny of her money, but would depend entirely on his own earnings. When the would-be father-in-law proposed to send him to Europe, Nirad did not agree, even though it meant that he would have to wait long. He had moreover told Rajaram Babu: "Whatever money you choose to donate for the founding of the hospital should be put down in the name of your daughter. When I take charge of the hospital I'll draw no remuneration for my work. I am a doctor. I don't have to worry about my livelihood."

Such extreme disinterestedness only confirmed Rajaram Babu's love and admiration for Nirad and gave Urmi cause for much pride. On the other hand, the fact that this pride had a legitimate cause turned Sarmila's mind against Nirad. 'Pshaw! Let's see how long these heroics last!' Henceforth, whenever Nirad was in the midst of one of his usual, profound discourses, Sarmila would suddenly get up and walk out of the room, her head mockingly cocked sideways, her steps audible from a considerable distance. For Urmi's sake she said nothing but her silence by its very irony was withering enough.

At first, every mail brought from Nirad four or five pages of long-winded counsel. After some time, however, there came a startling telegram, demanding a considerable sum of money, urgently needed for his study. Though the pride which Urmi had cherished as her supreme treasure received a blow, the telegram was also in a way secretly comforting. For, as the days passed and Nirad's absence was prolonged, her original nature had begun to seek ways of escape from the barricade of duty she had erected round it. Under various pretexts she would deceive herself and then reproach herself. Nirad's appeal for money, therefore, came as a consolation to her contrite mind.

Handing the telegram to the estate manager, Urmi said hesitatingly, "Kaka-babu, the money—"

"I can't make out what it means," said the manager. "All along we have been under the impression that your money was unacceptable to him." The manager did not like Nirad.

"But in a foreign land–" Urmi faltered, unable to finish the sentence.

"That the foreign soil can change our native character, I know well enough," said Kaka-babu. "But how are we going to keep pace with such changes?"

"But he might be landed in difficulties if the money is not sent to him," protested Urmi.

"Very well then, I'll send it. Don't be anxious. But mark my words, this is only the beginning, not the end of it."

That this was not the end was speedily proved when another call arrived for a still bigger sum–this time for reasons of health.

"I had better consult Sasanka Babu," said the manager, looking grave.

"Please, do not let Didi and others come to know of it," pleaded Urmi greatly flustered.

"I don't like to take all the responsibility on my shoulders."

"But all this money will in any case be his, one day."

"Before that we must see to it that it is not thrown away."

"But we must also consider his health."

"Ill-health is of various sorts. Exactly what he is suffering from is not known. Maybe, if he returned here the change of climate would restore him to health. We might arrange his passage back."

The proposal to get Nirad back greatly perturbed Urmi. She attributed it to her concern for his studies.

The Kaka was saying: "Well, let the money be sent this time,– though I fear it will only aggravate the doctor's malady."

Radhagovinda was a near relation of Urmi's. The innuendo in his words stirred a faint breath of suspicion in her mind. "Maybe, it's better to let Didi know." On the other hand, the question kept recurring to her, poking her:

"Why don't I feel dejected–as I should?"

About this time Sarmila's disease had begun to cause anxiety, the tragedy of her brother's case adding alarm to anxiety. A number of doctors were set on the trail of its mysterious source. Smiling her wearied smile, Sarmila remarked: "The culprit will elude the C.I.D., only the innocent will be harassed to death."

"Let the Inspectors carry on their legitimate investigation—but third degree methods, no, never!" Sasanka assured her.

Sasanka had two heavy contracts on hand, one with a jute mill on the Ganges' bank, the other at Tollygunge in the garden house of the Mirpur Zamindar. The workers' tenements at the jute mill which had to be completed within three months, besides the several tube-wells in different localities he had taken in hand, left him no time to spare. Between the pressure of his work and the frequent claims of Sarmila's illness on his time, he was in a state of constant anxiety.

In the many years of their married life he had never had to worry on account of his wife's health, with the result that this time the strain of her illness drove him into a state of almost childish flurry. Leaving his work unattended he would return home and sit helplessly by her side. Gently caressing her hair he would inquire how she felt that day.

"I'm alright," Sarmila would promptly answer. "Please, don't worry unnecessarily."

Encouraged by his own wishful thinking, Sasanka believed the obviously unbelievable and felt greatly relieved.

"I've been entrusted with a huge contract by the Raja of Dhenkanal, and have to discuss the plan with the Dewan. I'll return at the earliest—before the doctor comes."

"I beg of you," pleaded Sarmila anxiously, "don't let unnecessary hurry spoil your work. Don't I understand that your presence is needed there! Of course, you must go. If you don't, I'll only get worse. There are enough people to attend to me."

To build up a magnificent fortune had become Sasanka's obsession day and night. It was not wealth but the magnificence of it which drew him on. Man is made that way; he responds to the call of glory. One may despise wealth only when it barely and meagrely suffices; but the moment its summit is raised high, men flock to admire it. Not that they are any the better for it, but because they delight in watching the splendour of eminence. As Sasanka sat by his wife's side, his uneasy mind could not help apprehending where lay a possible obstacle to his career of achievement. Sarmila knew that this apprehension in her husband's mind was not due to any miserly greed but was rooted in a manly ambition to build up from the very bottom a tower of triumph. Considering his glory as her own, she did not like him to neglect his work in order to attend to her, however pleasing such attentions in themselves. She, therefore, constantly urged him to return to his duty.

Her own duties caused her endless anxiety. Now that she was laid up in bed, who knew what mess the servants were making–no doubt using bad ghee in cooking, neglecting to keep hot water in the bath at the appointed hour or to change the bed linen in time; no one to see if the drains had been properly cleaned. Well, she knew what confusion it meant if the clothes from the washer-man were not properly received and checked. Unable to bear the strain she would secretly leave her bed to see things for herself. The pain would increase, the temperature shoot up, and the doctor would be puzzled.

At last, she sent for her sister Urmimala. "Never mind your college for a few days–come to the rescue of my household, otherwise I can't even die in peace."

Those who have read the story so far will at this stage smile knowingly and declare, "We know the rest." Indeed, it does not need much intelligence to anticipate. What must happen does happen, and no more need happen. Nor, is it necessary to imagine that in the game of life Fortune will necessarily keep back her cards, throwing dust into Sarmila's eyes.

Urmi was enthusiastic at this opportunity of serving her sister and was ready, since there was no alternative, to set aside all other tasks. Moreover, so she argued, nursing a patient was quite in line with her future medical career. She got ready a leather-bound book of charts for recording graphically the daily variations of disease. She also made up her mind to read up from books all she could gather about her sister's illness, lest the attending physician look down upon her for her ignorance. Physiology being her subject in M.Sc., she would have no difficulty in following the therapeutic terminology. In short, having convinced herself that attending on her sister would mean no snapping of the thread of duty but would rather help her to pursue it the more arduously and steadfastly, she packed all her books and papers in a bag and presented herself at the Bhowanipore residence. She did not have to pore over the bulky medical manuals, for not even the specialists were able to diagnose the disease.

Imagining herself as the sole warden of the sick room, she very gravely announced to her sister: "Since I am here to see that the doctor's instructions are strictly carried out, you will have to listen to whatever I say."

Amused at the elaborate earnestness of her attitude, Sarmila replied, smiling: "Indeed, what teacher has coached you in such earnestness–this fanaticism of a new convert? As a matter of fact, I have called you here only because I must have someone to carry out my instructions. Your hospital is not yet ready, but my household is in full swing; so meanwhile, take charge of it so that your Didi may have some relief."

And so, she was relieved of her duty in the sick room at her Didi's own insistence.

Now, Urmi became the viceregent in the kingdom of her sister's household. Things were in chaos there and needed immediate measures. In the scheme of this household every activity of each member, high and low, was directed and subordinated to one great purpose, namely, the comfort and convenience of the gentleman who presided over it. That this gentleman was utterly helpless and pathetically incapable of looking after his own physical needs—this impression was too firmly rooted in Sarmila's mind to be ever dislodged. When she found that he had not even noticed the hole which his cigar had burnt in his sleeve, she was not a little amused, but was at the same time filled with a great tenderness. The engineer would bustle off in the morning to his duty in such a great hurry as to forget to turn the tap off after his wash, only to find on his return the bedroom floor one sheet of water and the carpet in a mess. At the very outset when the tap was being installed, Sarmila had objected, knowing that a tap so near the bed would only result in his hands in a daily recurrence of an all-round mess in the room. But the great engineer must set up every sort of complicated nuisance in the name of scientific amenities. Once, in a fit of originality he had contrived an entirely original model of a stove, with shutters and funnels on all sides for conserving heat and for the speedy discharge of ash, and fitted inside with a variety of special devices of cells and shelves for baking, grilling, boiling and what not. If, in the interest of peace and goodwill, the invention was accorded a warm domestic welcome, the reception was in words and manner only, not in any use made of it. Adult babies have their hobbies, which they forget in a day but which, if resisted, lead only to friction. Bored with the monotony of daily usage, they break into something spectacular, to which women need pay no more than lip-service, while free to do as they choose. This responsibility of husband-tending Sarmila had long enjoyed.

A long time, indeed. It was impossible for Sarmila to conceive of Sasanka's world without herself in it. But now, she was afraid that the courier of Death would intervene between that world and its presiding goddess. She even feared that after death her bodiless spirit would have no peace if Sasanka's bodily comforts were not well looked after. Fortunately, there was Urmi. Though not so gentle as her sister, Urmi could nevertheless, carry on the work, for after all hers was a woman's touch. Without the tender grace of such a touch the daily provision of a man's life is left dry and flavourless, devoid of charm. And so, as she watched Urmi's beautiful hands peel and cut an apple, rind and slice an orange, neatly pick out the seeds of a pomegranate and tastefully set everything on a plate of white stone, Sarmila seemed to realise her own self in her sister. A stream of directions would issue ceaselessly from her sick bed:

"Do fill his cigarette case, Urmi."

"Can't you see it won't occur to him to change his soiled kerchief?"

"He won't have the sense to ask the bearer to clean his shoes—see how stiff they look with their coating of cement and sand!"

"Do have the pillow cases changed, dear."

"Put away these paper scraps in the wastepaper basket."

"Do peep into his study, Urmi, I'm sure he has left the key of his cash box on the desk."

"Don't forget it's time to transplant the cauliflower seedlings."

"Please, ask the *mali* to prune the rose plants."

"Look at those daubs of lime on the back of his coat! Do wait a moment, why this hurry? Please, Urmi dear, brush them off."

Though Urmi was used to books rather than to domestic work, she thoroughly enjoyed her new duties. Having broken away from the rigid discipline of her life, these varied ministrations gave her a sense of freedom. The under-current of anxiety and devotion beneath the smooth running of this household was little realised by her, for the strain of its direction was borne by her sister. To Urmi it all seemed a play, a kind of holiday, occupation without an aim. Here was a world in itself, wholly different from her own old world; here no aim, no object to be achieved held up its warning finger before her; and yet the day was full of activity, delightfully varied. She had not to account for each mistake, each shortcoming. If her Didi tried to chide her, ever so mildly, Sasanka would laugh it all away, as though the very shortcomings of Urmi added a special relish to his enjoyment. Indeed, the fact that their little world had now lost its look of earnest responsibility, that in the new atmosphere of laxity, mistake and inadvertence no longer mattered, was to Sasanka a source of great relaxation and amusement. Life seemed a picnic now. The fact that Urmi never seemed worried, never looked miserable, never felt ashamed of little mishaps, but always overflowed with enthusiasm in whatever she did helped considerably to lighten the strain on Sasanka's mind of his own heavy responsibility of work. Nowadays, he was always eager to return home as soon as his work was over—sometimes, even when the work was not over.

It must be confessed that Urmi was no expert at household management. Nevertheless, it was evident that, if not by virtue of her work, by the charm of her personality she filled a great and longstanding void in this house. What this void was, it is difficult to define in words. And so, when Sasanka returned home these days, he experienced the buoyancy of a playful, holiday spirit in the atmosphere. This enjoyment was not of domestic comfort, nor was it merely in the atmosphere. It had a rapturous embodiment. Indeed, it was Urmi's own holiday spirit which filled the void in this house, making day and night radiant with her liveliness, sending waves of blood pulsing through the work-weary Sasanka. On the other hand, the unmistakable consciousness that she was a source of joy to Sasanka made Urmi happy. For the satisfaction that her mere presence could make another happy had long been denied to her, causing her no little humiliation.

The care and attention to his personal needs to which the master of the house had been so long accustomed, now began to seem to him of but secondary importance. He was pleased with everything now, delighted almost without any cause. He remonstrated with his wife:

"Why do you worry over trifles? An occasional change of routine does not necessarily mean inconvenience–in fact, it is quite a relief."

Sasanka's mind was now like a river in the interval between ebb and flow. The pressure of work had slowed down. The tempestuous protests that the work would suffer, the loss would be serious, *et cetera*, which had been so frequent before, were hardly audible now. At any such manifestation Urmi would blow out the solemnity with her laughter. If she found him looking unusually serious, she would inquire: "Has your bogy been here today–that green-turbaned broker, from God knows where–has he been frightening you?"

"How on earth did you know of him?" asked Sasanka in surprise.

"Oh, I know him very well. I found him sitting in the verandah that day. You had gone out, so I kept him engaged in conversation. He is from Bikanir; his wife was burnt to death when her mosquito-net caught fire. He is looking for another."

"In that case he will come here daily at the right time–just when I am out. As long as he has not discovered a wife, the dream will grow on him."

"Just let me know what you want of him. I believe I can get it out of him."

If nowadays, the fat figure of profit in Sasanka's income-ledger came for a while to a standstill in its numerical progress, he was not greatly perturbed. Never before had Sasanka Mazumdar's enthusiasm for listening-in to the evening radio been so pronounced. When Urmi dragged him to it, he did not spurn it as frivolous, nor think the time wasted. He even went to Dum Dum one early morning to watch the aeroplanes take off. Nor, was scientific curiosity the main attraction.

He learnt for the first time to go shopping in the New Market. It was Sarmila who used occasionally to visit the Market to buy fish, meat, fruits and vegetables. She looked upon this work as her own special responsibility and never dreamt nor even desired that Sasanka should accompany her on such errands. But Urmi never bought anything, she merely picked up things, handled them, looked them over and haggled with the shopkeeper. If Sasanka attempted to buy anything for her, she snatched away his purse and locked it up in her bag.

Urmi did not in the least share Sasanka's concern for his work. Sometimes, when she wasted too much of his time, he lost his temper with her; the result was so disastrous that to retrieve the tragedy he had to sacrifice twice as much time. Between the imminence of tears in Urmi's eyes and the urgent claims of his work he did his best to finish as much of his work as he could in his office before returning home. But even there he found it difficult to stay beyond the afternoon. If sometimes he was detained for any reason, he found awaiting him on return Urmi's stony, impenetrable silence. Sasanka was secretly thrilled at this expression of aggrieved affection in Urmi's eyes misty with suppressed tears.

Very innocently he would plead: "If you have sworn not to talk to me, I must respect your *satyagraha*, but for heaven's sake, Urmi, don't give up playing–it was not included in your vow." And forthwith he brought the tennis rackets. When about to win the set, he deliberately chose to lose it. Next morning on waking up, he would be seized with remorse for having wasted his time the previous day.

In the afternoon of a holiday, as he sat at his desk deeply absorbed in some difficult problem, a red-and-blue pencil in his right hand, the fingers of his left hand needlessly ruffling his hair, Urmi came and announced: "I've fixed it up with that broker of yours–he'll take me to see the Temple of Pareshnath. Come with me–please!"

"No, not today, please," pleaded Sasanka, "it's impossible to get away."

But Urmi was undaunted by the majesty of work.

"How can you," she protested, "without any compunction leave a young, helpless and unprotected girl in the hands of that green-turban? Is that what you call your chivalry?"

In the end, unable to resist, Sasanka left his desk and drove the car.

If Sarmila came to learn of any such outrage, she was greatly annoyed, for she considered it an unforgivable liberty on the part of a woman to intrude on man's field of activity. She had always treated Urmi as a child and thought her so even now; nevertheless, in no case was she going to let her turn her husband's office into a play-room. She sent for Urmi and talked to her severely. Her words might have borne fruit, if Sasanka, overhearing his wife's angry tone, had not come and stood behind the door, winking encouragingly at Urmi and beckoning to her with a pack of cards to slip away to his office to learn poker from him. It was no time for playing cards, nor had any such idea been in his mind. It was only to spare Urmi the painful humiliation of her sister's bitter scolding which hurt him almost more than it hurt Urmi. He himself might, by pleading, cajoling or mild reproof, restrain her from interfering with his work, but that Sarmila should take Urmi to task for it was more than he could bear.

Sarmila sent for him and remonstrated. "Why must you indulge her so much—at all hours of the day? Your work is bound to suffer."

"Ah, the poor lonely child," commiserated Sasanka, "if she finds no playmate, how can she live in this lonely house?"

So much for her childish pranks. But it also happened that when Sasanka sat engrossed in some architectural plan, Urmi would pull up a chair by his side and ask him to explain it to her. She was quick of understanding and could steer through mathematical formulae. Sasanka was delighted and would set her problems which she solved. She insisted on accompanying him when he went out on inspection in the steam launch of the jute company. And she not merely accompanied him, but challenged his figures and conclusions, thrilling him with her arguments, which Sasanka found more delightful than any poetry. So that now he was not afraid of bringing some of his office work home. Whether drafting plans or working out problems, she was at his side, listening to his explanation and following his arguments. Though the progress in Sasanka's work was rather slow, it seemed to him that the long hours spent at it were fruitfully employed.

Sarmila was scandalised. While she could appreciate Urmi's childish waywardness and might affectionately tolerate her shortcomings in the management of the household, she could not but strongly disapprove of her unrestrained frequent excursions into her husband's workaday world which she herself had looked upon as absolutely beyond the reach of the feminine mind. Sheer impertinence, it seemed to her–directly contravening the teaching of the *Bhagavat Gita* which enjoined that one should keep within the limits of one's own nature, one's *svadharma.*

Unable to restrain herself, she asked Urmi one day: "Can it be that you really enjoy all this tracing and drafting and calculating?"

"I do indeed–greatly, Didi."

"Really!" exclaimed Sarmila skeptically. "Or, is it only to please him that you pretend this interest?"

Well, why not? we might ask, since all that Sarmila desired was to make Sasanka happy. But while she would have done it by attending to his personal comforts, this particular way of making him happy did not accord with her conception of happiness. She would repeatedly send for her husband and expostulate:

"Why do you waste so much of your time with her? Your work suffers. She's a child, what will she understand of all this?"

"She understands no less than I do," replied Sasanka, thinking that praise of her sister must please his wife. The simpleton!

In the beginning, when in the excitement and pride of his work Sasanka had cooled in his attentions to his wife, Sarmila had not only accepted the fact as inevitable but had actually felt pride in it, and had steadily taught her devoted heart to restrain the ardour of its solicitude, saying, "Man belongs to the race of kings; he must perpetually extend his empire of heroic achievements, otherwise he would be less than woman; for while the natural grace and sweetness of woman, her inborn wealth of love, are sufficient in themselves for the fulfilment of her function in this world, man has to vindicate himself by constant battle and strife. In the old days kings marched out to new conquests, not always out of greed of territory, but to vindicate over again their proud claim to manliness. Far be it from woman to stand in the way of this pride!"

And so, Sarmila had not stood in the way; of her own accord she had effaced herself completely from the path to which he had set himself. Once, she had held him tight in the net of her devoted attachment, but gradually, at no little cost to her happiness, she had loosened the bonds, until she had learnt to serve him from behind the scenes.

And now, alas! she was shocked to see him sink lower day-by-day. From her sick bed she could not watch everything, but what she could sense was sufficient. Looking into Sasanka's face she could see that he was always in a kind of trance. That this mere slip of a girl should in a few days have shaken that stern worker out of his arduous striving–the ignominy was more agonising to Sarmila than the actual pain of her disease.

There was no doubt that the little details of his personal comfort to which Sasanka had been used so long were being neglected; for example, it would be suddenly noticed that his favourite dish was missing at the table. Some sort of excuse would, of course, be offered. But in the old days no excuse was ever tolerated in this house, no such inadvertence was ever overlooked, but was severely rebuked. What a great revolution, indeed, that in this very same disciplined household the direst negligence was now looked upon as more amusing than reprehensible! Whom to blame! If Urmi did as her sister desired and sat on her cane stool in the kitchen, supervising the culinary operations—while at the same time carrying on her investigations into the life-history of the cook—suddenly Sasanka would storm into the kitchen with his peremptory, "Come along! Have done with all this!"

"Why, what do you want me to do instead?"

"I'm off duty now. Come along, let's go and see the Victoria Memorial. I'll explain to you why it looks so ludicrously pretentious."

Urmi's impressionable mind found it hard to stick to her duties in face of so great a temptation. Sarmila was well aware that her sister's absence would make little material difference to the excellence of the cuisine, nevertheless, the solicitude of a feminine touch did impart grace and charm to a man's comfort. But what was the use of worrying when each day it became clearer that comfort hardly mattered to him any longer—he was so happy!

Thus, a sort of uneasiness grew upon and possessed Sarmila's mind. Tossing about in her sick-bed she kept on repeating to herself: 'This much I have learnt before death—whatever else I could do, I could not make him happy. I thought I should see myself in Urmi, but Urmi is not myself, she has her own individuality.' She looked through the window and thought: 'She cannot replace me, nor could I replace her. My absence would make some difference, but hers would create a void.'

In the midst of these thoughts she suddenly remembered that winter was approaching, and it was time for the warm clothing to be put out to dry in the sun. She sent for Urmi who was playing table-tennis with Sasanka.

"Here's the key, Urmi. Please, have all the winter clothes taken out and spread on the roof in the sun."

Hardly had Urmi turned the key in the lock when Sasanka turned up and said: "There's plenty of time for all that. Come and finish the game first."

"But Didi–"

"Alright, I'll get you your Didi's permission."

Didi did give her permission–with a deep sigh. Calling the maid-servant she asked her to put a cold compress on her head.

Although this spell of sudden freedom after a long confinement had tended to make Urmi forgetful of herself, there were times when she was suddenly reminded of her life's stern mission. She knew that she was not free; she was bound by her own self-imposed vow, bound also by that very vow to another individual, bound to his guardianship, bound to follow the daily routine he had set for her. She could in no way refute his life-long claim over her. It was easy enough to acknowledge this claim when Nirad was there. She seemed to draw strength from him. But now, while the heart was estranged, only the conscience was insistent, making the heart still more rebellious. The very difficulty of excusing her transgression made it possible for her to indulge it. In order, as it were, to drug this uneasiness with opium, she tried constantly to forget herself in fun and frolic with Sasanka, saying: "It'll be all right in the end. Let me make the most of this little holiday."

Another day, she would suddenly shake her head and taking out all her books and papers from the trunk sit and pore over them. Now, it was Sasanka's turn to snatch the books from her hands, shove them back into the trunk, and sit tight on the lid.

"How wicked of you, Sasankada!" Urmi protested. "Please, don't waste my time."

"I can't waste your time," retorted Sasanka, "without wasting my own as well. So, we are quits."

After a little pushing and jostling, Urmi had to give in. It didn't seem that she very much resented the fact either. Thus thwarted, her conscience, after a brief offensive of four or five days, gradually flagged.

"Please, don't imagine I am weak-minded," she warned Sasanka. "What I have resolved upon I shall carry out."

"That is?"

"That is, after getting my degree here, I shall proceed to Europe for medical study."

"And then?"

"And then, I shall found and maintain a hospital."

"Whom else will you maintain? That fellow Nirad Mukherjee, that insufferable—"

"Shut up!" cried Urmi, literally shutting his mouth with her palm. "If you talk like this, we'll fall out."

She struggled hard to keep her faith. 'I must be true, true to myself.' She thought that if she failed in the relationship which her father had established between her and Nirad, she would prove herself faithless. Her real trouble was lack of adequate inspiration from the other party. She was like a tree, well rooted in the soil, but bereft of any light of the sun, its leaves turning yellow. Sometimes, she found it intolerable and cried out:

"Why can't the fellow write as men write?"

Having received her early school training for many years in a convent, Urmi, whatever the other defects in her education, knew English well. Nirad was aware of it and was therefore, all the more keen to dazzle her with his mastery of that language. It would have been better if he had written in Bengali, for the poor fellow did not know how little English he knew. His sentences, packed with long, cumbrous words and phrases culled from books, creaked along like overloaded bullock-carts. Urmi felt like laughing but was too ashamed to do so and would reprove herself:

'It's snobbish to find fault with the English of a Bengali.'

When formerly Nirad used to lecture to her, as he always did, his presence and manner lent weight and dignity to his words, which struck her imagination as even mightier than they sounded. But there is little room for such effects in a long letter. His long-winded pomposities sounded silly and easily betrayed their lack of substance. All that she had grown used to while he was with her now began to jar upon her from a distance. The fellow was utterly devoid of any sense of humour. His letters exposed this want most glaringly and she could not help contrasting him with Sasanka.

What happened one day only emphasised this contrast. As she was rummaging for some clothes in her trunk, she discovered an unfinished knitted slipper at the bottom, which brought back to her the memory of an episode that had happened four years ago. Her brother Hemanta was living then. They had all gone up to Darjeeling. There was no end of fun. Hemanta and Sasanka between them seemed to have released a regular cataract of gaiety. Urmi, who had just learnt knitting from an aunt, had begun a pair of slippers intended as a birthday gift to her brother. It was a subject of constant chaffing by Sasanka. "Whatever else you may give to your brother, please, don't give him slippers. That way one insults one's elders, says Lord Manu."

"For whom has Lord Manu prescribed them then?" asked Urmi with a mischievous side-long glance.

"The ancient prescriptive right to be insulted," replied Sasanka gravely, "is the brother-in-law's. Moreover, you owe it to me, interest and all."

"Owe it to you? I don't remember."

"Nor can you. You were a mere child then and hardly of age to play the Puck in your sister's bridal chamber on the auspicious occasion of our wedding. The privilege your tender hands then missed of pulling the ears of this lucky chap now waits to be exercised in fashioning a pair of slippers for him."

The debt was, however, never paid, for that particular pair of slippers found its way to the feet of Urmi's brother.

Soon after, Urmi received a letter from Sasanka which caused her considerable amusement. The letter was still in the box. She opened it and re-read:

"You left yesterday. Before the memory of your visit could fade, a scandal has been associated with your name which it would be wrong of me to conceal from you.

"Many eyes have observed the slippers I habitually wear. What they have observed even better is the way my toe-nails jut out of the holes–like a wreath of moons breaking out of clouds. (*Vide* Bharat Chandra's *Annadamangal.* In case of doubt as to the authenticity of the simile, refer to *Didi.*) This morning in the office as Brindaban Nandi took the dust of my slippered feet, the dilapidated state of their dignity was exposed. Shocking! I asked my servant Mahesh what had happened to my new pair of slippers. On whose holy usurping feet had it found its refuge? He replied, scratching his head: 'When you went to Darjeeling with Urmi Mashi, the pair went with you. On your return only one slipper came back, the other–'here Mahesh grew red in the face. I also thundered at him to shut up, for there were other persons in the room. Stealing a pair of slippers is a base thing to do, but the human mind is weak and the temptation too great. Let us hope God forgives. Of course, when the theft is ingeniously carried out, it wipes away much of its shame. But to steal *one* slipper! Fie!

"I have suppressed the name of the thief. But if she allows her own natural sauciness to be provoked by this charge, she will only publicise it the more widely. If her conscience is clear, it may be worth while to create a scene even over one slipper. If now, you want to shut the mouth of that vile calumniator Mahesh, you had better have immediate recourse to a pair of hand-embroidered slippers. Fancy the fellow's cheek! Herewith, is enclosed the measure of my foot."

Urmi, delighted with the letter, had immediately set her hands to knitting a pair for Sasanka, but she could not finish it as she soon lost interest in knitting. Today when she discovered this unfinished slipper in her trunk, she resolved to present it, as it was, to Sasanka to mark the anniversary of their journey to Darjeeling, which was only a few weeks ahead. A deep sigh escaped her. Where were those light-winged days under that laughter-lit sky? All that lay in front of her was a prospect of a dreary life of duty, bleak and unrelieved like a desert.

It was the 26th of *Falgun*, the day of the Holi festival. Busy with his work, Sasanka had no time for this play and the day had been forgotten. Urmi went to where her sister lay in bed and putting the ceremonial mark of the red powder on her feet, *pranaamed* her. Then, she went in search of her brother-in-law and found him at his desk immersed in his work. Creeping behind him she smeared his head with the colour, which fell profusely on his file of papers as well. A regular skirmish ensued. The ink-pot being handy on the desk, Sasanka threw the red ink over Urmi's sari, and then catching hold of her hand, he snatched the powder wrapped in an end of her sari and rubbed it over her face. Then began an uproar of chasing and scuffling. Though it was getting late for lunch and Sasanka had not yet had his bath, the house went on ringing with the notes of Urmi's pealing laughter. It was only when Sarmila, concerned for Sasanka's health, began to send message after message that the hilarity came to an end.

The day had long receded, the night was far advanced. Overtopping the flowering branches of the *krishnachura* tree, the moon rose clear in the unclouded sky. In the sudden gusts of the spring breeze, the green denizens of the garden murmured and swayed, the web of light and shade at the foot of the trees blending in the harmony. Urmi sat by the window, silent and still. Sleep was not in her eyes, for the waves of excitement had not yet quieted down in her blood. The scent of the flowering mango tree filled her mind with its intoxication. The *madhavi* creeper thrilled with pain in the creative agony of its sap to burst into flower. Urmi's whole being too seemed filled with the same ecstasy. She went into the bathroom and poured water on her head and cooled the burning flesh with a wet towel. Then, she lay on her bed, tossing about, until sleep dragged her down into the world of dreams.

At about three in the morning she suddenly woke up. The moon was no longer visible from the window. The room was in darkness; outside, the row of areca palms seemed caught in a network of light and darkness. Urmi broke into a fit of sobbing. Unable to control it, she threw herself on her bed and hid her face into the pillow. It was the wail of the spirit; language cannot lend it either words or meaning. If asked, could she have explained from where came this flood of sorrow that overwhelmed her mind, sweeping away the day's record of duties, the night's repose of sleep?

When she woke in the morning, the sun was already in the room. She had missed her morning duty. Sarmila had excused her absence, attributing it to the strain of fatigue. What was this regret that had overcome and dejected Urmi and filled her with a sense of defeat! She went to her sister and said: "Didi, since I am not of much use to you here, I might as well return home, if you would permit me." Sarmila could no longer protest: 'No you can't go—please, don't!' She readily agreed. "Alright! You may go—since your studies suffer. Come and see us now and again when you have leisure."

Sasanka was out on duty. Taking advantage of his absence, Urmi left for her home that very day. When Sasanka returned from office he brought with him a set of instruments for mechanical drawing he had bought for Urmi, having promised to teach her the technique. Not finding her in her usual place, he came and asked Sarmila: "Where on earth has Urmi disappeared?"

Sarmila replied: "It was not convenient for her studies here, so she's gone home."

"But she had come prepared to put up with this inconvenience for a few days. Why then this objection today, all of a sudden?"

From her husband's tone, Sarmila divined that he suspected her as the cause. Without wasting any words on that score, she merely said: "Please, bring her back here–tell her I want her to return. I'm sure she won't object."

Returning home Urmi found awaiting her a long-overdue letter from Nirad. She was afraid to open it, knowing what a pile of guilt she had accumulated. So long, she had been citing her sister's illness as her excuse for indiscipline. The excuse had very nearly lost its validity, ever since Sasanka had insisted on engaging trained nurses for Sarmila both for day and night. In accordance with the doctors' instructions the nurses did not allow the relatives to frequent the patient's room. Urmi knew that her sister's illness would not carry weight with Nirad who would dismiss it with, "That's no excuse." Indeed, it was not, since her attendance was not needed. Full of repentance, she made up her mind to confess her wrongdoing and to beg for Nirad's forgiveness. She would swear never to go astray again, nor take any more liberties with the discipline of her life.

Before opening the letter, she took out again that photograph of

Nirad which she had not seen for so long, and placed it on her desk. She knew that if Sasanka saw it he would jeer at it. Never mind, she would remain unaffected by his ridicule. That would be her expiation. While in her sister's house, she had hitherto refrained from raising the topic of her impending marriage with Nirad, nor did anyone else there ever allude to it. The engagement had met with no one's approval in that house. Urmi now resolved, with clenched fists, to proclaim the fact in every act of hers. She put on her finger the engagement ring which she had so far kept hidden. It was a very cheap ornament which Nirad, by way of flaunting the pride of his "honest poverty", had valued far above any diamond. His manner had said: "The price of the ring is no measure of my value; it's my worth that lends value to the ring."

Having thus made due amends, Urmi very slowly opened the envelope. No sooner had she perused its contents than she gave a leap of joy. She felt like dancing, but not being used to that art, she snatched the *sitar* lying on her bed and, without bothering to tune it, began to draw all sorts of frenzies out of it. Just at that moment Sasanka entered the room. "What on earth is the matter?" he asked. "It seems the date of the wedding is fixed, after all!"

"Indeed, Sasankada, it's fixed."

"Fixed beyond any possibility of change?"

"Beyond all possibilities of change."

"Let me send for the pipers then and order sweets at Bhimnag's."

"You don't have to bother."

"What! Will you arrange everything yourself? Bravo Amazon! What about the wedding gifts?"

"The wedding gifts have gone from my own pocket."

"The fish being fried in its own oil, eh? I don't quite understand."

"Here, take this letter and read it."

She gave him the letter to read. Having finished it, Sasanka roared with laughter. Nirad had written that having discovered that it was not feasible to carry on in India the highly difficult line of research to which he had dedicated his life, it had become necessary for him to make a supreme sacrifice. He had no alterative but to release himself from his engagement to Urmi. A European lady had agreed to marry him and to devote herself to his work. But, of course, the mission was the same, whether it was carried on in India or over there. Hence, it would be no injustice to the spirit of Rajaram Babu's will if part of the money he had set apart for the mission were to be handed over to him. Indeed, such an act would but bring honour to the deceased.

"At any rate, it wouldn't be bad," commented Sasanka, "to help to keep this creature alive in that distant land. If you stop sending him money, there's the danger of the fellow turning up here one day, driven by hunger."

"If you are afraid of that," laughed Urmi, "you had better send him the money yourself. I won't give a penny."

"Sure, you won't change your mind anymore?" asked Sasanka. "Will the pride of the proud one last?"

"If I should change my mind, what's that to you, Sasankada?"

"To answer that question truthfully would only add to your conceit. For your own good, therefore, I'll keep quiet. But really, I wonder at the fellow's impertinence–what the English call cheek."

A great weight seemed to have been lifted off Urmi's mind–a burden of long standing. She hardly knew what to do with this joy of freedom. She tore up and threw away the programme of study. She flung the ring out of the window to the beggar in the lane who was asking for alms.

"Will any hawker buy these fat books with their pencil annotations?" she asked.

"First, let's hear what would happen, if no one bought them."

"The ghost of the dead and buried days may reside in them and may come and stand by my bed at dead of night, pointing its dread finger at me."

"If there be any such fear, I'll buy the books right away, without waiting for any hawker."

"What will you do with them?"

"Perform their last rites according to the Hindu *Shastras.* I would go as far as Gaya to consecrate their ashes, if that would set your mind at rest."

"No, that would be going too far."

"Very well, I'll build a pyramid in a corner of my library to lodge their mummy."

"But let me tell you, you can't go to your work today."

"Not at all?"

"Not at all."

"What am I to do instead?"

"Let's get into a car and just vanish."

"Go and get your sister's permission."

"I'll tell her after we return—though I'll get a good scolding. But then it won't matter."

"Right! I too am willing to stand your sister's scolding. I'll sweep you along at the rate of forty-five miles an hour, and won't mind bursting a tyre or running over a couple of our own species, even if it takes us as far as the jail—provided you promise thrice that at the end of our chariot-drive you will return to our house."

"Agreed, agreed, agreed!"

After the drive they returned to the Bhowanipore house, but the excitement of forty-five miles an hour still ran hot in their blood and would not subside. This turbulence of blood made them blind to all sense of responsibility, fear or shame.

For some days, Sasanka's work fell into a state of complete disorder. He knew that what he was doing was not right and that the price of neglect might prove to be very heavy. At night, he was haunted in bed by fearsome apprehensions in which all ominous possibilities seemed greatly exaggerated. But next day, he was once again "heedless of his trust", like the Yaksa of *Meghaduta.*

Alcohol taken once has to be taken again to drown the regret.

SASANKA

Thus, time passed. The eyes were frenzied, the mind infatuated. Urmi took long to realise what was happening to her, but one day she was rudely awakened to the reality.

For some unknown reason Urmi was afraid of Mathur-dada and had always avoided him. One day, Mathur came to her sister's room in the morning and stayed there till noon. Soon after, Sarmila sent for Urmi and with an expression at once calm and stern said to her: "Do you realise what havoc you have caused by distracting him from his work day after day?"

"Why, what has happened, Didi?" asked Urmi frightened.

"Mathur-dada has just informed me that your brother-in-law has grossly neglected his duties, leaving everything to Jawaharlal who has been helping himself to the building materials with both hands. It has come to light that large godowns have been so badly roofed that the rain pours through them as through a sieve, damaging the goods stored inside. Owing to the high reputation of our firm, the clients did not have the construction tested. And now, we are faced not only with the loss of our firm's reputation but with considerable financial loss as well. Mathur-dada is severing the partnership."

Urmi's heart sank, her face grew ashen. In a moment, as by a lightning flash, her heart's hidden secret was revealed to her. She realised now the full measure of intoxication which had unconsciously robbed her of her senses, of her power of discrimination. She had looked upon Sasanka's work as a sort of rival who must be thwarted, and from whose clutches she was ever impatient to snatch him away, to have him all to herself. Many a time when Sasanka was bathing, she had thoughtlessly dismissed visitors on business with a curt, "He can't see anybody now,"—only because she was afraid lest Sasanka should again after his bath get engrossed in work and Urmi's day be rendered fruitless for want of his leisure. The terrible picture of her infatuation rose full and clear before her eyes. Instantly, she flung herself at her sister's feet and began to repeat in hoarse and broken tones: "Kick me away from your house, drive me away from your presence, now, this very minute!"

The sister had made up her mind on no account to forgive Urmi, but now her heart melted. Gently caressing Urmi's head she said: "Don't worry. Some way out of the difficulty shall be found."

Urmi rose. "Why should you bear all the loss?" she cried. "I too have some means."

"Are you crazy?" broke in Sarmila. "Do you suppose I'm such a pauper as that? I have requested Mathur-dada not to make a fuss over this matter. I'll make up the loss. And now, listen, see that your brother-in-law does not come to know that I know anything about it."

Urmi again fell at her sister's feet. "Forgive me, Didi, please, forgive me!" she cried, beating her head.

"Who is to forgive whom, sister?" weariedly murmured Sarmila wiping her tears. "Life is so perplexing! We are baffled in our hopes, cheated of our loves."

After this incident Urmi did not leave her sister's side even for a moment, personally attending to every one of her needs, ministering medicine, serving food, helping her bathe, putting her to sleep. Once more she took to her books, poring over them, seated by her sister's bed. She dared not trust herself or Sasanka any more.

The result was that Sasanka took to visiting the sick-room. Only a male can be so clumsy in his infatuation as not to notice that his wife could plainly see through the motive of his frequent visits. Each time he bustled in Urmi blushed hot with shame. He invited Urmi to a football match to see the Mohun Bagan team play; the temptation did not work. He then brought the newspaper where in the advertisement column he had underlined Charlie Chaplin's name, but that also bore no fruit. When Urmi was less remote Sasanka did make an effort to attend to his work, but now even that was impossible.

However painful to her the sight of this unfortunate man, suffering so uselessly, Sarmila at first drew a secret pleasure from it. But she gradually noticed that his suffering was gaining on him, his face drying up, the black marks deepening under his eyes. It was obvious that with Urmi absent from the dining table, he did not relish his food and was slowly starving himself. The recent flood of gaiety that had inundated the house had suddenly ebbed, carrying away with it even the easy and peaceful tenor of their former days.

Once, Sasanka had been indifferent to his appearance. He used to have his hair cropped so short as almost to render the service of a comb superfluous. After many vehement attempts at remonstrating, Sarmila had in the end given him up as hopeless. But lately, Urmi's brief verdict couched in the form of a loud laugh had not been without effect. For the first time in his life Sasanka had begun to apply scented hair-oils to the new growth of hair on his head. But nowadays, his heart's wretchedness was so pitifully obvious in the unkempt state of his hair that it was no longer possible to make fun of it, open or secret. Love's tenderness proving stronger than its bitterness, Sarmila was torn with pity for him and contempt at her own callousness; the torment of her illness was intensified.

There was to be military tattoo on the Maidan of the troops stationed at the Fort. Timidly, Sasanka inquired: "Will you come, Urmi? I have booked good seats." Before Urmi could reply, Sarmila said: "Of course, she'll go. She's dying for a little outing."

Thus encouraged, Sasanka proposed after a couple of days: "Circus?" Urmi seemed only too eager. And then, "Botanical Gardens?" She hesitated, unwilling to leave her sister's side for so long. But the sister now advocated Sasanka's cause. Drudging with the masons the whole long day, getting messed all over with dust and sand–it was enough to drive one crazy. His health would break down if he didn't go out for a little fresh air. This plea was deemed sufficient to justify a trip as far as Rajganj.

'He cannot afford to lose her, for whose sake he does not mind risking the ruin of his work,' said Sarmila to herself.

Though no one ever told him in so many words, it seemed to Sasanka that what he was doing had the silent approval of all around him. He had convinced himself that Sarmila was in no way unhappy, that on the contrary, she felt happy in watching the happiness of this pair. This might have been impossible in the case of an ordinary woman, but then Sarmila was no ordinary woman. During the days of his government service, an artist had made a pencil sketch of his wife, which had till now remained buried in his portfolio. He now took it out and had it expensively framed by a European firm and hung it on the wall in his office, facing his desk. The gardener filled the vase in front with fresh flowers everyday.

At last, a day came when Sasanka, taking Urmi round the garden to see the sunflowers in bloom, suddenly seized her hand and confessed: "Surely, you know that I love you. As for your sister, she is a veritable goddess. I worship her as I could worship none else in this life. She is no creature of this earth, so infinitely superior is she to us."

Her sister had repeatedly confided to Urmi that her greatest consolation was that Urmi would be there to fill her place. Painful, no doubt, it was to imagine another woman in her place; on the other hand, she could not bear the thought of Sasanka dragging on a forlorn, wretched existence, without a woman to look after his comfort. She had also said that if he was thwarted in love, it would react even more ruinously on his business. Once the hunger of his heart was appeased, his work would resume its old order.

Sasanka's mind was in a delirium of exhilaration. He felt transported to a fairyland where all sense of responsibility faded in a stupor of happiness. Nowadays, he observed the sanctity of the Sunday as a holiday with the scrupulous adherence of a Christian. One day, he came and told Sarmila: "I've secured the steam-launch for the day from the Jute Sahibs. Tomorrow being Sunday, I propose to take Urmi to Diamond Harbour. We'll leave before day-break and return before dusk."

Something seemed to wring the very veins of Sarmila's heart; her forehead was wrinkled with pain. Sasanka noticed nothing.

"What about the food?" she mildly inquired.

"I've ordered it at a hotel."

There was a time when she had looked after such details. Then, Sasanka had been indifferent. Now it all seemed changed, topsy-turvy.

"Alright. You may go," she said. No sooner had the words left her mouth than Sasanka turned and hurriedly left, without caring to waste a moment. A desire to sob aloud overpowered Sarmila. She hid her face in the pillow and murmured over and over again: 'Why am I lingering?'

The next day, Sunday, was the anniversary of their wedding day, a day whose observance had never suffered a breach so far. This time, too, lying in her bed, she had planned all the arrangements, unknown to her husband. Nothing much. She would have made him put on the red *Banaras dhoti* he had worn at his wedding, herself clad in her wedding *sari*. She would have put a garland round his neck and made him sit and eat in front of her. Incense burning in the room, the gramophone in the adjoining room playing the familiar wedding music of the *sanai*–that was all. Every year on this day Sasanka had surprised her with some charming gift. This time too, she had felt sure that he had brought something to give her on the morrow.

But everything had turned bitter today. All alone in the room, she kept on murmuring: "False, false, all is false. What's the use of this farce!"

She had no sleep that night. Early in the morning she heard the car drive away from the gate. She broke into sobs. "Thou art but a myth, Lord!" she cried.

From now on, Sarmila's condition grew steadily and speedily worse. One day when the disease showed very grave symptoms, she sent for her husband. It was evening, the light in the room was faint. She motioned to the nurse to leave them alone. She made her husband sit beside her and, taking his hand in hers, said: "I have looked upon you as the Heaven-sent boon of my life. God did not grant me the power to prove worthy of you. I have done the best I could. For my many shortcomings I beg your forgiveness."

Silencing Sasanka, who was about to say something, she continued: "No, don't interrupt me. I leave Urmi to your care. She is my own sister; in her you will find me, and much else besides that you could not find in me. No, please keep still, don't say anything. That I have brought about your happiness before dying is to me the fulfilment of my good fortune."

From outside the nurse called: "The doctor has come."

"Please, bring him in," answered Sarmila.

The conversation stopped.

Sarmila's maternal uncle was an enthusiastic patron of all sorts of unorthodox systems of healing. Recently, he had become attached to a Sannyasi. When the doctors gave up Sarmila's case as hopeless, he insisted that the prescription of his Himalaya-returned Sannyasi should be given a trial. The medicine consisted of a powder made of a Tibetan root, to be taken with plenty of milk. Sasanka, who could never stand quacks, objected, but Sarmila pleaded: "It'll do no good, of course. But at any rate it'll please Uncle."

But the medicine did bear fruit. Her breathing trouble subsided and she no longer spat blood. Gradually, after a fortnight's treatment she was able to sit up. The doctors explained it by saying that sometimes, the imminence of death provokes so desperate a reaction in the body that the life is saved. However that might be, Sarmila's life was saved.

'How embarrassing!' thought Sarmila. 'What's to be done? Will life saved prove in the end a greater calamity than death?'

Urmi was busy packing. Her term of stay had drawn to its end. Sarmila went up to her.

"You can't leave," she said.

"Why, what do you mean?"

"I mean—is it so rare in our Hindu society for sisters to be co-wives?"

"Hush—for shame!"

"Afraid of a scandal? Are people's tongues of greater consequence than the voice of Fate?"

She sent for Sasanka and told him: "Let's migrate to Nepal. You were once offered job at the Royal Court there. You may get it now if you try. No one will malign us there."

Without giving anyone time to oppose her suggestion, Sarmila began to make preparations for departure. Morose and downcast, Urmi went about the house as though she would have liked to hide herself. Sasanka said to her: "If you abandon me now, you may well imagine what will happen to me."

"I'm unable to think, to decide for myself," replied Urmi. "Whatever you two decide, I'll accept."

The preparations took some days. When the day of departure

drew near, Urmi said: "Please, wait a week longer, while I go and consult uncle on a matter of business."

She left.

In her absence Mathur came to Sarmila looking very glum, and said: "You are going away at the right moment. After my last conversation with you, I arrived at a settlement with Sasanka of our mutual business relations, dividing the business without sharing liabilities. Lately, Sasanka has been going through the accounts with a view to winding up his own share of the business and it has come to light that not only has all your money been used up but it seems that this house too may have to be sold, to meet the liability."

"Did it never strike him that the crash was so imminent?" asked Sarmila.

"Some crashes," explained Mathur, "like the crash of lightning, are difficult to predict. They strike without a moment's warning. He was aware of his losses and could have repaired them in time, if the silly notion had not possessed him of resorting to quick expedients to restore his losses. Without consulting me he began to speculate in coal. The result was that he was in the end obliged to sell off in a falling market the goods bought when the market was soaring. Now, he has suddenly discovered that all he had has blown up like a rocket, leaving behind nothing but ashes. If now by God's grace he gets a job in Nepal, it may still be alright."

Sarmila was not afraid of poverty. On the contrary she knew that in the house of a needy husband her place would be all the more assured, for she was confident that she knew how to soften the rigours of want. Her ornaments would go a long way to keep off the starkness of poverty for some time. Urmi's portion, too, would be at the disposal of her husband if he married her—a faint suggestion of this thought did peep into her mind. But merely to exist is not enough. The fortune which her husband had built up so long by his own prowess, for whose sake she had, day after day, voluntarily suppressed many a claim of her heart, this embodiment of the joint dream of their lives now vanished like a mirage—the humiliation of it made her crumble into dust. She wished that death had spared her this dishonour.

'I have resigned myself to my fate,' she said to herself, 'but will he reconcile himself to the inexorable emptiness of poverty and dishonour? Will it not plant the bitterness of regret in his heart? He may find it hard one day to forgive her whose infatuation brought this all about; the very food served by her will taste like poison in his mouth. Chocked with shame by the stench of his own sottishness, he will only find fault with the alcohol. And if in the end he is driven to dependence on Urmi's income, the bitterness of his humiliation will turn every moment of her life into a hell.'

In the process of clearing his accounts with Mathur, Sasanka suddenly discovered that every penny of Sarmila's had been lost in his business, and that, without telling him anything about it, she had paid up the debt to Mathur. He recalled how, when he had resigned his Government post, he had built up his business with her money. Now again, leaving the ruin of his business behind, he was entering the harness of service, with the load of that same debt to Sarmila on his back. How would he ever repay the debt with the meagre income of a salaried post?

In about ten days' time they would be leaving for Nepal. That night he had not a wink of sleep. Before the day broke, he flung himself out of bed and bringing his fist down on the dressing table with all his might, cried out: "I will not go to Nepal." He swore: "Here in Calcutta we will stay on, the two of us along with Urmi—facing the full malicious glare of frowning, scowling society. And here in this very Calcutta I will build up once again the ruined edifice of my business."

Sarmila was busy making a list of articles to be taken on the journey or to be left behind. Suddenly, she heard her name called out, and ran to her husband, throwing the list down. Apprehensive of some sudden calamity she asked with a trembling heart, "Why, what's the matter?"

"I will not go to Nepal," came the reply. "I will defy society and stick it out here."

"Why, what has happened?" she inquired.

"Work," he replied.

Work! The same old word! Her heart began to beat fast.

"Don't think I am a coward, Sarmi. Could you imagine me so degraded as to run away from my responsibility?"

Drawing closer, Sarmila took his hand in hers.

"Do make your meaning clear," she said.

"Don't conceal the fact from me," cried Sasanka, "that I am once again in your debt."

"Alright, I won't," submitted Sarmila.

"From this very day," went on Sasanka, "I'll begin discharging the debt–as I did once before. Mark my words. I'll recover and drag up again what I have flung away into the abyss. Trust me again as you once gave me your trust."

Sarmila's head sank on her husband's breast.

"Let me also have your full trust," she murmured. "Teach me, train me, mould me so that I may become worthy of sharing your task."

From outside came the cry: "Letter!" Two letters came in, written in Urmi's hand. One of them was addressed to Sasanka:

"I am on my way to Bombay *en route* for Europe. I shall carry out father's wishes and return a doctor in about six or seven years' time. In the meantime the havoc I have caused in your home will have had time to repair itself. Don't worry about me. I can't help worrying about you."

The other letter was for Sarmila.

"Didi, a thousand *pranaams* at your feet. Forgive me the wrong I have done you unwittingly. If no wrong has been done–then that very knowledge will make me happy. I dare not hope for any greater happiness, nor indeed, do I know for certain wherein lies happiness. If happiness is not in store for me, let it be so. Let me only not err."

GLOSSARY

Annapurna	:	A name of the goddess Durga, conceived in the act of giving food to Shiva, her consort, and to the whole world. Sasankamauli is also one of the names of Shiva.
Da	:	Short for *Dada*, a term applied to elder brothers, elder cousins as well as (as in this case) to elder brother-in-law.
Debottar	:	Property endowed for religious purposes; *Shebait*, its trustee.
Di	:	Short for *Didi*, a term applied to elder sisters and elder cousins.
Gaya	:	The holy city in Bihar where Hindus go to perform last rites of the dead.
Kaka	:	Father's younger brother or cousin.
Kalapahar	:	A Bengali brahmin who renounced his religion and became a general under Muslim rulers and earned great notoriety as an iconoclast (16th century).
Khuki	:	A pet name for girls in Bengal.
Luchisthan	:	An untranslatable word. *Luchi* is a kind of fried pancake much favoured by Bengalis; *sthan* means place; *luchisthan* meaning a place which provides good food or material well-being. *Beluchisthan* (*be* meaning without), used as an antonym of *luchisthan*, is a pun on the

		word Baluchistan, the arid, rocky region to the north-west of India.
Makar	:	Fabulous marine animal described in Indian mythology as the mount of the goddess Ganga (Ganges); hence auspicious. The mouth of this animal appears as a decorative motif in Indian ornaments.
Mashi	:	Mother's sister. In Bengal servants usually address the mistress as *Mother.* The mistress's sister is hence referred to as *Mashi.*
Meghaduta	:	*The Cloud-Messenger,* the famous poem by Kalidasa.
Meghnadbadh Kavya	:	An epic in blank verse by Michael Madhusudan Dutta, the great predecessor of Tagore.
Pakhwaj	:	A kind of double drum.
Pranaam	:	The Hindu way of saluting one's elders is to touch their feet with one's hand and then to lift the hand to one's forehead.
Punjabi	:	A kind of upper garment worn by men; *Dhoti* is a lower garment.
Vidyut-lata	:	*Lit.* Lightning-creeper. *Nirad* literally means a cloud.

SACRIFICE & OTHER PLAYS

SANYASI OR THE ASCETIC

'Lead us from the unreal to the real'

Scene I

Sanyasi [*outside the cave*]. The division of days and nights is not for me, nor that of months and years. For me, the stream of time has stopped, on whose waves dances the world, like straws and twigs. In this dark cave I am alone, merged in myself,–and the eternal night is still, like a mountain lake afraid of its own depth. Water oozes and drips from the cracks, and in the pools float the ancient frogs. I sit chanting the incantation of nothingness. The world's limits recede, line after line.–The stars, like sparks of fire, flown from the anvil of time, are extinct; and that joy is mine which comes to the God Shiva, when, after aeons of dream, he wakes up to find himself alone in the heart of the infinite annihilation. I am free. I am the great Solitary One. When I was thy slave, O Nature, thou didst set my heart against itself, and madest it carry the fierce war of suicide through its world. Desires, that have no other ends, but to feed upon themselves and all that comes to their mouths, lashed me into fury. I ran about, madly chasing my shadow. Thou drovest me with thy lightning lashes of pleasure into the void of satiety. And the hungers, who are thy decoys, ever led me into the endless famine, where food turned into dust, and drink into vapour.

Till, when my world was spotted with tears and ashes, I took my oath, that I would have revenge upon thee, interminable Appearance, mistress of endless disguises. I took shelter in the darkness,—the castle of the Infinite,—and fought the deceitful light, day after day, till it lost all its weapons and lay powerless at my feet. Now, when I am free of fear and desires, when the mist has vanished, and my reason shines pure and bright, let me go out into the kingdom of lies, and sit upon its heart, untouched and unmoved.

Scene II

Sanyasi [*by the roadside*]. How small is this earth and confined, watched and followed by the persistent horizons. The trees, houses, and crowd of things are pressing upon my eyes. The light, like a cage, has shut out the dark eternity; and the hours hop and cry within its barriers, like prisoned birds. But why are these noisy men rushing on, and for what purpose? They seem always afraid of missing something,—the something that never comes to their hands.

[*The crowd passes.*]

[*Enter a* Village Elder *and two* Women.]

First woman. O my, O my! You *do* make me laugh.

Second woman. But who says you are old?

Village elder. There are fools who judge men by their outside.

First woman. How sad! We have been watching your outside from our infancy. It is just the same all through these years.

Village elder. Like the morning sun.

First woman. Yes, like the morning sun in its shining baldness.

Village elder. Ladies, you are overcritical in your taste. You notice things that are unessential.

Second woman. Leave off your chatter, Ananga. Let us hasten home, or my man will be angry.

First woman. Goodbye, sir. Please, judge us from our outside, we won't mind that.

Village Elder. Because you have no inside to speak of.

[*They go.*]

[*Enter three* Villagers.]

First villager. Insult me? The scoundrel! He shall regret it.

Second villager. He must be taught a thorough lesson.

First villager. A lesson that will follow him to his grave.

Third villager. Yes, brother, set your heart upon it. Never give him quarter.

Second villager. He has grown too big.

First villager. Big enough to burst at last.

Third villager. The ants, when they begin to grow wings, perish.

Second villager. But have you got a plan?

First villager. Not one, but hundreds. I will drive my plough-share over his household.–I will give him a donkey-ride through the town, with his cheeks painted white and black. I will make the world too hot for him, and–

[*They go.*]

[*Enter two* Students.]

First student. I am sure, Professor Madhab won in the debate.

Second student. No, it was Professor Janardan.

First student. Professor Madhab maintained his point to the last. He said that the subtle is the outcome of the gross.

Second student. But Professor Janardan conclusively proved that the subtle is the origin of the gross.

First student. Impossible.

Second student. It is clear as the day-light.

First student. Seeds come from the tree.

Second student. The tree comes from the seed.

First student. Sanyasi, which of these is true? Which is the original, the subtle or the gross?

Sanyasi. Neither.

Second student. Neither. Well, that sounds satisfactory.

Sanyasi. The origin is the end, and the end is the origin. It is a circle.—The distinction between the subtle and gross is in your ignorance.

First student. Well, it sounds very simple—and I think this was what my Master meant.

Second student. Certainly, this agrees more with what *my* master teaches.

[*They go out.*]

Sanyasi. These birds are word-peckers. When they pick up some wriggling nonsense, which can fill their mouth, they are happy.

[*Enter two* Flower-girls, *singing.*]

The weary hours pass by.
The flowers that blossom in the light
Fade and drop in the shadow.
I thought I would weave a garland
In the cool of the morning for my love.
But the morning wears on,
The flowers are not gathered.
And my love is lost.

A wayfarer. Why such regret, my darlings? When the garlands are ready, the necks will not be wanting.

First flower-girl. Nor the halter.

Second flower-girl. You are bold. Why do you come so close?

Wayfarer. You quarrel for nothing, my girl. I am far enough from you to allow an elephant to pass between us.

Second flower-girl. Indeed. Am I such a fright? I wouldn't have eaten you, if you had come.

[*They go out laughing.*]

[*Comes an old* Beggar.]

Beggar. Kind sirs, have pity on me. May God prosper you. Give me one handful from your plenty.

[*Enters a Soldier.*]

Soldier. Move away. Don't you see the Minister's son is coming?.

[*They go out.*]

Sanyasi. It is mid-day. The sun is growing strong. The sky looks like an overturned burning copper bowl. The earth breathes hot sighs, and the whirling sands dance by. What sights of man have I seen! Can I ever again shrink back into the smallness of these creatures, and become one of them? No, I am free. I have not this obstacle, this world round me. I live in a pure desolation.

[*Enter the girl* Vasanti *and a* Woman.]

Woman. Girl, you are Raghu's daughter, aren't you? You should keep away from this road. Don't you know it goes to the temple?

Vasanti. I am on the farthest side, Lady.

Woman. But I thought my cloth-end touched you. I am taking my offerings to the goddess,– I hope they are not polluted.

Vasanti. I assure you, your cloth did not touch me. [*The* Woman *goes.*] I am Vasanti, Raghu's daughter. May I come to you, father?

Sanyasi. Why not, child?

Vasanti. I am a pollution, as they call me.

Sanyasi. But they are all that,–a pollution. They roll in the dust of existence. Only he is pure who has washed away the world from his mind. But what have you done, daughter?

Vasanti. My father, who is dead, had defied their laws and their gods. He would not perform their rites.

Sanyasi. Why do you stand away from me?

Vasanti. Will you touch me?

Sanyasi. Yes, because nothing can touch me truly. I am ever away in the endless. You can sit here, if you wish.

Vasanti [*breaking into a sob*]. Never tell me to leave you, when once you have taken me near you.

Sanyasi. Wipe away your tears, child. I am a Sanyasi. I have neither hatred, nor attachment in my heart,—I never claim you as mine; therefore, I can never discard you. You are to me as this blue sky is,—you are,—yet you are not.

Vasanti. Father, I am deserted by gods and men alike.

Sanyasi. So am I. I have deserted both gods and men.

Vasanti. You have no mother?

Sanyasi. No.

Vasanti. Nor father?

Sanyasi. No.

Vasanti. Nor any friend?

Sanyasi. No.

Vasanti. Then, I shall be with you.—You won't leave me?

Sanyasi. I have done with leaving. You can stay near me, yet never coming near me.

Vasanti. I do not understand you, father. Tell me, is there no shelter for me in the whole world?

Sanyasi. Shelter? Don't you know this world is a bottomless chasm? The swarm of creatures, coming out from the hole of nothingness, seeks for shelter, and enters into the gaping mouth of this emptiness, and is lost. These are the ghosts of lies around you, who hold their market of illusions,—and the foods which they sell are shadows. They only deceive your hunger, but do not satisfy. Come away from here, child, come away.

Vasanti. But, father, they seem so happy in this world. Can we not watch them from the roadside?

Sanyasi. Alas, they do not understand. They cannot see that this world is death spread out to eternity.–It dies every moment, yet never comes to the end.–And we, the creatures of this world, live by feeding upon death.

Vasanti. Father, you frighten me.

[*Enters a* Traveller.]

Traveller. Can I get a shelter near this place?

Sanyasi. Shelter there is nowhere, my son, but in the depth of one's self.–Seek that; hold to it fast, if you would be saved.

Traveller. But I am tired, and want shelter.

Vasanti. My hut is not far from here. Will you come?

Traveller. But who are you?

Vasanti. Must you know me? I am Raghu's daughter.

Traveller. God bless you, child, but I cannot stay.

[*Goes.*]

[*Men come bearing somebody on a bed.*]

First bearer. He is still asleep.

Second bearer. How heavy the rascal is!

A traveller [*outside their group*]. Whom do you carry?

Third bearer. Bindé, the weaver, was sleeping as one dead, and we have taken him away.

Second bearer. But I am tired, brothers. Let us give him a shake, and waken him up.

Bindé [*wakes up*]. Ee, a, u–

Third bearer. What's that noise?

Bindé. I say. Who are you? Where am I being carried?

[*They put down the bed from their shoulders.*]

Third bearer. Can't you keep quiet, like all decent dead people?

Second bearer. The cheek of him! He must talk, even though he is dead.

Third bearer. It would be more proper of you, if you kept still.

Bindé. I am sorry to disappoint you, gentlemen, you have made a mistake.—I was not dead, but fast asleep.

Second bearer. I admire this fellow's impudence. Not only must he die, but argue.

Third bearer. He won't confess the truth. Let us go, and finish the rites of the dead.

Bindé. I swear by your beard, my brother, I am as alive as any of you.

[*They take him away, laughing.*]

Sanyasi. The girl has fallen asleep, with her arm beneath her little head; I think I must leave her now, and go. But, coward, must you run away,—run away from this tiny thing? These are nature's spiders' webs, they have danger merely for moths, and not for a Sanyasi like me.

Vasanti [*awaking with a start*]. Have you left me, Master?—Have you gone away?

Sanyasi. Why should I go away from you? What fear have I? Afraid of a shadow?

Vasanti. Do you hear the noise in the road?

Sanyasi. But stillness is in my soul.

[*Enters a young* Woman, *followed by* Men.]

Woman. Go now. Leave me. Don't talk to me of love.

First man. Why, what has been my crime?

Woman. You men have hearts of stone.

First man. Incredible. If our hearts were of stone, how could Cupid's darts make damage there?

Other man. Bravo. Well said.

Second man. Now, what is your answer to that, my dear?

Woman. Answer! You think you have said something very fine,—don't you? It is perfect rubbish.

First man. I leave it to your judgement, gentlemen. What I said was this, that if your hearts be of stone, how can—

Third man. Yes, yes, it has no answer at all.

First man. Let me explain it to you. She said, we men have hearts of stone, didn't she? Well, I said, in answer, if our hearts were truly of stone, how could Cupid's darts damage them? You understand?

Second man. Brother, I have been selling molasses in the town for the last twenty-four years,—do you think I cannot understand what you say?

[*They go out.*]

Sanyasi. What are you doing, my child?

Vasanti. I am looking at your broad palm, father. My hand is a little bird that finds its nest here. Your palm is great, like the great earth which holds all. These lines are the rivers, and these are hills.

[*Puts her cheek upon it.*]

Sanyasi. Your touch is soft, my daughter, like the touch of sleep. It seems to me this touch has something of the great darkness, which touches one's soul with the wand of the eternal.—But, child, you are the moth of the daylight. You have your birds and flowers and fields—what can you find in me, who have my centre in the One and my circumference nowhere?

Vasanti. I do not want anything else. Your love is enough for me.

Sanyasi. The girl imagines I love her,—foolish heart. She is happy in that thought. Let her nourish it. For they have been brought up in illusions, and they must have illusions to console them.

Vasanti. Father, this creeper trailing on the grass, seeking some tree to twine itself round, is my creeper. I have tended it and watered it from the time when it had pushed up only two little leaves into the air, like an infant's cry. This creeper is me,–it has grown by the road-side, it can be so easily crushed. Do you see these beautiful little flowers, pale blue with white spots in their hearts,– these white spots are their dreams. Let me gently brush your forehead with these flowers. To me, things that are beautiful are the keys to all that I have not seen and not known.

Sanyasi. No, no, the beautiful is mere phantasy. To him who knows, the dust and the flower are the same.–But what languor is this that is creeping into my blood and drawing before my eyes a thin mist veil of all the rainbow colours? Is it nature herself weaving her dreams round me, clouding my senses? (*Suddenly, he tears the creeper, and rises up.*) No more of this; for this is death. What game of yours is this with me, little girl? I am a sanyasi, I have cut all my knots, I am free,–No, no, not those tears. I cannot bear them.–But where was hidden in my heart this snake, this anger, that hissed out of its dark with its fang? No, they are not dead,– they outlive starvation. These hell-creatures clatter their skeletons and dance in my heart, when their mistress, the great witch, plays upon her magic flute.–Weep not, child, come to me. You seem to me like a cry of a lost world, like the song of a wandering star. You bring to my mind something, which is infinitely more than this Nature,–more than the sun and stars. It is as great as the darkness. I understand it not. I have never known it, therefore, I fear it. I must leave you.–Go back whence you came,–the messenger of the unknown.

Vasanti. Leave me not, father,–I have none else but you.

Sanyasi. I must go, I thought that I had known,–but I do not know. Yet, I must know. I leave you, to know who you are.

Vasanti. Father, if you leave me, I shall die.

Sanyasi. Let go my hand. Do not touch me. I must be free.–

[*He runs away.*]

Scene III

[The Sanyasi is seen, sitting upon a boulder in a mountain path.]

[A shepherd boy passes by, singing.]

Do not turn away your face, my love,
The spring has bared open its breast.
The flowers breathe their secrets in the dark.
The rustle of the forest leaves comes across the sky,
Like the sobs of the night.
Come, love, show me your face.

Sanyasi. The gold of the evening is melting in the heart of the blue sea. The forest, on the hillside, is drinking the last cup of the daylight. On the left, the village huts are seen through the trees with their evening lamps lighted, like a veiled mother watching by her sleeping children. Nature, thou art my slave. Thou hast spread thy many-coloured carpet in the great hall where I sit alone, like a king, and watch thee dance with thy starry necklace twinkling on thy breast.

[Shepherd girls pass by, singing.]

The music comes from across the dark river and calls me.
I was in the house and happy,
But the flute sounded in the still air of night,
And a pain pierced my heart.
Oh, tell me the way who know it,–
Tell me the way to him.
I will go to him with my one little flower,
And leave it at his feet,
And tell him that his music is one with my love.

[They go.]

Sanyasi. I think such an evening had come to me only once before in all my births. Then, its cup overbrimmed with love and music, and I sat with someone, the memory of whose face is in that setting star of the evening.—But where is my little girl, with her dark sad eyes, big with tears? Is she there, sitting outside her hut, watching that same star through the immense loneliness of the evening? But the star must set, the evening close her eyes in the night, and tears must cease and sobs be stilled in sleep. No, I will not go back. Let the world-dreams take their own shape. Let me not trouble its course and create new phantasies. I will see, and think, and know.

[*Enters a ragged* Girl.]

Girl. Are you there, father?

Sanyasi. Come, child, sit by me. I wish I could own that call of yours. Someone did call me father, once, and the voice was somewhat like yours. The father answers now,—but where is that call?

Girl. Who are you?

Sanyasi. I am a sanyasi. Tell me, child, what is your father?

Girl. He gathers sticks from the forest.

Sanyasi. And you have a mother?

Girl. No. She died when I was a child.

Sanyasi. Do you love your father?

Girl. I love him more than anything else in the world. I have no one else but him.

Sanyasi. I understand you. Give me your little hand,— let me hold it in my palm,—in this big palm of mine.

Girl. Sanyasi, do you read palms? Can you read in my palm all that I am and shall be?

Sanyasi. I think I can read, but dimly know its meaning. One day, I shall know it.

Girl. Now I must go to meet my father.

Sanyasi. Where?

Girl. Where the road goes into the forest. He will miss me, if he does not find me there.

Sanyasi. Bring your head near to me, child. Let me give you my kiss of blessing, before you go.

[*Girl goes.*]

[A Mother *enters, with two children.*]

Mother. How stout and chubby Misri's children are. They are something to look at. But the more I feed you, the more you seem to grow thin everyday.

First girl. But why do you always blame us for that, mother? Can we help it?

Mother. Don't I tell you to take plenty of rest? But you must always be running about.

Second girl. But mother, we run about on your errands.

Mother. How dare you answer me like that?

Sanyasi. Where are you going, daughter?

Mother. My salutation, father. We are going home.

Sanyasi. How many are you?

Mother. My mother-in-law, and my husband and two other children, beside these.

Sanyasi. How do you spend your days?

Mother. I hardly know how my days pass. My man goes to the field, and I have my house to look after. Then, in the evening, I sit to spin with my elder girls. [*To the girls*] Go and salute the sanyasi. Bless them, father.

[*They go.*]

[*Enter two* Men.]

First man. Friend, go back from here. Do not come any further.

Second man. Yes, I know. Friends meet in this earth by chance, and the chance carries us on together some portion of the way, and then comes the moment when we must part.

Second friend. Let us carry away with us the hope that we part to meet again.

First friend. Our meetings and partings belong to all the movements of the world. Stars do not take special notice of us.

Second friend. Let us salute those stars which *did* throw us together. If for a moment, still it has been much.

First friend. Look back for a minute before you go. Can you see that faint glimmer of the water in the dark, and those *casuarina* trees on the sandy bank? Our village is all one heap of dark shadows. You can only see the lights. Can you guess which of those lights are ours?

Second friend. Yes. I think I can.

First friend. That light is the last farewell look of our past days upon their parting guest. A little further on, and there will remain one blot of darkness.

[*They go away.*]

Sanyasi. The night grows dark and desolate. It sits like a woman forsaken,–those stars are her tears, turned into fire. O my child, the sorrow of your little heart has filled, forever, all the nights of my life with its sadness. Your dear caressing hand has left its touch in this night air,–I feel it on my fore-head,–it is damp with your tears. My darling, your sobs that pursued me, when I fled away, have clung to my heart. I shall carry them to my death.

Scene IV

[*In the village path.*]

Sanyasi. Let my vows of sanyasi go. I break my staff and my alms-bowl. This stately ship, this world, which is crossing the sea of time,—let it take me up again, let me join once more the pilgrims. O the fool, who wanted to seek safety in swimming alone and gave up the light of the sun and stars, to pick his way with his glow-worm's lamp! The bird flies in the sky, not to fly away into the emptiness, but to come back again to this great earth.—I am free. I am free from the bodiless chain of the Nay. I am free among things, and forms and purpose. The finite is the true infinite, and love knows its truth. My girl, you are the spirit of all that is,—I can never leave you.

[*Enters a* Village Elder.]

Sanyasi. Do you know, brother, where Raghu's daughter is?
Village Elder. She has left her village, and we are glad.
Sanyasi. Where has she gone?
Village Elder. Do you ask where? It is all one to her where she goes.
[*Goes out.*]

Sanyasi. My darling has gone to seek a somewhere in the emptiness of nowhere. She must find me.

[*A crowd of* Villagers *enter.*]

First man. So, our King's son is going to be married tonight.
Second man. Can you tell me, when is the wedding hour?
Third man. The wedding hour is only for the bridegroom and the bride. What have we got to do with it?
A woman. But won't they give us cakes for the happy day?
First man. Cakes? You *are* silly. My uncle lives in the town—I have

heard from him that we shall have curds and parched rice.

Second man. Grand.

Fourth man. But we shall have a great deal more water than curds. You may be sure of that.

First man. Moti, you are a dull fellow. Water in the curds at a prince's wedding!

Fourth man. But we are not princes ourselves, Panchu. For us, poor people, the curds have the trick of turning into water most parts.

First man. Look there. That son of the charcoal-burner is still busy with his work. We mustn't allow that.

Second man. We shall burn him into charcoal, if he does not come out.

Sanyasi. Do you know, any of you, where is Raghu's daughter?

The woman. She has gone away.

Sanyasi. Where?

Woman. That we don't know.

First man. But we are sure that she is not the bride for our prince.

[*They laugh and go out.*]

[*Enters a* Woman, *with a child.*]

Woman. My obeisance to you, father. Let my child touch your feet with his head. He is sick. Bless him, father.

Sanyasi. But, daughter, I am no longer a sanyasi. Do not mock me with your salutation.

Woman. Then, who are you? What are you doing?

Sanyasi. I am seeking.

Woman. Seeking whom?

Sanyasi. Seeking my lost world back.—Do you know Raghu's daughter? Where is she?

Woman. Raghu's daughter? She is dead.

Sanyasi. No, she cannot be dead. No. No.

Woman. But what is her death to you, Sanyasi?

Sanyasi. Not only to me; it would be death to all.
Woman. I do not understand you.
Sanyasi. She can never be dead.

MALINI

Act I

The Balcony of the Palace facing the street.

Malini. The moment has come for me, and my life, like the dew drop upon a lotus leaf, is trembling upon the heart of this great time. I shut my eyes and seem to hear the tumult of the sky, and there is an anguish in my heart, I know not for what.

[*Enters* Queen.]

Queen. My child, what is this? Why do you forget to put on dresses that befit your beauty and youth? Where are your ornaments? My beautiful dawn, how can you absent the touch of gold from your limbs?

Malini. Mother, there are some who are born poor, even in a king's house. Wealth does not cling to those whose destiny it is to find riches in poverty.

Queen. That the child whose only language was the baby cry should talk to me in such riddles!—My heart quakes in fear when I listen to you. Where did you pick up your new creed, which goes against all our holy books? My child, they say that the Buddhist monks, from whom you take your lessons, practise black arts; that they cast their spells upon men's minds, confounding them with lies. But I ask you, is religion a thing that one has to find by seeking? Is it not like sunlight, given to you for all days? I am a simple woman. I do not understand men's creeds and dogmas. I only know that women's true objects of worship come to their own arms, without asking, in the shape of their husbands and their children.

[*Enters* King.]

King. My daughter, storm clouds are gathering over the King's house. Go no farther along your perilous path. Pause, if only for a short time.

Queen. What dark words are these?

King. My foolish child, if you must bring your new creed into this land of the old, let it not come like a sudden flood threatening those who dwell on the bank. Keep your faith to your own self. Rake not up public hatred and mockery against it.

Queen. Do not chide my girl, and teach her the crookedness of your diplomacy. If my child should choose her own teachers and pursue her own path, I do not know who can blame her.

King. Queen, my people are agitated, they clamour for my daughter's banishment.

Queen. Banishment? Of your own daughter?

King. The Brahmins, frightened at her heresy, have combined, and–

Queen. Heresy, indeed. Are all truths confined only in the musty, old books? Let them fling away their worm-eaten creeds, and come and take their lessons from this child. I tell you King, she is not a common girl,–she is a pure flame of fire. So, the divine spirit has taken birth in her. Do not despise her, less some day you strike your forehead, and weep, and find her no more.

Malini. Father, grant to your people their request. The great moment has come. Banish me.

King. Why, child? What want do you feel in your father's house?

Malini. Listen to me, father. Those, who cry for my banishment, cry for me. Mother, I have no words in which to tell you what I have in my mind. Leave me without regret, like the tree that sheds its flowers unheeding. Let me go out to all men,–for the world has claimed me from the King's hands.

King. Child, I do not understand you.

Malini. Father, you are a King. Be strong and fulfil your mission.

Queen. Child, is there no place for you here, where you were born? Is the burden of the world waiting for your little shoulders?

Malini. I dream, while I am awake, that the wind is wild, and the water is troubled; the night is dark, and the boat is moored in the haven. Where is the captain, who shall take the wanderers home? I feel I know the path, and the boat will thrill with life at my touch, and speed on.

Queen. Do you hear, King? Whose words are these? Do they come from this little girl? Is she your daughter, and have I borne her?

King. Yes, even as the night bears the dawn,—the dawn that is not of the night, but of all the world.

Queen. King, have you nothing to keep her bound to your house,—this image of light?—My darling, your hair has come loose on your shoulders. Let me bind it up.—Do they talk of banishment, King? If this be a part of their creed, then let come the new religion, and let those Brahmins be taught afresh what is truth.

King. Queen, let us take away our child from this balcony. Do you see the crowd gathering in the street?

[*They all go out.*]

[*Enter a crowd of* Brahmins, *in the street, before the palace balcony. They shout.*]

Brahmins. Banishment of the King's daughter!

Kemankar. Friends, keep your resolution firm. The woman, as an enemy, is to be dreaded more than all others. For reason is futile against her and forces are ashamed; man's power gladly surrenders itself to her powerlessness, and she takes her shelter in the strongholds of our own hearts.

First Brahmin. We must have audience with our King, to tell him that a snake has raised its poisonous hood from his own nest, and is aiming at the heart of our sacred religion.

Supriya. Religion? I *am* stupid. I do not understand you. Tell me, sir, is it your religion that claims the banishment of an innocent girl?

First Brahmin. You are a marplot, Supriya, you are ever a hindrance to all our enterprises.

Second Brahmin. We have united in defence of our faith, and you come like a subtle rift in the wall, like a thin smile on the compressed lips of contempt.

Supriya. You think that, by the force of numbers, you will determine truth, and drown reason by your united shouts?

First Brahmin. This is rank insolence, Supriya.

Supriya. The insolence is not mine but theirs who shape their scripture to fit their own narrow hearts.

Second Brahmin. Drive him out. He is none of us.

First Brahmin. We have all agreed upon the banishment of the Princess.–He who thinks differently, let him leave this assembly.

Supriya. Brahmins, it was a mistake on your part to elect me as one of your league. I am neither your shadow, nor an echo of your texts. I never admit that truth sides with the shrillest voice and I am ashamed to own as mine a creed that depends on force for its existence. [*To* Kemankar] Dear friend, let me go.

Kemankar. No, I will not. I know you are firm in your action, only doubting when you debate. Keep silence, my friend; for the time is evil.

Supriya. Of all things the blind certitude of stupidity is the hardest to bear. To think of saving your religion by banishing a girl from her home! But let me know what is her offence. Does she not maintain that truth and love are the body and soul of religion? If so, is that not the essence of all creeds?

Kemankar. Religion is one in its essence, but different in its forms. The water is one, yet by its different banks it is bounded and preserved for different peoples. What if you have a well-spring of your own in your heart, spurn not your neighbours who must go for their draught of water to their ancestral pond with the green of its gradual slopes mellowed by ages and its ancient trees bearing eternal fruit.

Supriya. I shall follow you, my friend, as I have ever done in my life, and not argue.

[*Enters* Third Brahmin.]

Third Brahmin. I have good news. Our words have prevailed, and the King's army is about to take our side openly.

Second Brahmin. The army?–I do not quite like it.

First Brahmin. Nor do I. It smells of rebellion.

Second Brahmin. Kemankar, I am not for such extreme measures.

First Brahmin. Our faith will give us victory, not our arms. Let us make penance, and recite sacred verses. Let us call on the names of our guardian gods.

Second Brahmin. Come, Goddess, whose wrath is the sole weapon of thy worshippers, deign to take form and crush even to dust the blind pride of unbelievers. Prove to us the strength of our faith, and lead us to victory.

All. We invoke thee, Mother, descend from thy heavenly heights and do thy work among mortals.

[*Enters* Malini.]

Malini. I have come.

[*They all bow to her, except* Kemankar *and* Supriya, *who stand aloof and watch.*]

Second Brahmin. Goddess.–Thou hast come at last, as a daughter of man, withdrawing all thy terrible power into the tender beauty of a girl. Whence hast thou come, Mother? What is thy wish?

Malini. I have come down to my exile at your call.

Second Brahmin. To exile from heaven, because thy children of Earth have called thee?

First Brahmin. Forgive us, Mother. Utter ruin threatens this world and it cries aloud for thy help.

Malini. I will never desert you. I always knew that your doors were open for me. The cry went from you for my banishment and I woke up, amidst the wealth and pleasure of the King's house.

Kemankar. The Princess.

All. The King's daughter.

Malini. I am exiled from my home, so that I may make your home my own. Yet, tell me truly, have you need of me? When I lived in seclusion, a lonely girl, did you call to me from the outer world? Was it no dream of mine?

First brahmin. Mother, you have come, and taken your seat in the heart of our hearts.

Malini. I was born in a King's house, never once looking out from my window. I had heard that it was a sorrowing world,—the world out of my reach. But I did not know where it felt its pain. Teach me to find this out.

First Brahmin. Your sweet voice brings tears to our eyes.

Malini. The moon has just come out of those clouds. Great peace is in the sky. It seems to gather all the world in its arms, under the fold of one vast moonlight. There goes the road, losing itself among the solemn trees with their still shadows. There are the houses, and there the temple; the river bank in the distance looks dim and desolate. I seem to have come down, like a sudden shower from a cloud of dreams, into this world of men, by the roadside.

First Brahmin. You are the divine soul of this world.

Second Brahmin. Why did not our tongues burst in pain, when they shouted for your banishment?

First Brahmin. Come, Brahmins, let us restore our Mother to her home.

[*They shout.*]

Victory to the Mother of the world! Victory to the Mother in the heart of the Man's daughter!

[Malini *goes, surrounded by them.*]

Kemankar. Let the illusion vanish. Where are you going, Supriya, like one walking in his sleep?

Supriya. Leave hold of me, let me go.

Kemankar. Control yourself. Will you, too, fly into the fire with the rest of the blinded swarm?

Supriya. Was it a dream, Kemankar?

Kemankar. It was nothing but a dream. Open your eyes, and wake up.

Supriya. Your hope of heaven is false, Kemankar. Vainly have I wandered in the wilderness of doctrines. I never found peace. The God, who belongs to the multitude and the God of the books are not my own God. These never answered my questions and never consoled me. But, at last, I have found the divine breathing and alive in the living world of men.

Kemankar. Alas, my friend, it is a fearful moment when a man's heart deceives him. Then, blind desire becomes his gospel and fancy usurps the dread throne of his gods. Is yonder moon, lying asleep among soft fleecy clouds, the true emblem of everlasting reality? The naked day will come tomorrow, and the hungry crowd begin again to drag the sea of existence with their thousand nets. And then, this moon-lit night will hardly be remembered, but as a thin film of unreality made of sleep and shadows and delusions. The magic web, woven of the elusive charms of a woman, is like that,—and can it take the place of highest truth?

Can any creed, born of your fancy, satisfy the gaping thirst of the mid-day, when it is wide awake in its burning heat?

Supriya. Alas, I know not.

Kemankar. Then, shake yourself up from your dreams, and look before you. The ancient house is on fire, whose nurslings are the ages. The spirits of our forefathers are hovering over the impending ruins, like crying birds over their perishing nests. Is this the time for vacillation, when the night is dark, the enemies knocking at the gate, the citizens asleep, and men drunken with delusions laying their hands upon their brothers' throats?

Supriya. I will stand by you.

Kemankar. I must go away from here.

Supriya. Where? And for what?

Kemankar. To foreign lands. I shall bring soldiers from outside. For this conflagration cries for blood, to be quenched.

Supriya. But our own soldiers are ready.

Kemankar. Vain is all hope of help from them. They, like moths, are already leaping into the fire. Do you not hear how they are shouting like fools? The whole town has gone mad, and is lighting her festival lamps at the funeral pyre of her own sacred faith.

Supriya. If you must go, take me with you.

Kemankar. No. You remain here, to watch and keep me informed. But, friend, let your heart be not drawn away from me by the novelty of the falsehood.

Supriya. Falsehood is new, but our friendship is old. We have ever been together from our childhood. This is our first separation.

Kemankar. May it prove our last! In evil times the strongest bonds give way. Brothers strike brothers and friends turn against friends. I go out into the dark, and in the darkness of night I shall come back to the gate. Shall I find my friend watching for me, with the lamp lighted? I take away that hope with me.

[*They go.*]

[*Enter* King, *with the* Prince, *in the balcony.*]

King. I fear I must decide to banish my daughter.

Prince. Yes, sire, delay will be dangerous.

King. Gently, my son, gently. Never doubt that I will do my duty. Be sure I will banish her.

[Prince *goes.*]

[*Enters* Queen.]

Queen. Tell me, King, where is she? Have you hidden her, even from me?

King. Whom?

Queen. My Malini.

King. What? Is she not in her room?

Queen. No, I cannot find her. Go with your soldiers and search for her through all the town, from house-to-house. The citizens have stolen her. Banish them all. Empty the whole town, till they return her.

King. I will bring her back,—even if my Kingdom goes to ruin.

[*The* Brahmins *and soldiers bring* Malini, *with torches lighted.*]

Queen. My darling, my cruel child. I never keep my eyes off you,—how could you evade me, and go out?

Second Brahmin. Do not be angry with her, Queen. She came to our home to give us her blessings.

First Brahmin. Is she only yours? And does she not belong to us as well?

Second Brahmin. Our little mother, do not forget us. You are our star, to lead us across the pathless sea of life.

Malini. My door has been opened for you. These walls will never more separate us.

Brahmins. Blessed are we, and the land where we were born.

[*They go.*]

Malini. Mother, I have brought the outer world into your house, I seem to have lost the bounds of my body. I am one with the life of this world.

Queen. Yes, child. Now, you shall never need to go out. Bring in the world to you, and to your mother.–It is close upon the second watch of the night. Sit here. Calm yourself. This flaming life in you is burning out all sleep from your eyes.

Malini [*embracing her mother*]. Mother, I am tired. My body is trembling. So vast is this world.–Mother dear, sing me to sleep. Tears come to my eyes, and a sadness descends upon my heart.

Act II

The Palace Garden

Malini. What can I say to you? I do not know how to argue. I have not read your books.

Supriya. I am learned only among the fools of learning. I have left all arguments and books behind me. Lead me, princess, and I shall follow you, as the shadow follows the lamp.

Malini. But, Brahmin, when you question me, I lose all my power and do not know how to answer you. It is a wonder to me to see that even you, who knows everything, come to me with your questions.

Supriya. Not for knowledge I come to you. Let me forget all that I have ever known. Roads there are, without number, but the light is missing.

Malini. Alas, sir, the more you ask me, the more I feel my poverty. Where is that voice in me, which came down from heaven, like an unseen flash of lightning, into my heart? Why did you not come that day, but keep away in doubt? Now that I have met the world face-to-face my heart has grown timid, and I do not know how to hold the helm of the great ship that I must guide. I feel I am alone, and the world is large, and ways are many, and the light from the sky comes of a sudden to vanish the next moment. You who are wise and learned, will you help me?

Supriya. I shall deem myself fortunate, if you ask my help.

Malini. There are times when despair comes to choke all the life-currents; when suddenly, amidst crowds of men, my eyes turn upon myself and I am frightened. Will you befriend me in those moments of blankness, and utter me one word of hope that will bring me back to life.

Supriya. I shall keep myself ready. I shall make my heart simple and pure, and my mind peaceful, to be able truly to serve you.

[*Enters* Attendant.]

Attendant. The citizens have come, asking to see you.

Malini. Not today. Ask their pardon for me. I must have time to fill my exhausted mind, and have rest to get rid of weariness.

[Attendant *goes.*]

Tell me again about Kemankar, your friend. I long to know what your life has been and its trials.

Supriya. Kemankar, is my friend, my brother, my master. His mind has been firm and strong, from early days, while my thoughts are always flickering with doubts. Yet, he has ever kept me close to his heart, as the moon does its dark spots. But, however strong a ship may be, if it harbours a small hole in its bottom, it must sink.—That I would make you sink, Kemankar, was in the law of nature.

Malini. You made him sink?

Supriya. Yes, I did. The day when the rebellion slunk away in shame before the light in your face and the music in the air that touched you, Kemankar alone was unmoved. He left me behind him, and said that he must go to the foreign land to bring soldiers, and uproot the new creed from the sacred soil of Kashi.–You know what followed. You made me live again in a new land of birth. 'Love for all life' was a mere word, waiting from the old time to be made real,–and I saw that truth in you in flesh. My heart cried for my friend, but he was away, out of my reach; then came his letter, in which he wrote that he was coming with a foreign army at his back, to wash away the new faith in blood, and to punish you with death.–I could wait no longer. I showed the letter to the King.

Malini. Why did you forget yourself, Supriya? Why did fear overcome you? Have I not room enough in my house for him and his soldiers?

[*Enters* King.]

King. Come to my arms, Supriya, I went at a fit time to surprise Kemankar and to capture him. An hour later, and a thunderbolt would have burst upon my house in my sleep. You are my friend, Supriya, come–

Supriya. God forgive me.

King. Do you not know, that a King's love is not unsubstantial? I give you leave to ask for any reward that comes to your mind. Tell me, what do you want?

Supriya. Nothing, sire, nothing. I shall live, begging from door-to-door.

King. Only ask me, and you shall have provinces worthy to tempt a king.

Supriya. They do not tempt me.

King. I understand you. I know towards what moon you raise your hands. Mad youth, be brave to ask even that which seems so impossible. Why are you silent? Do you remember the day when you prayed for my Malini's banishment? Will you repeat that prayer to me, to lead my daughter to exile from her father's house?–My daughter, do you know that you owe your life to this noble youth? And is it hard for you to pay off that debt with your–?

Supriya. For pity's sake, sire, no more of this. Worshippers there are many who by life-long devotion have gained the highest fulfilment of their desire. Could I be counted one of them I should be happy. But to accept it from the King's hands as the reward of treachery? Lady mine, you have the plenitude and peace of your greatness; you know not the secret cravings of a poverty-stricken soul. I dare not ask from you an atom more than that pity of love which you have for every creature in the world.

Malini. Father, what is your punishment for the captive?

King. He shall die.

Malini. On my knees I beg from you his pardon.

King. But he is a rebel, my child.

Supriya. Do you judge him, King? He also judged you, when he came to punish you, not to rob your kindgom.

Malini. Spare him his life, father. Then only will you have the right to bestow on him your friendship, who has saved you from a great peril.

King. What do you say, Supriya? Shall I restore a friend to his friend's arms?

Supriya. That will be king-like in its grace.

King. It will come in its time, and you will find back your friend. But a King's generosity must not stop there. I must give you something which exceeds your hope,–yet not as a mere reward. You have won my heart, and my heart is ready to offer you its best treasure.–My child, where was this shyness in you before now? Your dawn had no tint of rose,–its light was white and dazzling. But today a tearful mist of tenderness sweetly tempers it for mortal eyes. [*To* Supriya] Leave my feet, rise up and come to my heart. Happiness is pressing it like pain. Leave me now for a while. I want to be alone with my Malini. [Supriya *goes.*] I feel I have found back my child once again,—not the bright star of the sky, but the sweet flower that blossoms on earthly soil. She is my daughter, the darling of my heart.

[*Enters* Attendant.]

Attendant. The captive, Kemankar, is at the door.

King. Bring him in. Here comes he, with his eyes fixed, his proud head held high, a brooding shadow on his forehead, like a thunder cloud motionless in a suspended storm.

Malini. The iron chain is ashamed of itself upon those limbs. The insult to greatness is its own insult. He looks like a god defying his captivity.

[*Enters* Kemankar *in chains.*]

King. What punishment do you expect from my hands?

Kemankar. Death.

King. But if I pardon you?

Kemankar. Then, I shall have time again to complete the work I began.

King. You seem out of love with your life. Tell me your last wish, if you have any.

Kemankar. I want to see my friend, Supriya, before I die.

King [*to the* Attendant]. Ask Supriya to come.

Malini. There is a power in that face that frightens me. Father, do not let Supriya come.

King. Your fear is baseless, child.

[Supriya *enters, and walks towards* Kemankar, *with arms extended.*]

Kemankar. No, no, not yet. First, let us have our say, and then the greeting of love.—Come closer to me. You know I am poor in words,—and my time is short. My trial is over, but not yours. Tell me, why have you done this?

Supriya. Friend, you will not understand me. I had to keep my faith, even at the cost of my love.

Kemankar. I understand you, Supriya. I have seen that girl's face, glowing with an inner light, looking like a voice becoming visible. You offered, to the fire of those eyes, the faith in your fathers' creed, the faith in your country's good, and built up a new one on the foundation of a treason.

Supriya. Friend, you are right. My faith has come to me perfected in the form of that woman. Your sacred books were dumb to me. I have read, by the help of the light of those eyes, the ancient book of creation, and I have known that true faith is there, where there is man, where there is love. It comes from the mother in her devotion, and it goes back to her from her child. It descends in the gift of a giver and it appears in the heart of him who takes it. I accepted the bond of this faith which reveals the infinite in man, when I set my eyes upon that face full of light and love and peace of hidden wisdom.

Kemankar. I also once set my eyes on that face, and for a moment dreamt that religion had come at last, in the form of a woman, to lead man's heart to heaven. For a moment, music broke out from the very ribs of my breast and all my life's hopes blossomed in their fulness. Yet, did not I break through these meshes of illusion to wander in foreign lands? Did not I suffer humiliation from unworthy hands in patience, and bear the pain of separation from you, who have been my friend from my infancy? And what have you been doing meanwhile? You sat in the shade of the King's garden, and spent your sweet leisure in idly weaving a lie to condone your infatuation and calling it a religion.

Supriya. My friend, is not this world wide enough to hold men whose natures are widely different? Those countless stars of the sky, do they fight for the mastery of the One? Cannot faiths hold their separate lights in peace for the separate worlds of minds that need them?

Kemankar. Words, mere words. To let falsehood and truth live side-by-side in amity, the infinite world is not wide enough. That the corn ripening for the food of man should make room for thorny weeds, love is not so hatefully all-loving. That one should be allowed to sap the sure ground of friendship with betrayal of trust, could tolerance be so traitorously wide as that? That one should die like a thief to defend his faith and the other live in honour and wealth who betrayed it–no, no, the world is not so stony-hard as to bear without pain such hideous contradictions in its bosom.

Supriya [*to* Malini]. All these hurts and insults I accept in your name, my lady. Kemankar, you are paying your life for your faith,–I am paying more. It is your love, dearer than my life.

Kemankar. No more of this prating. All truths must be tested in death's court. My friend, do you remember our student days when we used to wrangle the whole night through, to come at last to our teacher, in the morning, to know in a moment which of us was right? Let that morning break now. Let us go there to that land of the final, and stand before death with all our questions, where the changing mist of doubts will vanish as a breath, and the mountain peaks of eternal truth will appear, and we two fools will look at each other and laugh.–Dear friend, bring before death that which you deem your best and immortal.

Supriya. Friend, let it be as you wish.

Kemankar. Then, come to my heart. You had wandered far from your comrade, in the infinite distance,–now, dear friend, come eternally close to me, and accept from one, who loves you, the gift of death. [*Strikes* Supriya *with his chains, and* Supriya *falls.*]

Kemankar [*embracing the dead body of* Supriya]. Now, call your executioner.

King [*rising up*]. Where is my sword?

Malini. Father, forgive Kemankar!

SACRIFICE

A temple of the Goddess Kali in Tripura.

[*Enters* Gunavati, *the Queen.*]

Gunavati. Have I offended thee, dread Mother? Thou grantest children to the beggar woman, who sells them to live, and to the adulteress, who kills them to save herself from infamy, and here I am, the Queen, with all the world lying at my feet, hankering in vain for the baby-touch at my bosom, to feel the stir of a dearer life within my life. What sin have I committed, Mother, to merit this, to be banished from the mothers' heaven?

[*Enters* Raghupati, *the priest.*]

O Master, have I ever been remiss in my worship? And my husband, is he not godlike in his purity? Then why has the Goddess, who weaves the web of this world-illusion, assigned my place in the barren waste of childlessness?

Raghupati. Our Mother is all caprice, she knows no law, our sorrows and joys are mere freaks of her mind. Have patience, daughter, today we shall offer special sacrifice in your name to please her.

Gunavati. Accept my grateful obeisance, father. My offerings are already on their way to the temple,—red bunches of hybiscus and beasts of sacrifice.

[*They go out.*]

[*Enter* Govinda, *the King;* Jaising, *the servant of temple; and* Aparna, *the beggar girl.*]

Jaising. What is your wish, sire?

Govinda. Is it true that this poor girl's pet goat has been brought by force to the temple to be killed? Will Mother accept such a gift with grace?

Jaising. King, how are we to know whence the servants collect our daily offerings of worship? But, my child, why is this weeping? Is it worthy of you to shed tears for that which Mother herself has taken?

Aparna. Mother! I am his mother. If I return late to my hut, he refuses his grass, and bleats, with his eyes on the road. I take him up in my arms, when I come, and share my food with him. He knows no mother but me.

Jaising. Sire, could I make the goat live again, by giving up a portion of my life, gladly would I do it. But how can I restore that which Mother herself has taken?

Aparna. Mother has taken? It is a lie. Not mother, but demon.

Jaising. O, the blasphemy!

Aparna. Mother, art thou there to rob a poor girl of her love? Then, where is the throne, before which to condemn thee? Tell me, King.

Govinda. I am silent, my child. I have no answer.

Aparna. This blood-streak running down the steps, is it his? O my darling, when you trembled and cried for dear life, why did your call not reach my heart through the whole deaf world?

Jaising [*To the image*]. I have served thee from my infancy, Mother Kali, yet I understand thee not. Does pity only belong to weak mortals, and not to gods? Come with me, my child, let me do for you what I can. Help must come from man, when it is denied from gods.

[*All go out but the King.*]

[*Enter* Raghupati; Nakshatra, *who is the King's brother; and the courtiers.*]

All. Victory be to the King!

Govinda. Know you all, that I forbid shedding of blood in the temple from today forever.

Minister. You forbid sacrifice to the Goddess?

General Nayan Rai. Forbid sacrifice?

Nakshatra. How terrible! Forbid sacrifice?

Raghupati. Is it a dream?

Govinda. No dream, father. It is awakening. Mother came to me, in a girl's disguise, and told me that blood she cannot suffer.

Raghupati. She has been drinking blood for ages. Whence comes this loathing all of a sudden?

Govinda. No, she never drank blood, she kept her face averted.

Raghupati. I warn you, think and consider. You have no power to alter laws laid down in scriptures.

Govinda. God's words are above all laws.

Raghupati. Do not add pride to your folly. Do you have the effrontery to say that *you* alone have heard God's words, and not I?

Nakshatra. It is strange, that the King should have heard from gods and not the priest.

Govinda. God's words are ever ringing in the world, and he who is wilfully deaf cannot hear them.

Raghupati. Atheist! Apostate!

Govinda. Father, go to your morning service, and declare to all worshippers that hence-forward they will be punished with banishment who shed creatures' blood in their worship of the Mother of all creatures.

Raghupati. Is this your last word?

Govinda. Yes.

Raghupati. Then, curse upon you! Do you, in your enormous pride, imagine that the Goddess, dwelling in your land, is your subject? Do you presume to bind her with your laws and rob her of her dues? You shall never do it. I declare it,–I who am her servant.

[*Goes.*]

Nayan Rai. Pardon me, sire, but have you the right?

Minister. King, is it too late to revoke your order?

Govinda. We dare not delay to uproot sin from our realm.

Minister. Sin can never have such a long lease of life. Could they be sinful,—the rites that have grown old at the feet of the Goddess?

[*The King is silent.*]

Nakshatra. Indeed, they could not be.

Minister. Our ancestors have performed these rites with reverence; can you have the heart to insult them?

[*The King remains silent.*]

Nayan Rai. That which has the sanction of ages, do you have the right to remove it?

Govinda. No more doubts and disputes. Go and spread my order in all my lands.

Minister. But, sire, the Queen has offered her sacrifice for this morning's worship; it has come near the temple gate.

Govinda. Send it back.

[*He goes.*]

Minister. What is this?

Nakshatra. Are we, then, to come down to the level of Buddhists, and treat animals as if they have their right to live? Preposterous! [*They all go out.*]

[*Enters* Raghupati—Jaising *following him with a jar of water to wash his feet.*]

Jaising. Father.

Raghupati. Go!

Jaising. Here is some water.

Raghupati. No need of it!

Jaising. Your clothes.

Raghupati. Take them away!

Jaising. Have I done anything to offend you?

Raghupati. Leave me alone. The shadows of evil have thickened. The King's throne is raising its insolent head above the temple altar. Ye Gods of these degenerate days, are ye ready to obey the King's laws with bowed heads, fawning upon him like his courtiers?

Jaising. Whatever has happened, father?

Raghupati. I cannot find words to say. Ask the Mother Goddess who has been defied.

Jaising. Defied? By whom?

Raghupati. By King Govinda.

Jaising. King Govinda defied Mother Kali?

Raghupati. Defied you and me, all scriptures, all countries, all time, defied Mahakali, the Goddess of the endless stream of time,—sitting upon that puny little throne of his.

Jaising. King Govinda?

Raghupati. Yes, yes, your King Govinda, the darling of your heart. Ungrateful! I have given all my love to bring you up, and yet, King Govinda is dearer to you than I am.

Jaising. The child raises its arms to the full moon, sitting upon his father's lap. You are my father and my full moon is King Govinda. Then is it true, what I hear from people, that our King forbids all sacrifice in the temple? But in this we cannot obey him.

Raghupati. Banishment is for him who does not obey.

Jaising. It is no calamity to be banished from a land where Mother's worship remains incomplete. No, so long as I live, the service of the temple shall be fully performed.

[*They go out.*]

[*Enter* Gunavati *and her* Attendant.]

Gunavati. What is it you say? The Queen's sacrifice turned away from the temple gate? Is there a man in this land who carries more than one head on his shoulders, that he could dare think of it? Who is that doomed creature?

Attendant. I am afraid to name him.

Gunavati. Afraid to name him, when I ask you? Whom do you fear more than me?

Attendant. Pardon me.

Gunavati. Give my salutation to the priest, and ask him to come.

[Attendant *goes out.*]

[*Enters* Govinda.]

Gunavati. Have you heard, King? My offerings have been sent back from Mother's temple.

Govinda. I know it.

Gunavati. You know it, and yet bear the insult?

Govinda. I beg to ask your pardon for the culprit.

Gunavati. I know, King, your heart is merciful, but this is no mercy. It is feebleness. If your kindness hampers you, leave the punishment in my hand. Only, tell me, who is he?

Govinda. It is I, my Queen. My crime is in nothing else but having given you pain.

Gunavati. I do not understand you.

Govinda. From today, shedding of blood in gods' temples is forbidden in my land.

Gunavati. Who forbids it?

Govinda. Mother herself.

Gunavati. Who heard it?

Govinda. I.

Gunavati. You! That makes me laugh. The Queen of all the world comes to the gate of Tripura's King with her petition.

Govinda. Not with her petition, but with her sorrow.

Gunavati. Your dominion is outside the temple limit. Do not send your commands there, where they are impertinent.

Govinda. The command is not mine, it is Mother's.

Gunavati. If you have no doubt in your decision, do not cross my faith. Let me perform my worship according to my light.

Govinda. I promised my Goddess to prevent sacrifice of life in her temple, and I must carry it out.

Gunavati. I also promised my Goddess the blood of three hundred kids and one hundred buffaloes, and I will carry it out. You may leave me now.

Govinda. As you wish.

[*He goes out.*]

[*Enters* Raghupati.]

Gunavati. My offerings have been turned back from the temple, father.

Raghupati. The worship offered by the most ragged of all beggars is not less precious than yours, Queen. But the misfortune is that Mother has been deprived.

Gunavati. What will come of all this, father?

Raghupati. That is only known to her who fashions this world with her dreams. But this is certain, that the throne which casts its shadow upon Mother's shrine will burst like a bubble, vanishing in the void.

Gunavati. Have mercy and save us, father.

Raghupati. Ha, ha! I am to save you,—you, the consort of a King who boasts of his kingdom on the Earth and in Heaven as well, before whom the gods and the Brahmins must—Oh, shame! Oh, the evil age, when the Brahmin's futile curse recoils upon himself, to sting him into madness.

[*About to tear his sacrificial thread.*]

Gunavati [*preventing him*]. Have mercy upon me.

Raghupati. Then give back to Brahmins what is theirs by right.

Gunavati. Yes, I will. Go, master, to your worship, and nothing will hinder you.

Raghupati. Indeed your favour overwhelms me. At the merest glance of your eyes gods are saved from ignominy and the Brahmin is restored to his sacred offices. Thrive and grow fat and sleek till the dire day of judgement comes.

[*Goes out.*]

[*Re-enters King* Govinda.]

Govinda. My Queen, the shadow of your angry brows hides all light from my heart.

Gunavati. Go! Do not bring a curse upon this house.

Govinda. Woman's smile removes all curse from the house, her love is God's grace.

Gunavati. Go, and never show your face to me again.

Govinda. I shall come back, my Queen, when you remember me.

Gunavati. [*clinging to the King's feet*]. Pardon me, King. Have you become so hard, that you forget to respect woman's pride? Do you not know, beloved, that thwarted love takes the disguise of anger?

Govinda. I would die, if I lost my trust in you. I know, my love, that clouds are for moments only, and the sun is for all days.

Gunavati. Yes, the clouds will pass by, God's thunder will return to his armoury, and the sun of all days will shine upon the traditions of all time. Yes, my King, order it so, that Brahmins be restored to their rights, the Goddess to her offerings, and the King's authority to its earthly limits.

Govinda. It is not the Brahmin's right to violate the eternal good. Creature's blood is not the offering for gods. And it is within the rights of the King and the peasant alike to maintain truth and righteousness.

Gunavati. I prostrate myself on the ground before you; I beg at your feet. The custom that comes through all ages is not the King's own. Like the heaven's air, it belongs to all men. Yet your Queen begs it of you, with clasped hands, in the name of your people. Can you still remain silent, proud man, refusing entreaties of love in favour of duty which is doubtful? Then go, go, go from me.

[*They go.*]

[*Enter* Raghupati, Jaising *and* Nayan Rai.]

Raghupati. General, your devotion to Mother is well-known.

Nayan Rai. It runs through generations of my ancestors.

Raghupati. Let this sacred love give you indomitable courage. Let it make your sword-blade mighty as God's thunder, and win its place above all powers and positions of this world.

Nayan Rai. The Brahmin's blessings will never be in vain.

Raghupati. Then, I bid you collect your soldiers and strike Mother's enemy down to the dust.

Nayan Rai. Tell me, father, who is the enemy?

Raghupati. Govinda.

Nayan Rai. Our King?

Raghupati. Yes, attack him with all your force.

Nayan Rai. It is evil advice. Father, is this to try me?

Raghupati. Yes, it is to try you, to know for certain whose servant you are. Give up all hesitation. Know that the Goddess calls, and all earthly bonds must be severed.

Nayan Rai. I have no hesitation in my mind. I stand firm in my post, where my Goddess has placed me.

Raghupati. You are brave.

Nayan Rai. Am I the basest of Mother's servants, that the order should come for me to turn traitor? She herself stands upon the faith of man's heart. Can she ask me to break it? Then, today comes to dust the King, and tomorrow the Goddess herself.

Jaising. Noble words.

Raghupati. The King, who has turned traitor to Mother, has lost all claims to your allegiance.

Nayan Rai. Drive me not, father, into a wilderness of debates. I know only one path,—the straight path of faith and truth. This stupid servant of Mother shall never swerve from that highway of honour.

[*Goes out.*]

Jaising. Let us be strong in our faith as he is, master. Why ask the aid of soldiers? We have the strength within ourselves for the task given to us from above. Open the temple gate wide, father. Sound the drum. Come, come, O citizens, to worship her, who takes all fear away from our hearts. Come, Mother's children.

[Citizens *come.*]

First Citizen. Come, come, we are called.

All. Victory to Mother!

[*They sing and dance.*]

The dread Mother dances naked in the battlefield,
Her lolling tongue burns like a red flame of fire,
Her dark tresses fly in the sky, sweeping away the sun and stars,
Red streams of blood run from her cloud-black limbs,
And the world trembles and cracks under her tread.

Jaising. Do you see the beasts of sacrifice coming towards the temple, driven by the Queen's attendants?

[*They cry.*]

Victory to Mother! Victory to our Queen!

Raghupati. Jaising, make haste and get ready for the worship.
Jaising. Everything is ready, father.
Raghupati. Send a man to call Prince Nakshatra in my name.

[Jaising *goes.*]

[Citizens *sing and dance, enters King* Govinda.]

Govinda. Silence, Raghupati! Do you dare to disregard my order?
Raghupati. Yes, I do.
Govinda. Then, you are not for my land.
Raghupati. No, my land is there, where the King's crown kisses the dust. Ho! Citizens! Let Mother's offerings be brought in here.

[*They beat drums.*]

Govinda. Silence! [*To his attendants*] Ask my General to come. Raghupati, you drive me to call soldiers to defend God's right. I feel the shame of it; for the force of arms only reveals man's weakness.

[*Enter General* Nayan Rai *and* Chandpal, *who is the second in command of the army.*]

Govinda. Stand here with your soldiers to prevent sacrifice of life in the temple.
Nayan. Pardon me, sire. The King's servant is powerless in the temple of God.
Govinda. General, it is not for you to question my order. You are to carry out my words. Their merits and demerits belong only to me.
Nayan. I am your servant, my King, but I am a man above all. I have reason and my religion. I have my King,–and also my God.
Govinda. Then, surrender your sword to Chandpal. He will protect the temple from pollution of blood.
Nayan Rai. Why to Chandpal? This sword was given to my forefathers

by your royal ancestors. If you want it back, I will give it up to you. Be witness, my fathers, who are in the heroes' paradise, the sword that you made sacred with your loyal faith and bravery, I surrender to my King.

[*Goes out.*]

Raghupati. The Brahmin's curse has begun its work already.

[*Enters* Jaising.]

Jaising. The beasts have been made ready for the sacrifice.

Govinda. Sacrifice?

Jaising [*on his knees*]. King, listen to my earnest entreaties. Do not stand in the way, hiding the Goddess, man as you are.

Raghupati. Shame, Jaising. Rise up and ask my pardon. I am your Master. Your place is at my feet, not the King's. Fool! Do you ask King's sanction to do God's service? Leave alone the worship and the sacrifice. Let us wait and see how his pride prevails in the end. Come away.

[*They go out.*]

[*Enters* Aparna, *the beggar girl.*]

Aparna. Where is Jaising? He is not here, but only you,—the image whom nothing can move. You rob us of all our best without uttering a word. We pine for love, and die beggars for want of it. Yet, it comes to you unasked, though you need it not. Like a grave, you hoard it under your miserly stone, keeping it from the use of the yearning world. Jaising, what happiness do you find from her? What can she speak to you? O my heart, my famished heart!

[*Enters* Raghupati.]

Raghupati. Who are you?

Aparna. I am a beggar girl. Where is Jaising?

Raghupati. Leave this place at once. I know you are haunting this temple, to steal Jaising's heart from the Goddess.

Aparna. Has the Goddess anything to fear from me? I fear her.

[*She goes out.*]

[*Enter* Jaising *and Prince* Nakshatra.]

Nakshatra. Why have you called me?

Raghupati. Last night, the Goddess told me in a dream, that you shall become King within a week.

Nakshatra. Ha, ha, this is news, indeed.

Raghupati. Yes, you shall be King.

Nakshatra. I cannot believe it.

Raghupati. You doubt my words?

Nakshatra. I do not want to doubt them. But suppose, by chance, it never comes to pass.

Raghupati. No, it shall be true.

Nakshatra. But, tell me, how can it ever become true?

Raghupati. The Goddess thirsts for King's blood.

Nakshatra. King's blood?

Raghupati. You must offer it to her before you can be King.

Nakshatra. I know not where to get it.

Raghupati. There is King Govinda.—Jaising, keep still.—Do you understand? Kill him in secret. Bring his blood, while warm, to the altar.—Jaising, leave this place, if you cannot remain still,—

Nakshatra. But he is my brother, and I love him.

Raghupati. Your sacrifice will be all the more precious.

Nakshatra. But, father, I am content to remain as I am. I do not want the kingdom.

Raghupati. There is no escape for you, because the Goddess commands it. She is thirsting for blood from the King's house. If your brother is to live, then you must die.

Nakshatra. Have pity on me, father.

Raghupati. You shall never be free in life, or in death, until her bidding is done.

Nakshatra. Advise me, then, how to do it.

Raghupati. Wait in silence. I will tell you what to do, when the time comes. And now, go.

[Nakshatra *goes.*]

Jaising. What is it that I heard? Merciful Mother, is it your bidding? To ask brother to kill brother? Master, how could you say that it was Mother's own wish?

Raghupati. There was no other means but this to serve my Goddess.

Jaising. Means? Why means? Mother, have you not your own sword to wield with your own hand? Must your wish burrow underground, like a thief, to steal in secret? Oh, the sin!

Raghupati. What do you know about sin?

Jaising. What I have learnt from you.

Raghupati. Then, come and learn your lesson once again from me. Sin has no meaning in reality. To kill is but to kill, it is neither sin nor anything else. Do you not know that the dust of this Earth is made of countless killings? Old Time is ever writing the chronicle of the transient life of creatures in letters of blood. Killing is in the wilderness, in the habitations of man, in birds' nests, in insects' holes, in the sea, in the sky; there is killing for life, for sport, for nothing whatever. The world is ceaselessly killing; and the great Goddess Kali, the spirit of ever changing time, is standing with her thirsty tongue hanging down from her mouth, with her cup in hand, into which is running the red life-blood of the world, like juice from the crushed cluster of grapes.

Jaising. Stop, Master. Is then love a falsehood and mercy a mockery, and the one thing true, from the beginning of time, the lust for destruction? Would it not have destroyed itself long ago? You are playing with my heart, my Master. Look there, she is gazing at me. My blood-thirsty Mother, wilt thou accept my blood? Is it so delicious to thee? Master, did you call me? The Mother, who is thirsting for our love, you accuse of blood-thirstiness!

Raghupati. Then, let the sacrifice be stopped in the Temple.

Jaising. Yes, let it be stopped.–No, no, Master, you know what is right and what is wrong. The heart's laws are not the laws of scripture. Eyes cannot see with their own light,–the light must come from the outside. Tell me, Father, is it true that the Goddess seeks King's blood?

Raghupati. Alas, child, have you lost your faith in me?

Jaising. My world stands upon my faith in you. If the Goddess must have King's blood, let me bring it to her. I will never allow a brother to kill his brother.

Raghupati. But there can be no evil in carrying out God's wishes.

Jaising. No, it must be good, and I will earn the merit of it.

Raghupati. But, my boy, I have reared you from your childhood, and you have grown close to my heart. I can never bear to lose you, by any chance.

Jaising. I will not let your love for me be soiled with sin. Release Prince Nakshatra from his promise.

Raghupati. I will think, and decide tomorrow.

[*He goes.*]

Jaising. Deeds are better, however cruel they may be, than the hell of thinking and doubting. You are true, my Master, to kill is no sin, to kill a brother is no sin, to kill a king is no sin.–Where do you go, my brothers? To the fair at Nishipur? There the women are to dance? Oh, this world is pleasant! And the dancing limbs of the girls are beautiful. In what careless merriment the crowds flow through the roads, making the sky ring with their laughter and song. I will follow them.

[*Enters* Raghupati.]

Raghupati. Jaising.

Jaising. I do not know you. I drift with the crowd. Why ask me to stop? Go your own way.

Raghupati. Jaising.

Jaising. The road is straight before me. With an alms bowl in hand and the beggar girl as my sweetheart I shall walk on. Who says that the world's ways are devious? Anyhow we reach the end,—the end where all laws and rules are no more, where the errors and hurts of life are forgotten. What is the use of all these scriptures, and the teacher and his instructions?—My Master, my Father, what wild words are these of mine? I was living in a dream. There stands the temple, cruel and immovable as truth. What was your order, my teacher? I have not forgotten it. (*Bringing out the knife*) I am sharpening your words in my mind, till they become one with this knife in keenness. Have you any other order to give me?

Raghupati. My boy, my darling, how can I tell you how deep is my love for you?

Jaising. No, Master, do not tell me of love. Let me think only of duty. Love, like the green grass and the trees and life's music, is only for the surface of the world. It comes and vanishes like a dream. But underneath is duty, like the rude layers of stone, like a huge load that nothing can move.

[*They go out.*]

[*Enter King* Govinda *and* Chandpal.]

Chandpal. Sire, I warn you to be careful.

Govinda. Why? What do you mean?

Chandpal. I have overheard a conspiracy to take away your life.

Govinda. Who wants my life?

Chandpal. I am afraid to tell you, lest the news becomes to you more deadly than the knife itself. It was Prince Nakshatra, who—

Govinda. Nakshatra?

Chandpal. He has promised to Raghupati to bring your blood to the Goddess.

Govinda. To the Goddess? Then, I cannot blame him. For a man loses his humanity when it concerns his gods. You go to your work and leave me alone.

[Chandpal *goes out.*]

(*Addressing the image*) Accept these flowers, Goddess, and let your creatures live in peace. Mother, those who are weak in this world are so helpless, and those who are strong are so cruel. Greed is pitiless, ignorance blind, and pride takes no heed when it crushes the small under its foot. Mother, do not raise your sword and lick your lips for blood; do not set brother against brother, and woman against man. If it is your desire to strike me by the hand of one I love, then let it be fulfilled. For the sin has to ripen to its ugliest limits, before it can burst and die a hideous death.

[Jaising *rushes in.*]

Jaising. Tell me, Goddess, dost thou truly want King's blood? Ask it in thine own voice, and thou shalt have it.

A Voice. I want King's blood.

Jaising. King, say your last prayer, for your time has come.

Govinda. What makes you say it, Jaising?

Jaising. Did you not hear what the Goddess said?

Govinda. It was not the Goddess. I heard the familiar voice of Raghupati.

Jaising. Drive me not from doubt to doubt. It is all the same, whether the voice comes from the Goddess, or from my master.—

[*He unsheathes his knife, and then throws it away.*]

Listen to the cry of thy children, Mother. Let there be only flowers for thy offerings,—no more blood. They are red even as blood,—these bunches of hybiscus. They have come out of the heart-burst of the Earth, pained at the slaughter of her children. Accept this. Thou must accept this. I defy thy anger. Blood thou shalt never have. Redden thine eyes. Raise thy sword. Bring thy furies of destruction. I do not fear thee King, leave this Temple to its Goddess, and go to your men.

[Govinda *goes.*]

Alas, alas, in a moment I gave up all that I had, my Master, my Goddess.

[Raghupati *comes.*]

Raghupati. I have heard all. Traitor, you have betrayed your Master.

Jaising. Punish me, Father.

Raghupati. What punishment will you have?

Jaising. Punish me with my life.

Raghupati. No, that is nothing. Take your oath touching the feet of the Goddess.

Jaising. I touch her feet.

Raghupati. Say, I will bring kingly blood to the altar of the Goddess, before it is midnight.

Jaising. I will bring kingly blood to the altar of the Goddess, before it is midnight.

[*They go out.*]

[*Enters* Gunavati.]

Gunavati. I failed. I have hoped that, if I remained hard and cold for some days, he would surrender. Such faith I had in my power, vain woman that I am. I showed my sullen anger, and remained away from him; but it was fruitless. Woman's anger is like a diamond's glitter; it only shines, but cannot burn. I would rather it were like thunder, bursting upon the King's house, startling him up from his sleep, and dashing his pride to the ground.

[*Enters the boy* Druva.]

Gunavati. Where are you going?

Druva. I am called by the King.

[*Goes out.*]

Gunavati. There goes the darling of the King's heart. He has robbed my unborn children of their father's love, usurped their right to the first place in the King's breast. O Mother Kali, your creation is infinite and full of wonders, only send a child to my arms in merest whim, a tiny little warm living flesh to fill my lap, and I shall offer you whatever you wish. [*Enters* Nakshatra.] Prince Nakshatra, why are you so excited?

Nakshatra. Tell me what you want of me.

Gunavati. The thief that steals the crown awaiting you,—remove him. Do you understand?

Nakshatra. Yes, except who the thief is.

Gunavati. That boy, Druva. Do you not see how he is growing in the King's lap, till one day he reaches the crown?

Nakshatra. Yes. I have often thought of it. I have seen my brother putting his crown on the boy's head in play.

Gunavati. Playing with the crown is a dangerous game. If you do not remove the player, he will make a game of you.

Nakshatra. Yes, I like it not.

Gunavati. Offer him to Kali. Have you not heard that Mother is thirsting for blood?

Nakshatra. But sister, this is not my business.

Gunavati. Fool, can you feel yourself safe, so long as Mother is not appeased? Blood she must have; save your own, if you can.

Nakshatra. But she wants King's blood.

Gunavati. Who told you that?

Nakshatra. I know it from one to whom the Goddess herself sends her dreams.

Gunavati. Then, that boy must die for the King. His blood is more precious to your brother than his own, and the King can only be saved by paying the price, which is more than his life.

Nakshatra. I understand.

Gunavati. Then lose no time. Run after him. He is not gone far. But remember. Offer him in my name.

Nakshatra. Yes, I will.

Gunavati. The Queen's offerings have been turned back from Mother's gate. Pray to her that she may forgive me.

[*They go out.*]

[*Enters* Jaising.]

Jaising. Goddess, is there any little thing, that yet remains, out of the wreck of thee? If there be but a faintest spark of thy light in the remotest of the stars of evening, answer my cry, though thy voice be the feeblest. Say to me, 'Child, here I am.'—No, she is nowhere. She is naught. But take pity upon Jaising, O Illusion! Art thou so irredeemably false, that not even my love can send the slightest tremor of life through thy nothingness? O fool, for whom have you upturned your cup of life, emptying it to the last drop? For this unanswering void,—truthless, merciless, and motherless?

[*Enters* Aparna.]

Aparna, they drive you away from the Temple; yet you come back over and over again. For you are true, and truth cannot be banished. We enshrine falsehood in our Temple, with all devotion; yet she is never there. Leave me not, Aparna. Sit here by my side. Why are you so sad, my darling? Do you miss some god, who is God no longer? But is there any need of God in this little world of ours? Let us be fearlessly godless and come closer to each other. They want our blood. And for this, they have come down to the dust of our Earth, leaving their magnificence of Heaven. For in their heaven there are no men, no creatures, who can suffer. No, my girl, there is no Goddess.

Aparna. Then, leave this temple, and come away with me.

Jaising. Leave this temple? Yes, I will leave. Alas, Aparna, I must leave. Yet, I cannot leave it, before I have paid my last dues to the–But let that be. Come closer to me, my love. Whisper something to my ears, which will overflow this life with sweetness, flooding death itself.

Aparna. Words do not flow when the heart is full.

Jaising. Then, lean your head on my breast. Let the silence of two eternities, life and death, touch each other.–But no more of this. I must go.

Aparna. Jaising, do not be cruel. Can you not feel what I have suffered?

Jaising. Am I cruel? Is this your last word to me? Cruel, as that block of stone, whom I called Goddess? Aparna, my beloved, if you were the Goddess, you would know what fire is this that burns my heart. But you *are* my Goddess. Do you know how I know it?

Aparna. Tell me.

Jaising. You bring to me your sacrifice every moment, as a mother does to her child. God must be all sacrifice, pouring out his life in all creation.

Aparna. Jaising, come, let us leave this Temple and go away together.

Jaising. Save me, Aparna, have mercy upon me and leave me. I have only one object in my life. Do not usurp its place.

[*Rushes out.*]

Aparna. Again and again I have suffered. But my strength is gone. My heart breaks.

[*She goes out.*]

[*Enter* Raghupati *and Prince* Nakshatra.]

Raghupati. Prince, where have you kept the boy?

Nakshatra. He is in the room where the vessels for worship are kept. He has cried himself to sleep. I think I shall never be able to bear it, when he wakes up again.

Raghupati. Jaising was of the same age when he came to me. And I remember how he cried till he slept at the feet of the Goddess,—the temple lamp dimly shining on his tear-stained child-face. It was a stormy evening like this.

Nakshatra. Father, delay not. I wish to finish it all, while he is sleeping. His cry pierces my heart like a knife.

Raghupati. I will drug him to sleep, if he wakes up.

Nakshatra. The King will soon find it out, if you are not quick. For, in the evening, he leaves the care of his kingdom to come to this boy.

Raghupati. Have more faith in the Goddess. The victim is now in her own hands and it shall never escape.

Nakshatra. But Chandpal is so watchful.

Raghupati. Not more so than our Mother.

Nakshatra. I thought I saw a shadow pass by.

Raghupati. The shadow of your own fear.

Nakshatra. Do we not hear the sound of a cry?

Raghupati. The sound of your own heart. Shake off your despondency, Prince. Let us drink this wine duly consecrated. So long as the purpose remains in the mind, it looms large and fearful. In action it becomes small. The vapour is dark and diffused. It dissolves into water drops that are small and sparkling. Prince, it is nothing. It takes only a moment,—not more than it does to snuff a candle.

Nakshatra. I think we should not be too rash. Leave this work till tomorrow night.

Raghupati. Tonight is as good as tomorrow night, perhaps better.

Nakshatra. Listen to the sound of footsteps.

Raghupati. I do not hear it.

Nakshatra. See there,—the light.

Raghupati. The King comes. I fear we have delayed too long.

[*King* Govinda *comes with attendants.*]

Govinda. Make them prisoners. [*To* Raghupati] Have you anything to say?

Raghupati. Nothing.

Govinda. Do you admit your crime?

Raghupati. Crime? Yes, my crime was that, in my weakness, I delayed in carrying out Mother's service. The punishment comes from the Goddess. You are merely her instrument.

Govinda. According to my law, my soldiers shall escort you to exile, Raghupati, where you shall spend eight years of your life.

Raghupati. King, I never bent my knees to any mortal in my life. I am a Brahmin. Your caste is lower than mine. Yet, in all humility, I pray to you, give me only one day's time.

Govinda. I grant it.

Raghupati [*mockingly*]. You are the King of all kings. Your majesty and mercy are alike immeasurable. Whereas I am a mere worm, hiding in the dust.

[*He goes out.*]

Govinda. Nakshatra, admit your guilt.

Nakshatra. I am guilty, sire, and I dare not ask for your pardon.

Govinda. Prince, I know you are tender of heart. Tell me, who beguiled you with evil counsel?

Nakshatra. I will not take other names, King. My guilt is my own. You have pardoned your foolish brother more than once, and once more he begs to be pardoned.

Govinda. Nakshatra, leave my feet. The judge is still more bound by his laws than his prisoner.

Attendants. Sire, remember that he is your brother, and pardon him.

Govinda. Let me remember that I am a king. Nakshatra shall remain in exile for eight years, in the house we have built, by the sacred river, outside the limits of Tripura. [*Taking* Nakshatra's *hands*] The punishment is not yours only, brother, but also mine,—the more so because I cannot share it bodily.

[*They all go out.*]

[*Enter* Raghupati *and* Jaising.]

Raghupati. My pride wallows in the mire. I have shamed my Brahminhood. I am no longer your master, my child. Yesterday, I had the authority to command you. Today, I can only beg your favour. Life's days are mere tinsel, most trifling of God's gifts, and I had to beg for one of those days from the King with bent knees. Let that one day be not in vain. Let its infamous black brows be red with King's blood before it dies. Why do you not speak, my boy? Though I forsake my place as your master, yet have I not the right to claim your obedience as your father,—I who am more than a father to you, because father to an orphan? You are still silent, my child? Then, let my knees bend to you, who were smaller than my knees when you first came to my arms.

Jaising. Father, do not torture the heart that is already broken. If the Goddess thirsts for kingly blood, I will bring it to her before tonight. I will pay all my debts, yes, every farthing. Keep ready for my return. I will delay not.

[*Goes out.*]

[*Storm outside.*]

Raghupati. She is awake at last, the Terrible. Her curses go shrieking through the town. The hungry furies are shaking the cracking branches of the world tree with all their might, for the stars to break and drop. My Mother, why didst thou keep thine own people in doubt and dishonour so long? Leave it not for thy servant to raise thy sword. Let thy mighty arm do its own work!— I hear steps.

[*Enters* Aparna.]

Aparna. Where is Jaising?

Raghupati. Away evil omen. [Aparna *goes out.*] But if Jaising never comes back? No, he will not break his promise. Victory to thee, Great Kali, the giver of all success!—But if he meet with obstruction? If he be caught and lose his life at the guards' hands?—Victory to thee, watchful Goddess, Mother invincible! Do not allow thy repute to be lost, and thine enemies to laugh at thee. If thy children must lose their pride and faith in their Mother, and bow down their heads in shame before the rebels, who then shall remain in this orphaned world to carry their banner?—I hear his steps. But so soon? Is he coming back foiled in his purpose? No, that cannot be. Thy miracle needs not time, O Mistress of all time, terrible with thy necklace of human skulls.

[*Rushes in* Jaising.]

Jaising, where is the blood?

Jaising. It is with me. Let go my hands. Let me offer it myself [*Entering the temple*] Must thou have kingly blood, Great Mother, who nourishest the world at thy breast with life?—I am of the royal caste, a Kshatriya. My ancestors have sat upon thrones, and there are rulers of men in my mother's line. I have kingly blood in my veins. Take it, and quench thy thirst forever.

[*Stabs himself and falls.*]

Raghupati. Jaising! O cruel, ungrateful! You have done the blackest crime. You kill your father! Jaising, forgive me, my darling. Come back to my heart, my heart's one treasure! Let me die in your place.

[*Enters* Aparna.]

Aparna. It will madden me. Where is Jaising? Where is he?

Raghupati. Come, Aparna, come, my child, call him with all your love. Call him back to life. Take him to you, away from me, only let him live.

[Aparna *enters the temple and swoons.*]

Raghupati [*beating his forehead on the temple floor*]. Give him, give him, give him.—Give him back to me! [*Stands up addressing the image.*] Look how she stands there, the silly stone,—deaf, dumb, blind,—the whole sorrowing world weeping at her door,—the noblest hearts wrecking themselves at her stony feet. Give me back my Jaising. Oh, it is all in vain. Our bitterest cries wander in emptiness,—the emptiness that we vainly try to fill with these stony images of delusion. Away with them! Away with these our impotent dreams, that harden into stones, burdening our world.

[*He throws away the image, and comes out into the courtyard.*]

[*Enters* Gunavati.]

Gunavati. Victory to thee, great Goddess! But, where is the Goddess?

Raghupati. Goddess there is none.

Gunavati. Bring her back, father. I have brought her my offerings. I have come at last, to appease her anger with my own heart's blood. Let her know that the Queen is true to her promise. Have pity on me, and bring back the Goddess only for this night. Tell me,—where is she?

Raghupati. She is nowhere,—neither above, nor below.

Gunavati. Master, was not the Goddess here in the temple?

Raghupati. Goddess?—If there were any true Goddess anywhere in the world, could she bear this thing to usurp her name?

Gunavati. Do not torture me. Tell me truly. Is there no Goddess?

Raghupati. No, there is none.

Gunavati. Then, who was here?

Raghupati. Nothing, nothing.

[Aparna *comes out from the temple.*]

Aparna. Father.

Raghupati. My sweet child! 'Father,'—did you say? Do you rebuke me with that name? My son, whom I have killed, has left that one dear call behind him in your sweet voice.

Aparna. Father, leave this temple. Let us go away from here.

[*Enters the King.*]

Govinda. Where is the Goddess?

Raghupati. The Goddess is nowhere.

Govinda. But what blood-stream is this?

Raghupati. King, Jaising, who loved you so dearly, has killed himself.

Govinda. Killed himself? Why?

Raghupati. To kill the falsehood, that sucks the life-blood of man.

Govinda. Jaising is great. He has conquered death. My flowers are for him.

Gunavati. My King.

Govinda. Yes, my love.

Gunavati. The Goddess is no more.

Govinda. She has burst her cruel prison of stone, and come back to woman's heart.

Aparna. Father, come away.

Raghupati. Come, child. Come, Mother. I have found thee. Thou art the last gift of Jaising.

THE KING AND THE QUEEN

Act I

The Palace Garden. King Vikram *and Queen* Sumitra.

Vikram. Why have you delayed in coming to me for so long, my love?

Sumitra. Do you not know, my King, that I am utterly yours, wherever I am? It was your house, and its service, that kept me away from your presence, but not from you.

Vikram. Leave the house, and its service, alone. My heart cannot spare you for my world, I am jealous of its claims.

Sumitra. No, King. I have my place in your heart, as your beloved, and in your world, as your Queen.

Vikram. Alas, my darling, where have vanished those days of unalloyed joy, when we first met in love; when our world awoke not,—only the flush of the early dawn of our union broke through our hearts in over-flowing silence? You had sweet shyness in your eyelids, like a dew drop on the tip of a flower-petal, and the smile flickered on your lips like a timid evening lamp in the breeze. I remember the eager embrace of your love, when the morning broke and we had to part, and your unwilling steps, heavy with languor, that took you away from me. Where were the house, and its service, and the cares of your world?

Sumitra. But then, we were scarcely more than a boy and a girl; and today, we are the King and the Queen.

Vikram. The King and the Queen? Mere names. We are more than that; we are lovers.

Sumitra. You are my King, my husband, and I am content to follow your steps. Do not shame me by putting me before your kingship.

Vikram. Do you not want my love?

Sumitra. Love me truly by not making your love extravagant; for truth can afford to be simple.

Vikram. I do not understand woman's heart.

Sumitra. King, if you thriftlessly squander your all upon me, then I shall be deprived.

Vikram. No more vain words, Queen. The birds' nests are silent with love. Let lips keep guard upon lips, and allow not words to clamour.

[*Enters* Attendant.]

Attendant. The minister begs audience, to discuss a grave matter of state.

Vikram. No, not now.

[Attendant *goes.*]

Sumitra. Sire, ask him to come.

Vikram. The state and its matter can wait. But sweet leisure comes rarely. It is frail, like a flower. Respite from duty is a part of duty.

Sumitra. Sire, I beg of you, attend to your work.

Vikram. Again, cruel woman. Do you imagine that I always follow you to win your unwilling favour, drop by drop? I leave you and go.

[He *goes.*]

[*Enters* Devadatta, *the King's Brahmin friend.*]

Sumitra. Tell me, sir, what is that noise outside the gate?

Devadatta. That noise? Command me, and with the help of soldiers I shall drive away that noise, ragged and hungry.

Sumitra. Do not mock me. Tell me what has happened.

Devadatta. Nothing. It is merely hunger,–the vulgar hunger of poverty. The famished horde of barbarians is rudely clamouring, making the drowsy cuckoos in your royal garden start up in fear.

Sumitra. Tell me, father, who are hungry?

Devadatta. It is their ill-fate. The King's poor subjects have been practising long to live upon half a meal a day, but they have not yet become experts in complete starvation. It is amazing.

Sumitra. But, father, the land is smiling with ripe corn. Why should the King's subjects die of hunger?

Devadatta. The corn is his, whose is the land,–it is not for the poor. They, like intruding dogs at the King's feast, crouch in the corner for their crumbs, or kicks.

Sumitra. Does it mean, that there is no King in this land?

Devadatta. Not one, but hundreds.

Sumitra. Are not the King's officers watchful?

Devadatta. Who can blame your officers? They came penniless from the alien land. Is it to bless the King's subjects with their empty hands?

Sumitra. From the alien land? Are they my relatives?

Devadatta. Yes, Queen.

Sumitra. What about Jaisen?

Devadatta. He rules the province of Singarh with such scrupulous care, that all the rubbish, in the shape of food and raiment, has been cleared away; only the skin and bones remain.

Sumitra. And Shila?

Devadatta. He keeps his eyes upon the trade; he relieves all merchants of their excessive profits, taking the burden upon his own broad shoulders.

Sumitra. And Ajit?

Devadatta. He lives in Vijaykote. He smiles sweetly, strokes the land on its back with his caressing hand, and whatever comes to his touch gathers with care.

Sumitra. What shame is this. I must remove this refuse from my father's land and save my people. Leave me now, the King comes. [*Enters the King.*] I am the mother of my people. I cannot bear their cry. Save them, King.

Vikram. What do you want me to do?

Sumitra. Turn those out from your kingdom, who are oppressing the land.

Vikram. Do you know who they are?

Sumitra. Yes, I know.

Vikram. They are your own cousins.

Sumitra. They are not a whit more my own than my people. They are robbers, who, under the cover of your throne, seek for their victims.

Vikram. They are Jaisen, Shila, Ajit.

Sumitra. My country must be rid of them.

Vikram. They will not move without fight.

Sumitra. Then fight them, sire.

Vikram. Fight? But let me conquer *you* first, and then I shall have time to conquer my enemies.

Sumitra. Allow me, King, as your Queen. I will save your subjects myself.

[*Goes.*]

Vikram. This is how you make my heart distraught. You sit alone upon your peak of greatness, where I do not reach you. You go to attend your own God, and I go seeking you in vain.

[*Enters* Devadatta.]

Devadatta. Where is the Queen, sire? Why are you alone?

Vikram. Brahmin, this is all your conspiracy. You come here to talk of the state news to the Queen?

Devadatta. The state is shouting its own news loud enough to reach the Queen's ears. It has come to that pass, when it takes no heed, lest your rest be broken. Do not be afraid of me, King. I have come to ask my Brahmin's dues from the Queen. For, my wife is out of humour, her larder is empty, and in the house there are a number of empty stomachs.

[*He goes.*]

Vikram. I wish all happiness to my people. Why should there be suffering, and injustice? Why should the strong cast his vulture's eyes upon the poor man's comforts, pitifully small? [*Enters* Minister.] Banish all the foreign robbers from my kingdom, this moment. I must not hear the cry of the oppressed for a day longer.

Minister. But, King, the evil that has been slowly growing for long, you cannot uproot in a day.

Vikram. Strike at its root with vigour, and fell it with your axe in a day,—the tree that has taken a hundred years to grow.

Minister. But we want arms and soldiers.

Vikram. Where is my general?

Minister. He himself is a foreigner.

Vikram. Then, invite the hungry people. Open my treasure; stop this cry with food; send them away with money,—And if they want to have my kingdom, let them do so in peace, and be happy.

[*He goes.*]

[*Enter* Sumitra *and* Devadatta.]

Minister. Queen, my humble salutation to you.

Sumitra. We cannot allow misery to go unchecked in our land.

Minister. What are your commands, Queen?

Sumitra. Call immediately, in my name, all our chiefs who are foreigners.

Minister. I have done so already. I have taken upon myself to invite them into the Capital, in the King's name, without asking for his sanction, for fear of refusal.

Sumitra. When did you send your messengers?

Minister. It will soon be a month hence. I am expecting their answers every moment. But I am afraid they will not respond.

Sumitra. Not respond to the King's call?

Devadatta. The King has become a piece of wild rumour, which they can believe, or not, as they like.

Sumitra. Keep your soldiers ready, Minister, for these people. They shall have to answer to me, as my relatives.

[*The* Minister *goes.*]

Devadatta. Queen, they will not come.

Sumitra. Then, the King shall fight them.

Devadatta. The King will not fight.

Sumitra. Then, I will.

Devadatta. You!

Sumitra. I will go to my brother Kumarsen, Kashmir's King, and with his help fight these rebels, who are a disgrace to Kashmir. Father, help me to escape from this kingdom, and do your duty, if things come to the worst.

Devadatta. I salute thee, Mother of the people.

[*He goes.*]

[*Enters* Vikram.]

Vikram. Why do you go away, Queen? My hungry desire is revealed to you in its naked poverty. Do you, therefore, go away from me in derision?

Sumitra. I feel shamed to share alone your heart, which is for all men.

Vikram. Is it absolutely true, Queen, that you stand on your giddy height, and I grovel in the dust? No. I know my power. There is an unconquerable force in my nature, which I have turned into love for you.

Sumitra. Hate me, King, hate me. Forget me. I shall bear it bravely,–but do not wreck your manhood against a woman's charms.

Vikram. So much love, yet such neglect? Your very indifference, like a cruel knife, cuts into my bosom, laying bare the warm bleeding love,–and then, to fling it into the dust!

Sumitra. I throw myself at your feet, my beloved. Have you not forgiven your Queen, again and again, for wrongs done? Then, why is this wrath, sire, when I am blameless?

Vikram. Rise up, my love. Come to my heart. Shut my life from all else for a moment, with your encircling arms, rounding it into a world completely your own.

A voice from outside. Queen.

Sumitra. It is Devadatta.–Yes, father, what is the message?

[*Enters* Devadatta.]

Devadatta. They have defied the King's call,–the foreign governors of the provinces,–and they are preparing for rebellion.

Sumitra. Do you hear, King?

Vikram. Brahmin, the palace garden is not the council-house.

Devadatta. Sire, we rarely meet our King in the council-house, because it is not the palace garden.

Sumitra. The miserable dogs, grown fat upon the King's table sweepings, dare dream of barking against their master? King, is it time for debating in the council chamber? Is not the course clear before you? Go with your soldiers and crush these miscreants.

Vikram. But our general himself is a foreigner.

Sumitra. Go yourself.

Vikram. Am I your misfortune, Queen,–a bad dream, a thorn in your flesh? No. I will never move a step from here. I will offer them terms of peace. Who is it that has caused this mischief? The Brahmin and the woman conspired to wake up the sleeping snake from its hole. Those who are too feeble to protect themselves are the most thoughtless in causing disasters to others.

Sumitra. O the unfortunate land, and the unfortunate woman who is the Queen of this land.

Vikram. Where are you going?

Sumitra. I am going to leave you.

Vikram. Leave me?

Sumitra. Yes, I am going to fight the rebels.

Vikram. Woman, you mock me.

Sumitra. I take my farewell.

Vikram. You dare not leave me.

Sumitra. I dare not stay by your side, when I weaken you.

Vikram. Go, proud woman. I will never ask you to turn back,—but claim no help from me.

[Sumitra *goes.*]

Devadatta. King, you allow her to go alone?

Vikram. She is not going. I do not believe her words.

Devadatta. I think she is in earnest.

Vikram. It is her woman's wiles. She threatens me, while she wants to spur me into action; and I despise her methods. She must not think that she can play with my love. She shall regret it. O my friend, must I learn my lesson at last, that love is not for the King,—and learn it from that woman, whom I love like my doom? Devadatta, you have grown with me from infancy,—can you not forget, for a moment, that I am a king, and feel that I have a man's heart that knows pain?

Devadatta. My heart is yours, my friend, which is not only ready to receive your love, but your anger.

Vikram. But why do you invite the snake into my nest?

Devadatta. Your house was on fire,—I merely brought the news, and wakened you up. Am I to blame for that?

Vikram. What is the use of waking? When all are mere dreams, let me choose my own little dream, if I can, and then die. Fifty years hence, who will remember the joys and sorrows of this moment? Go, Devadatta, leave me to my kingly loneliness of pain.

[*Enters a* Courtier *who is a foreigner.*]

Courtier. We ask justice from your hands, King,—we, who came to this land with the Queen.

Vikram. Justice for what?

Courtier. It has come to our ears, that false accusations against us are brought before you, for no other cause than that we are foreigners.

Vikram. Who knows, if they are not true? But so long as I trust you, can you not remain silent? Have I ever insulted you with the least suspicion—the suspicions that are bred like maggots in the rotten hearts of cowards? Treason I do not fear. I can crush it under my feet. But I fear to nourish littleness in my own mind.—You can leave me now.

[*The* Courtier *goes.*]

[*Enter* Minister *and* Devadatta.]

Minister. Sire, the Queen has left the palace, riding on her horse.

Vikram. What do you say? Left my palace?

Minister. Yes, King.

Vikram. Why did you not stop her?

Minister. She left in secret.

Vikram. Who brought you the news?

Minister. The priest. He saw her riding before the palace temple.

Vikram. Send for him.

Minister. But sire, she cannot be far. She has only just left. You can yet bring her back.

Vikram. Bringing her back is not important. The great fact is, that she left me.–Left me! And all the King's soldiers and forts, and prisons and iron chains, could not keep fast this little heart of a woman.

Minister. Alas, King. Calumny, like a flood-burst, when the dyke is broken, will rush in from all sides.

Vikram. Calumny! Let the people's tongues rot with their own poison.

Devadatta. In the days of eclipse, men dare look at the mid-day sun through their broken pieces of glass, blackened with soot. Great Queen, your name will be soiled, tossed from mouth-to-mouth, but your light will ever shine far above all soiling.

Vikram. Bring the priest to me. [Minister *goes.*] I can yet go to seek her, and bring her back. But is this my eternal task? That she should always avoid me, and I should ever run after the fugitive heart? Take you flight, woman, day and night, homeless, loveless, without rest and peace. [*Enters* Priest.] Go, go, I have heard enough, I do not want to know more. [*The* Priest *is about to go.*] Come back.–Tell me, did she come down to the temple to pray, with tears in her eyes?

Priest. No, sire. Only, for a moment, she checked her horse and turned her face to the temple, bowing her head low,–then rode away fast as lightning. I cannot say, if she had tears in her eyes. The light from the temple was dim.

Vikram. Tears in her eyes? You could not even imagine such enormity? Enough. You may go. [*The* Priest *goes.*] My God, you know that all the wrong that I have done to her, was that I loved her. I was willing to lose my heaven and my kingdom for her love. But they have not betrayed me, only she has.

[*Enters* Minister.]

Minister. Sire, I have sent messengers on horse-back in pursuit of her.

Vikram. Call them back. The dream has fled away. Where can your messengers find it? Get ready my army. I will go to war myself, and crush the rebellion.

Minister. As you command.

[*Goes away.*]

Vikram. Devadatta, why do you sit silent and sad? The thief has fled, leaving the booty behind, and now I pick up my freedom. This is a moment of rejoicing to me. False, false friend, false are my words. Cruel pain pierces my heart.

Devadatta. You shall have no time for pain, or for love, now,–your life will become one stream of purpose, and carry your kingly heart to its great conquest.

Vikram. But I am not yet completely freed in my heart. I still believe she will soon come back to me, when she finds that the world is not her lover, and that man's heart is the only world for a woman. She will know what she has spurned, when she misses it; and my time will come when, her pride gone, she comes back, and jealously begins to woo me.

[*Enters* Attendant.]

Attendant. A letter from the Queen.

[*Gives the letter, and goes.*]

Vikram. She relents already. [*Reads the letter.*] Only this. Just two lines, to say that she is going to her brother in Kashmir, to ask him to help her to quell the rebellion in my kingdom. This is insult! Help from Kashmir!

Devadatta. Lose no time to forestall her,–and let that be your revenge.

Vikram. My revenge? You shall know it.

Act II

Tent in Kashmir. Vikram *and the* General.

General. Pardon me, King, if I dare offer you advice in the interest of your kingdom.

Vikram. Speak to me.

General. The rebellion in our land has been quelled. The rebels themselves are fighting on your side. Why waste our strength and time in Kashmir, when your presence in your own Capital is so urgently needed?

Vikram. The fight here is not over yet.

General. But Kumarsen, the Queen's brother, is already punished for his sister's temerity. His army is routed, he is hiding for his life. His uncle, Chandrasen, is only too eager to be seated upon the vacant throne. Make him the King, and leave this unfortunate country to peace.

Vikram. It is not for punishment, that I stay here; it is for fight. The fight has become like a picture to a painter. I must add bold lines, blend strong colours, and perfect it everyday. My mind grows more and more immersed in it, as it blossoms into forms; and I leave it with a sigh, when it is finished. The destruction is merely its materials, out of which it takes its shape. It is a creation. It is beautiful, as red bunches of *palash*, that break out like a drunken fury, yet every one of its flowers delicately perfect.

General. But, Sire, this cannot go on for ever. You have other duties. The minister has been sending me message after message, entreating me to help you to see how this war is ruining your country.

Vikram. I cannot see anything else in the world but what is growing under my masterly hands. Oh, the music of swords. Oh, the great battles, that clasp your breast tight like hard embraces of love. Go, General, you have other works to do,—your advices flash out best on the points of your swords. [General *goes.*] This is deliverance. The bondage has fled of itself, leaving the prisoner free. Revenge is stronger than the thin wine of love. Revenge is freedom,—freedom from the coils of cloying sweetness.

[*Enters* General.]

General. I can espy a carriage coming towards our tent, perhaps bringing an envoy of peace. It has no escort of armed soldiers.

Vikram. Peace must follow the war. The time for it has not yet come.

General. Let us hear the messenger first, and then,—

Vikram. And then continue the war.

[*Enters a* Soldier.]

Vikram. What do you say?

Soldier. The Queen has come.

Vikram. Which Queen?

Soldier. Our Queen, Sumitra.

Vikram. Go, General, see who has come. [*The* General *and the* Soldier *go.*] This is the third time that she has come, vainly attempting to coax me away, since I have carried war into Kashmir. But these are no dreams—these battles. To wake up suddenly, and then find again the same palace gardens, the flowers, the Queen, the long days made of sighs and small favours. No, a thousand times, no. She has come to make me captive, to take me as her trophy from the war-field into her palace hall. She may as well try to capture the thunderstorms.

[*Enters* General.]

General. Yes, sire, it is our own Queen, who wants to see you. It breaks my heart when I cannot allow her to come freely into your presence.

Vikram. This is neither the time, nor the place, to see a woman.

General. But, sire.

Vikram. No, no. Tell my guards to keep a strict watch at my tent door,–not for enemies, but for women.

[General *goes.*]

[*Enters* Shankar.]

Shankar. I am Shankar,–King Kumarsen's servant. You have kept me captive in your tent.

Vikram. Yes, I know you.

Shankar. Your Queen waits outside your tent.

Vikram. She will have to wait for me farther away.

Shankar. It makes me blush to say, that she has come humbly to ask your pardon; or, if that is impossible, to accept her punishment from your hand. For, she owns that she alone was to blame,– and she asks you, in the name of all that is sacred, to spare her brother's country and her brother.

Vikram. But you must know, old man, it is war,–and this war is with her brother, and not herself. I have no time to discuss the rights and wrongs of the question with a woman. But, being a man, you ought to know that when once a war is started, rightly or wrongly, it is our man's pride that must carry it on to the end.

Shankar. But do you know, sire, you are carrying on this war with a woman, and she is your Queen. Our King is merely espousing her cause, being her brother. I ask you, is it king-like, or man-like, to magnify a domestic quarrel into a war, carrying it from country to country?

Vikram. I warn you, old man, your tongue is becoming dangerous. You may tell the Queen, in my name, that when her brother, Kumarsen, owns his defeat and surrenders himself into our hands, the question of pardoning will then be discussed.

Shankar. That is as impossible as for the morning sun to kiss the dust of the western horizon. My King will never surrender himself alive into your hands, and his sister will never suffer it.

Vikram. Then, the war must continue. But do you not think that bravery ceases to be bravery at a certain point, and becomes mere fool-hardiness? Your King can never escape me. I have surrounded him on all sides, and he knows it.

Shankar. Yes, he knows it and also knows that there is a great gap.

Vikram. What do you mean?

Shankar. I mean death,—the triumphal gate through which he will escape you, if I know him right. And there waits his revenge.

[*He goes.*]

[*Enters* Attendant.]

Attendant. Sire, Chandrasen, and his wife Revati, Kumarsen's uncle and aunt, have come to see you.

Vikram. Ask them in.

[*Enter* Chandrasen *and* Revati.]

Vikram. My obeisance to you both.

Chandrasen. May you live long.

Revati. May you be victorious.

Chandrasen. What punishment have you decided for him?

Vikram. If he surrenders, I shall pardon him.

Revati. Only this, and nothing more? If tame pardon comes at the end, then why is there such preparation? Kings are not overgrown children, and war is no mere child's play.

Vikram. To rob was not my purpose, but to restore my honour. The head that bears the crown cannot bear insult.

Chandrasen. My son, forgive him. For he is neither mature in age, nor in wisdom. You may deprive him of his right to the throne, or banish him, but spare him his life.

Vikram. I never wished to take his life.

Revati. Then, why such an army and arms? You kill the soldiers, who have done you no harm, and spare him who is guilty?

Vikram. I do not understand you.

Chandrasen. It is nothing. She is angry with Kumarsen for having brought our country into trouble, and for giving you just cause for anger, who are so nearly related to us.

Vikram. Justice will be meted out to him, when he is captured.

Revati. I have come to ask you never to suspect that we are hiding him. It is the people. Burn their crops and their villages,—drive them with hunger, and then they will bring him out.

Chandrasen. Gently, wife, gently. Come to the palace, son, the reception of Kashmir awaits you there.

Vikram. You go there now, and I shall follow you. [*They go out.*] Oh, the red flame of hell-fire. The greed and hatred in a woman's heart. Did I catch a glimpse of my own face in her face, I wonder? Are there lines like those on my forehead, the burnt tracks made by a hidden fire? Have my lips grown as thin and curved at both ends as hers, like some murderer's knife? No, my passion is for war,—it is neither for greed, nor for cruelty; its fire is like love's fire, that knows no restraint, that counts no cost, that burns itself, and all that it touches, either into a flame, or to ashes.

[*Enters* Attendant.]

Attendant. The Brahmin, Devadatta, has come, awaiting your pleasure.

Vikram. Devadatta has come? Bring him in,–No, no, stop. Let me think,–I know him. He has come to turn me back from the battle-field. Brahmin, you undermined the river banks, and now, when the water overflows, you piously pray that it may irrigate your fields, and then tamely go back. Will it not wash away your houses, and ruin the country? The joy of the terrible is blind,–its term of life is short, and it must gather its plunder in fearful haste, like a mad elephant uprooting the lotus from the pond. Wise councils will come, in their turn, when the great force is spent,–No, I must not see the Brahmin.

[*Enters* Amaru, *the chieftain of Trichur hills.*]

Amaru. Sire, I have come at your bidding, and I own you as my King.

Vikram. You are the chief of this place?

Amaru. Yes. I am the chief of Trichur. You are the King of many kings, and I am your servant. I have a daughter, whose name is Ila. She is young and comely. Do not think me vain, when I say that she is worthy to be your spouse. She is waiting outside. Permit me, King, and I shall send her to you as the best greeting of this land of flowers.

[*He goes out.*]

[*Enters* Ila *with her* Attendant.]

Vikram. Ah! She comes, as a surprise of dawn, when the moment before it seemed like a dark night. Come, maiden, you have made the battle-field forget itself. Kashmir has shot her best arrow, at last, to pierce the heart of the war-god. You make me feel that my eyes had been wandering among the wilderness of things, to find at last their fulfilment. But why do you stand so silent, with your eyes on the ground? I can almost see a trembling of pain in your limbs, whose intensity makes it invisible.

Ila [*kneeling*]. I have heard that you are a great King. Be pleased to grant me my prayer.

Vikram. Rise up, fair maiden. This Earth is not worthy to be touched by your feet. Why do you kneel in the dust? There is nothing that I cannot grant you.

Ila. My father has given me to you. I beg myself back from your hands. You have wealth untold, and territories unlimited,–go and leave me behind in the dust; there is nothing that you can want.

Vikram. Is there, indeed, nothing that I can want? How shall I show you my heart? Where is its wealth? Where are its territories? It is empty. Had I no kingdom, but only you–

Ila. Then, first take my life,–as you take that of the wild deer of the forest, piercing her heart with your arrows,–

Vikram. But why, child,–why such contempt for me? Am I so utterly unworthy of you? I have won kingdoms with the might of my arms. Can I not hope to beg your heart for me?

Ila. But my heart is not mine. I have given it to one who left me months ago, promising to come back and meet me in the shade of our ancient forest. Days pass, and I wait, and the silence of the forest grows wistful. If he find me not, when he comes back! If he go away forever, and the forest shadows keep their ancient watch for the love-meeting that remains eternally unfulfilled! King, do not take me away,–leave me for him, who has left me, to find me again.

Vikram. What a fortunate man is he. But I warn you, girl, gods are jealous of our love. Listen to my secret. There was a time when I despised the whole world, and only loved. I woke up from my dream, and found that the world was there,–only my love burst as a bubble. What is his name, for whom you wait?

Ila. He is Kashmir's King. His name is Kumarsen.

Vikram. Kumarsen!

Ila. Do you know him? He is known to all. Kashmir has given its heart to him.

Vikram. Kumarsen? Kashmir's King?

Ila. Yes. He must be your friend.

Vikram. But do you not know, that the sun of his fortune has set? Give up all hope of him. He is like a hunted animal, running and hiding from one hole to another. The poorest beggar in these hills is happier than he.

Ila. I hardly understand you, King.

Vikram. You, women, sit in the seclusion of your hearts, and only love. You do not know how the roaring torrent of the world passes by, and we, men, are carried away in its waves in all directions. With your sad, big eyes, filled with tears, you sit and watch, clinging to flimsy hope. But learn to despair, my child.

Ila. Tell me the truth, King. Do not deceive me. I am so very little and so trivial. But I am all his own. Where,–in what homeless wilds,–is my lover roaming? I will go to seek him,–I, who never have been out of my house. Show me the way,–

Vikram. His enemy's soldiers are after him,–he is doomed.

Ila. But are you not his friend? Will you not save him? A king is in danger, and will you suffer it as a King? Are you not honour-bound to succour him? I know that all the world loved him. But where are they, in his time of misfortune? Sire, you are great in power, but what is your power for, if you do not help the great? Can you keep yourself aloof? Then, show me the way,–I will offer my life for him,–the one, weak woman.

Vikram. Love him, love him with all you have–Love him, who is the King of your precious heart. I have lost my love's heaven myself,–but let me have the happiness to make you happy. I will not covet your love.–The withered branch cannot hope to blossom with borrowed flowers. Trust me. I am your friend. I will bring him to you.

Ila. Noble King. I owe you my life and my heaven of happiness.

Vikram. Go, and be ready with your bridal dress. I will change the tune of my music. (Ila *goes.*) This war is growing tiresome. But peace is insipid. Homeless fugitive, you are more fortunate than I am. Woman's love, like heaven's watchful eyes, follows you wherever you go in this world, making your defeat a triumph and misfortune splendid, like sunset clouds.

[*Enters* Devadatta.]

Devadatta. Save me from my pursuers.

King. Who are they?

Devadatta. They are your guards, King. They kept me under strict watch for this ever-lasting half-hour. I talked to them of art and letters; they were amused. They thought I was playing the fool to please them. Then, I began to recite to them the best lyrics of Kalidas,—and it soothed this pair of yokels to sleep. In perfect disgust, I left their tent to come to you.

King. These guards should be punished for their want of taste in going off to sleep when the prisoner recited Kalidas.

Devadatta. We shall think of the punishment later on. In the meanwhile, we must leave this miserable war and go back home. Once, I used to think that only they died of love's separation, who were the favoured of fortune, delicately nurtured. But since I left home to come here, I have discovered that even a poor Brahmin is not too small to fall a victim to angered love.

Vikram. Love and death are not too careful in their choice of victims. They are impartial. Yes, friend, let us go back home. Only I have one thing to do, before I leave this place. Try to find out, from the chief of Trichur, Kumarsen's hiding-place. Tell him, when you find him, that I am no longer his enemy. And, friend, if somebody else is there with him,—if you meet her,—

Devadatta. Yes, yes, I know. She is ever in our thoughts, yet she is beyond our words. She, who is noble, her sorrow has to be great.

Vikram. Friend, you have come to me, like the first sudden breeze of spring. Now, my flowers will follow, with all the memories of the past happy years.

[Devadatta *goes.*]

[*Enters* Chandrasen.]

Vikram. I have glad tidings for you. I have pardoned Kumarsen.

Chandrasen. You may have pardoned him,—but now that I represent Kashmir, he must await his country's judgement at my hands. He shall have his punishment from me.

Vikram. What punishment?

Chandrasen. He shall be deprived of his throne.

Vikram. Impossible. His throne I will restore to him.

Chandrasen. What right have you in Kashmir's throne?

Vikram. The right of the victorious. This throne is now mine, and I will give it to him.

Chandrasen. *You* give it to him! Do I not know proud Kumarsen, from his infancy? Do you think he will accept his father's throne as a gift from you? He can bear your vengeance, but not your generosity.

[*Enters a* Messenger.]

Messenger. The news has reached us that Kumarsen is coming in a closed carriage to surrender himself.

[*Goes out.*]

Chandrasen. Incredible! The lion comes to beg his chains! Is life so precious?

Vikram. But why does he come in a closed carriage?

Chandrasen. How can he show himself? The eyes of the crowd in the streets will pierce him, like arrows, to the quick. King, put out the lamp, when he comes, receive him in darkness. Do not let him suffer the insult of the light.

[*Enters* Devadatta.]

Devadatta. I hear that the King, Kumarsen, is coming to see you of his own will.

Vikram. I will receive him with solemn rituals,—with you as our priest. Ask my general to employ his soldiers to make preparation for a wedding festival.

[*Enter the* Brahmin Elders.]

All. Victory be to you.

First Elder. We hear that you have invited our King, to restore him to his throne,—Therefore, we have come to bless you for the joy that you have given to Kashmir.

[*They bless him, and* Vikram *bows to them.*
The Brahmins *go out. Enters* Shankar.]

Shankar [*to* Chandrasen]. Sire, is it true that Kumarsen is coming to surrender himself to his enemies?

Chandrasen. Yes, it is true.

Shankar. Worse than a thousand lies. O my beloved King, I am your old servant, I have suffered pain that only God knows, yet never complained. But how can I bear this? That you should travel through all the roads of Kashmir, to enter your cage of prison? Why did not your servant die before this day?

[*Enters a* Soldier.]

Soldier. The carriage is at the door.

Vikram. Have they no instruments at hand,—flutes and drums? Let them strike a glad tune. [*Coming near the door*] I welcome you, my kingly friend, with all my heart.

[*Enters* Sumitra, *with a covered tray in her hands.*]

Vikram. Sumitra. My Queen!

Sumitra. King Vikram, day and night you sought him in hills and forests, spreading devastation, neglecting your people and your honour, and today he sends through me to you his coveted head,—the head upon which death sits even more majestic than his crown.

Vikram. My Queen.

Sumitra. Sire, no longer your Queen; for merciful death has claimed me.

[*Falls and dies.*]

Shankar. My King, my Mother, my darling boy, you have done well. You have come to your eternal throne. God has allowed me to live for so long to witness this glory. And now, my days are done, and your servant will follow you.

[*Enters* Ila, *dressed in a bridal dress.*]

Ila. King, I hear the bridal music. Where is my lover? I am ready.

SHESHER KABITA

The Last Poems of Rabindranath Tagore

1

Before me stretches the ocean of peace:
helmsman, launch me.
Be my eternal companion,
take me in your arms.
The road to eternity will be lit
by the pole star.

Bestower of freedom,
your forgiveness, your mercy
shall sustain me forever
as I journey towards eternity.

May mortal bonds decay,
may the great universe embrace me
and in my heart know without fear
the great unknown.

Shantiniketan: 3 December 1939

2

Death like Rahu
casts shadows only
but cannot sap life's divine ambrosia:
entrapped by this material world
this I know for sure.

The eternal value of love
cannot be stolen
by any plunderer lurking
in secret caves of the universe:
this I know for sure.

What I found as most true
hid inherent falsehood in guise:
this disgrace of life
the laws of universe will not bear,
this I know for sure.

Everything moves by the ceaseless force of change:
this is the law of time.
Death appears changeless
and cannot therefore be true:
this I know for sure.

He who knows this world exists
realises himself,
as a witness of all that exists,

his truth is in the truth of that ultimate self:
this I know for sure.

Shantiniketan: 7 May 1940

3

Bird,
why do you forget your song at times?
Why not sing on?
A songless dawn is futile:
are you not aware of this?

The first touch of dawn
trembles on green trees:
in that tremor is your song
that wakes amongst the leaves.
You are the one this morning loves:
are you not aware of this?

The goddess of awakening is there:
she waits for me
her anchal spread:
are you not aware of this?

Do not deprive her
of the gift of your song.
After the dreams of a sorrowful night
your morning song
brings the message of a new life:
are you not aware of this?

Shantiniketan: 17 February 1941

4

The sun flames
on this lonely afternoon.
I stare at the vacant chair.
I find no consolation there.
In its breast
echoes the haunting voice of despair.

The voice of emptiness is filled with pity:
the message escapes.
Like the tragic eyes of a dog without its master
laments a heart that cannot understand
what happened and why.
All day and night its eyes search in vain.
The chair speaks with greater sorrow,
the dumb pain of the void
spreads in this room without you.

Shantiniketan: 26 March 1941

5

If I can once again
I shall find that chair
in whose embrace remains
the loving message of a distant land.

Escaped dreams of the past
shall crowd there again,
their half-heard murmurs
shall build a nest again.

Recalling pleasant memories,
making awakening sweet,
the flute that is now silent
shall bring back its melodies.

Arms outstretched near the window,
on the fragrant path of spring,
the footsteps of that great silence
shall be heard at night.

With the love of a distant land
she who has waited for long
will sustain her nearness forever,
her whispers resound in my ears.

She, whom words failed,
who spoke only with her eyes,

this chair will keep awake forever
memories of her tristful voice.

Shantiniketan: 6 April 1941

6

There comes the man supreme:
the world is thrilled,
grassblades quiver,
conches resound in the heavens,
gongs of victory sound on earth.
This sacred moment brings the great birth.

The forts of the moonless night
are ruins today.
On the hilltops dawn echoes:
fear not, fear not.
Hopes of a new life emerge.
Hail the new man:
the cosmos reverberates with this cry.

Shantiniketan: 1 Baisakh 1348

7

Life is sacred I know:
but its actual form I have never grasped.
From some mysterious fountainhead
it breaks
and travels down some wandering route
I cannot trace.
It gains a new purity each morning
from the dawn:
a million miles away
I fill this golden vessel with its lustre.

That life gave voice to the day and night:
it worshipped the unseen with wild flowers
and lit clay lamps
in the silent dusk.
My heart offered it
the first love of my life.
All routine loves
touched by its golden wand
are awake today:
my love for her,
for these flowers,
all these are its very own
by its touch.

At birth the book is brought, its pages blank:
it slowly fills with words each day.

Stringing bead after bead about oneself
the portrait emerges at day's end.
The painter recognises himself
by his own signature.
Then, he lines through the words, the forms
with an indifferent stroke of black.
Only a few words in gold remain distinct:
they wake radiant beside the pole star.

Shantiniketan: 25 April 1941

8

In the fifth year of marriage
with the intimacy of a youth
full of mysteries,
secret juices ripen within the heart:
from the buds to clusters of fruit,
from stalk to fragile petal
spreads a golden glow.
A strange fragrance tempts guests in,
a restrained beauty
entrances the wanderer.

For five years the flowering creepers of spring
have filled with nectar the chalice of love:
drunk with honey
the garrulous black bee buzzes.
A serene joy welcomes the uninvited
and those who came when they heard.
In the first year of marriage
from all corners of the Earth
the flute played the *shahana raga*,
the sound of laughter echoed everywhere.
Today, a brief smile breaks on the face of dawn
in soundless humour.
The flute captures the resonance of the *kannada*
as the seven stars call for meditation.

In five years this dream of pleasure flowered
and brought a paradise of fulfilment in life.

The *vasant pancham raga* that played first
has now achieved fulfilment, too.
As you walk the flowering forest bed
your anklets ring with the tremulous raga of spring.

Shantiniketan: 25 April 1941

9

Goddess of language:
I carve your image single-minded
in this lonely courtyard.
Lumps of clay
lie scattered:
unfinished, voiceless,
they stare at the vacant
without hope.
At the feet of your proud image
they lie humbled,
not knowing why they are there.

Yet, more pitiful than them are those
who had once found form
but as time passed
lost all meaning.
Where were you invited?
They cannot answer.
To build which dream
they bore the debt of dust
and came
to the door of mankind?
From which lost paradise
this portrait of Urvashi
did the poet want to capture
on this mortal canvas?
For this you were called,

kept with care in this gallery of paintings
and then forgotten one day.

The primaeval dust you belong to
with supreme indifference claimed you
in its soundless chariot racing into the unknown.

This is good.
This tired acclaim,
crippled, waste today,
these routine humiliations
dog the steps of time
and interrupt its journey.
Spurned, insulted,
you find peace at last
when you become one with the dust again.

Shantiniketan: 3 May 1941

10

On this birthday I feel lost.
I want my friends to pledge
the touch of their hands,
this Earth's ultimate love,
so that I can take with me life's supreme grace,
the last blessings of my fellow men.

My bag is empty today,
I have given away
all there was to give.
If something comes in return–
some love, some forgiveness–
I shall take them with me
when I set sail in my raft
towards that silent festival of the end.

Shantiniketan: 6 May 1941

11

On the bank of the Rupnarayan
I woke
and realised this world
was no dream.
With alphabets of blood
I saw my self defined.
I recognised my self
through endless suffering,
countless wounds.
Truth is cruel:
I love its cruelty
for it never lies.
Life is a *tapasya* of pain till death:
to gain the terrible value of truth,
settle all debts by death.

Shantiniketan: 13 May 1941

12

At this festival of gifts on your birthday
strange and colourful is this
courtyard of the early dawn.
With countless flowers and leaves
life offers its gifts with abandon.
Nature keeps a watch on her treasures
from time to time:
you are now a witness to her affluence.
When the giver and the taker are united,
a divine desire
is fulfilled today.
The poet of the universe, amazed,
blesses you:
as a witness for his verse, you have come
rain-washed
in this clear *shravan* sky.

Shantiniketan: 13 July 1941

13

The first day's sun
asked
the world's first emergence:
Who are you?
There was no answer.

Years passed.
The last day's sun
asked a final question
near the shores of the western sea
amidst the silence of dusk:
Who are you?
There was no answer.

Calcutta: 27 July 1941

14

Often, the dark night of sorrow
has come to my door
armed with only one weapon:
the fearful visage of pain, macabre threats of terror–
deceptive in the dark.
Whenever I believed in that mask of terror
I suffered meaningless defeat.
This game of loss and victory, these apparitions of life:
stumbling ahead from childhood, dogged by this fear
I have heard the mockery of suffering.
This strange restless vision of terror:
crafted in the dark by the skilled hands of death.

Calcutta: 29 July 1941

15

You have riddled the path of your creation
with strange nets of deceit,
O deceitful one.
Snares of false beliefs you have skilfully laid
in our simple lives.
With such delusions you have marked the great:
for him you have not kept the secret night.
Your stars
light his way
towards his inner self,
a path for ever clear,
by his simple faith
made radiant all the way.
Apparently tortuous, he is actually simple:
and this is his pride.
Others think he is deluding himself.
But he finds truth
bathed in the inner light within himself.
Nothing can deceive him.
His last reward he carries
to his coffer.
He who can effortlessly bear your guiles
receives at your hand
his imperishable right to peace.

Calcutta: 30 July 1941